RELEVANCY IN ELEMENTARY CURRICULUM

Books by the Same Authors published by Discovery Publishing House

Science Curriculum

Elementary Curriculum

Elementary Curriculum Improvement

Language Arts Curriculum

Philosophy and Curriculum

Psychology and Curriculum

Improving School Administration

School Curriculum and Administration

Teaching English Successfully

Teaching Language Arts Successfully

Teaching Mathematics Successfully

Teaching Reading Successfully

Teaching Science Successfully

Teaching Social Studies Successfully

Teaching Mathematics in Elementary Schools

Teaching Science in Elementary Schools

Teaching Social Studies in Elementary Schools

RELEVANCY IN ELEMENTARY CURRICULUM

By

Prof. Marlow Ediger

Professor Emeritus in Education

Truman State University

201 W. 22nd, Box 417

North Newton KS 67117

USA

&

Dr. Digumarti Bhaskara Rao

M.Sc., M.A., M.A., M.Ed., Ph.D.

Reader

R.V.R. College of Education

Guntur–522 006

Andhra Pradesh

India

DPH

DISCOVERY PUBLISHING HOUSE

NEW DELHI-110002

First Published-2004
Reprint 2005
Reprinted-2006
ISBN 81-7141-751-5

Published by

DISCOVERY PUBLISHING HOUSE
4831/24, Ansari Road, Prahlad Street,
Darya Ganj, New Delhi-110002 (India)
Phone: 23279245 • Fax: 91-11-23253475
E-mail:dphtemp@indiatimes.com

Printed at:

Tarun Offset Printers, Delhi-53

Dedicated

to

the popular surgeon

and

great humanist

Dr. MADDINENI GOPALA KRISHNA

Secretary & Correspondent

R.V.R. & J.C. College of Engineering

Guntur

&

Secretary

Nagarjuna Education Society

Guntur–522 006

Preface

Relevancy in Elementary Curriculum is written for the use in preservice as well as inservice professional education of teachers, principals, and supervisors. Hopefully, in using this textbook, continuous improvement of the elementary school curriculum will be in evidence. Professionals engaged, directly or indirectly, in the teaching of elementary school pupils must develop a relevant curriculum for boys and girls. Each child must be guided in realizing his or her optimum achievement level. Thus, the teacher, as well as principals and supervisors, must be concerned with selecting objectives which all pupils individually can achieve. Learning activities should guide pupils in achieving the desired objectives. These learning activities should be interesting, meaningful and purposeful for all pupils. Provision definitely needs to be made for individual differences. It is, of course, important to evaluate pupil achievement to determine if objectives have been realized. If objectives have not been achieved, the professional educator needs to determine why this happened.

Relevancy in Elementary Curriculum may be utilized in preparing professional teachers for the elementary school. This book may also be utilized by curriculum designers and textbook writers alongwith teachers and administrators in improving the status of elementary education.

Prof. Marlow Ediger

Dr. Digumarti Bhaskara Rao

Contents

The Pupil, Learning and Society

The teacher of elementary school curriculum needs to be well versed in principles of learning. When following these criteria or guidelines, pupils can be assisted in achieving to their optimum. Too often, teachers have violated important principles of learning when teaching pupils thus underachievement has become a part of learners. A good environment for learning is provided when the teacher follows acceptable guidelines in teaching pupils.

Purpose in Learning

The teacher needs to develop or maintain purpose for learning within pupils. Pupils may learn very little from ongoing learning activities if they "see" little or no purpose in what is being learned. Learners must sense a reason for learning selected facts, concepts, and generalizations. Too, frequently, the classroom teacher has merely assigned a certain number of pages for pupils to read from a textbook with no readiness activities involving purpose for reading. The teacher, perhaps, merely stated the following: "read pages 110 to 113 for tomorrow and answer questions five, six and seven at the end of the chapter." It is no wonder that many learners fail to sense purpose for reading.

If pupils are to read content from a basal reader, for example, the teacher can guide pupils in a discussion pertaining to the related pictures in the textbook. Pictures from the teacher's file could also be utilized. As these pictures are being discussed, the teacher could print the related new words on the chalkboard that pupils will be encountering in their reading. These words should be printed in neat manuscript style and their meaning discussed. Pupils can then obtain a mental image of these words from the chalkboard and utilize these learnings in recognizing new words which they will meet in print. They should also be able to recall the meanings of the new words when reading so that meaningful learning may take place. As the pictures and related new words are being discussed, pupils should ask questions and identify problem areas. Pupils can then read to find information to answer these questions or problem areas. Thus, a purpose is involved in reading and that is to get needed information which the learner desires. Students learn more if they sense that a purpose is involved in learning than if no reasons exist for participating in a given learning activity.

Interest in Learning

It is important for teachers to select learning activities which capture the interests of pupils. Pupils should learn more if they are interested in a given learning activity as compared to having a lack of interest. Too often, teachers have not considered the interests of pupils when selecting appropriate learning activities. Thus, learners do not achieve to their optimum. The teacher can construct an interest inventory whereby pupils can respond in checking what is of interest to them. For example, on this interest inventory, all pupils could check their hobby or hobbies from those listed by the teacher. Space should be left for writing in their hobby or hobbies if they are not listed. Hobbies which pupils have can become a definite part of ongoing learning activities in a given unit. For example, stamps from a collection, pertaining to a unit of study on Great Britain, can become a part of the learning activities on that country. Or, a rock collection could become a definite part of a science unit pertaining to the changing surface of the earth. On the interest inventory, some pupils may indicate positive attitudes toward listening to music of other lands. Certainly these musical recordings can be brought into selected social studies units when they relate to the nations or areas of the world being studied. Teachers need to study various interest inventories and develop an instrument which would give data on ways of capturing the interests of pupils.

Pupils, generally, will show little interest in a given learning activity which is excessively complex. For example, pupils who read well below grade level will not be interested in reading content from books which are written for the grade level they are presently in. The words, terms, and ideas being presented from these textbooks will not be on the understanding level of pupils. Thus, interest in learning will lag. Nor will talented and gifted learners generally be interested in content which is written well below their present achievement level in reading. These learners will generally be bored and feel a lack of challenge in learning activities which have excessively low standards.

Some learning activities have a tendency to capture pupil interest more as compared to other kinds of activities. Well selected films, filmstrips, pictures, slides, excursions, and records can generate much pupil interest if properly introduced. Pupils from different achievement levels in a group can generally benefit from these learning activities. They can interpret and gain content on different achievement levels.

Learning activities involving discussions can make for a lack of interest on the part of learners if the ideas being discussed contain excessively difficult vocabulary terms which learners do not understand or if the discussion activity is carried on for too long a period of time.

Meaning Attached to Learning

To benefit adequately from ongoing learning activities, pupils need to understand that which is being learned. Too, frequently, pupils have memorized facts, statements, and conclusions without really understanding or attaching meaning to what has been learned. Or, pupils have memorized content for a test resulting in a rapid rate of forgetting. If pupils attach meaning to what has been learned, an improved retention rate should thus result. All teachers should be highly interested in having pupils retain as much as possible of what has been learned.

For learning to be meaningful for pupils, the teacher must assess the learner in terms of his present achievement level. Thus, in initiating or introducing a unit, the teacher should develop some kind of pretest which will assist in determining present achievement levels of pupils. This could involve the use of a variety of evaluation techniques. Paper-pencil tests could be used as well as discussions. Not all evaluation, of course, should be done through the use of paper-pencil tests. Tests such as these will not adequately measure how well pupils can utilize a microscope in science or how well pupils can construct and make models related to ongoing social studies units.

Once pupils have been pretested, the teacher needs to adjust objectives in a unit of study. The objectives should then be attainable for pupils. Careful selection of learning activities or determining an appropriate instructional sequence for learners is then important. If the objectives are too difficult for pupils to realize, meaningful learning will then not occur. Learning activities which are too difficult for pupils make for a lack of meaningful learnings on the part of children. The teacher needs to pay careful attention to proper sequence when pupils are pursuing ongoing learning activities. The teacher may "jump" too far ahead of pupils if careful attention is not paid to proper sequence in ongoing learning activities. The other extreme in sequence could pertain to the teacher duplicating what learners already have mastered or learned in previous units of study. Thus, it is important that the teacher think in terms of good sequence when providing learning activities for pupils.

The teacher can be misled in providing for meaningful learning activities for pupils if the type of pretest utilized is not in harmony with the learner's present achievement level. For example, a first grade pupil will not reveal what he knows in a given unit of study if he is asked to respond in writing to essay items in a pretest situation. Nor would he reveal present achievement levels, generally, if he were asked to read and respond to complex true-false, multiple-choice, completion, or matching items. Each child must be pretested using an appropriate evaluation technique which is in harmony with child growth and development characteristics.

Motivating the Learner

Pupils who lack motivation will not have the necessary energy level to become actively involved and benefit fully from ongoing learning activities. The teacher must think of strategies which assist learners to achieve to their optimum due to appropriate motivation. Forcing learners to memorize a given set of facts, generally, would make for situations where learners lack motivation. In some situations, teachers want to depend upon scolding or embarrassing learners in order to "encourage" learning. Sooner or later, teachers discover that under such circumstances pupils learn to dislike learning, teachers, as well as the school as an institution. Pupils may come to the conclusion that school is an unhappy place and learning is something to be shunned. A few teachers still feel that pupils learn only when they are forced to and that learning occurs only in situations involving drudgery. These teachers may think and feel that learning cannot be enjoyable for children and in their deeds emphasizes that "learning" can come about largely when experiences for children are made unpleasant through regurgitation of facts, rote learning, and drill.

The teacher rather needs to think of stimulating pupils so that an inward desire to learn will result. A good bulletin board developed at different intervals when units are taught can do much to assist pupils in asking questions whereby a desire exists to get data in answer to these questions. In developing these bulletin board displays, the teacher needs to think of possible questions pupils may raise pertaining to the pictures contained thereon. Can the bulletin board display help develop an inward desire to learn on the part of pupils? This question needs to be answered in the affirmative by classroom teachers. The teacher can also develop interesting learning centres pertaining to different units of study. This should assist learners in identifying important problem areas thus motivating pupils in developing an inward desire to learn. The teacher can also utilize films and filmstrips in teaching. These aids to learning must be on the understanding level of pupils and have content which would stimulate pupil curiosity. Learning activities need to be selected carefully by teachers so that pupil motivation for learning will be at its optimum.

Providing for Individual Differences

Too frequently, all pupils in a classroom are on the same page at the same time when a given textbook is utilized in the classroom. Situations such as these do not provide for individual differences within a classroom. For some time, educators have recognized that pupils differ from each other in capacity, achievement, interests, energy level, and home background, among other factors. Common sense would say that not all learners then can be at the same place at the same time when utilizing textbooks for a given lesson or lessons.

Some pupils learn more from a particular learning activity as compared to others. For example, a third grade pupil with below average achievement may not benefit as much as possible from a third grade textbook since it is generally written for average achievers. However, this same pupil may learn much from studying and discussing content from audio-visual aids which pertain to ongoing units of study. Pupils have different learning styles. It behooves the classroom teacher to select learning activities which provide for different learning styles within a classroom.

In addition to different learning styles, pupils achieve at various rates of speed. There are many different approaches and methods available to the teacher to use in order that individual differences within a classroom can be provided for. For example, in the individualized reading programme, each pupil would select his own library book to read. A pupil may be in the fifth grade, but he is reading on the third grade level. Thus, a library book is selected by this child which is on his reading level. He also selects a book which contains content which is interesting and meaningful. Another student who is in the fifth grade may be a talented and gifted learner. This student may select and read library books which are on the seventh and eighth grade levels. He should select library books which are interesting and challenging. Having completed reading a library book, the pupil reveals how well he has comprehended the contents of that book. Once learners have selected a library book, they read at their own unique rate of speed. Child A should not compare himself with Child B in terms of difficulty of the library book being read or in terms of rate of speed in reading. Each child is unique with his own interests, capacity, and achievement. Following the completion of reading a library book, the child may have a conference with his teacher. The teacher must eventually get to know the contents of various library books well. He will need to assess the child's comprehension in gaining ideas from reading. Questions asked by the teacher should not destroy interest in reading; rather, the learner should be stimulated in wanting to engage in reading more complex library books with continued improvement in the area of comprehension. In the conference, the teacher can assess each pupil's interest and enthusiasm for reading. The teacher can also evaluate the breadth of content pupils are reading when selecting various library books for the individualized reading programme.

In discussing individualized reading, the authors have attempted to describe how pupils can select library books which vary in complexity as far as reading levels are concerned. Each pupil, then, ideally selects a library book which is on his reading level. The classroom setting needs to have an ample number of library books dealing with various reading achievement levels. Each learner also will differ from others in the rate he is reading content. Each child in a class needs to be successful in achievement so that optimal growth can also take place.

Balance Among Objectives

It is important for the teacher to think in terms of some kind of balance among objectives. If a teacher only emphasizes cognitive domain objectives which deal with the use of the intellect, pupils will not develop as well as possible in other facets of development. Cognitive objectives, of course, are of utmost importance for pupils to achieve; however, psychomotor and affective domain objectives should also be stressed. Psychomotor domain objectives deal primarily with the use of the muscles such as in making and constructing objects and models, repairing objects and items, dramatizing situations, performing folk dances, and playing games. Affective domain objectives pertain to attitudinal development of pupils. All pupils need to have positive attitudes toward learning. Positive attitudes will assist learners to achieve at their optimal rate in cognitive and psychomotor domain objectives. Each pupil should develop positive attitudes toward himself as an individual so that an adequate self concept may result. Certainly, learners need to have wholesome attitudes toward others so that good human relations can then be in evidence. A lack of respect toward classmates generally results in behavioural problems. Feelings of respect toward others are the heart of democratic living. Pupils should develop wholesome attitudes toward others. All individuals desire to be respected.

Cognitive domain objectives are important for learners to achieve. An ample number of understandings need to be developed and understood so that critical and creative thinking can be emphasized in problem solving activities. Life in society demands that individuals become highly proficient in problem solving. All human beings face problems in life which require the best solutions possible. There is no better place to emphasize problem solving than in the elementary school years. The environment in school can be structured for pupils so that problem solving activities can be stressed. The teacher needs to structure an interesting learning environment in the classroom which will guide learners to identify important problems. In introducing a unit, an attractive bulletin board display can capture pupil curiosity whereby questions are asked to begin learning activities which involve the problem solving approach. These questions need to be adequately delimited so that related data or information can be gathered. Further stages of problem solving can then be stressed such as developing and testing hypotheses, and revising the original hypotheses if necessary. The teacher needs to think of numerous learning activities that stimulate pupil curiosity which is basic to identifying problems or questions when using the problem solving approach. Thus, it is important for the teacher to stress cognitive, as well as psychomotor and affective domain objectives. One domain of objectives such as the affective or attitudinal dimension may hinder or help achievement in the other domains—the cognitive and psychomotor.

A different classification scheme which may be utilized in an attempt to provide for balance among objectives is understandings, skills and attitudes. When studying a unit on Great Britain, for example, learners need to develop important understandings pertaining to agriculture, manufacturing, urban living, family living, transportation, and communication. Pupils, of course, would not understand the people of Great Britain unless generalizations are developed pertaining to the above named areas.

Pupils also need to develop an adequate number of skills such as reading, writing, speaking, listening, using the card catalog, using reference materials, making and constructing objects and models, and working effectively in groups.

Attitudinal objectives would deal with the same category as affective domain objectives. Again, it is of utmost importance for pupils to develop wholesome attitudes toward themselves and others so that an adequate self concept exists and good human relations are in evidence.

Success in Learning

The teacher must select objectives, learning activities, and evaluation techniques which assist learners in developing feelings of success. Nothing is gained by having pupils develop feelings of failure. Much money is wasted each year in "teaching" pupils when they experience failure and frustration. The teacher's task is to teach pupils rather than failing or flunking individuals in the elementary school. Too often teachers have felt that their role is to pass or fail pupils rather than guide them to achieve to their optimum. A teacher may think and feel that he has high standards for pupils when rigid standards are utilized to determine grades that pupils should receive. All teachers should realize that tests can be written which are excessively difficult and all learners in a class could receive failing marks or grades. Tests can be written which are excessively easy and most learners could get very high or excellent marks or grades. What is important is that pupils realize objectives through carefully selected learning activities. The objectives may need to be properly adjusted after a pretest has been administered in beginning a new unit of study.

Pupils who experience excessive failure generally develop an inadequate self concept. They feel they can't achieve well because of experiencing much failure; thus, a lack of successful accomplishment results.

Learning activities need to be adjusted to the present achievement level of each child. Careful attention needs to be paid to sequence so that pupils may experience success in ongoing learning activities. Teachers need to reward pupils with praise if each pupil is doing better than formerly. All pupils then can receive praise regardless of capacity or present achievement levels. Praise for improved performance generally spurs pupils on to greater efforts.

Respect for Pupils

It is of utmost importance for teachers to respect all pupils under his or her influence. As was mentioned previously, pupils differ from each other in capacity and achievement. Thus the teacher needs to respect pupils regardless of capacity and achievement levels. The slow learner, as well as average and talented achievers, need to be assisted in realizing their optimum achievement. Provisions need to be made in the classroom which will provide for each individual pupil.

Pupil come to school from different socio-economic levels. Some of these pupils wear more expensive clothing than others. Some are neat and tidy. Others wear old clothing which may not be as clean as the teacher would desire it to be. However, the teacher must realize that pupils can come from unfortunate home situations. An adequate income may be the lot of some parents. Misfortune such as illness, death, unemployment, and dissension may afflict a considerable number of homes in a given community. Thus, the child in such an environment cannot achieve to his optimum. He may worry so much over the home environment that little time is left for thought, study, and learning. By having much knowledge about each individual pupil, the teacher can use this information to do a better job of teaching. Certainly, the information, used properly by the teacher, should assist in providing for individual differences. Teachers become much more tolerant and understanding of learners if they understand each child's home background and experiences.

A child in the elementary school may speak nonstandard English due to models presented in the home environment. Too frequently, teachers have felt that nonstandard English should be criticized so that pupils will want to speak standard English. Teachers may have corrected pupil's spoken language until there is little desire left to speak, especially in the teacher's presence. Pupils will gradually learn standard English when listening to the teacher who presents an example or model to follow. Learners may also get examples pertaining to the speaking of standard English when listening to recordings, tapes, films, and the voices of others who speak English which is generally acceptable to middle class Americans. Pupils should not be forced to change from nonstandard to standard English. Generally, forced changes placed on learners make for negative attitudes toward the teacher and school.

The teacher should respect pupils who come from minority groups such as those who speak a foreign language in the home or those who come from homes whose religious preferences are different from that of others in the class setting. Pupils of different races need to be accepted as individuals who deserve the best in education and other opportunities regardless of creed or religion. Learners should be assisted in developing an adequate self-concept so that optimal contributions can come from all in a democratic society.

Studying Trends in Society

By carefully studying trends in American society, educators can get valuable assistance in determining what should be taught in the elementary school. Too frequently, textbooks utilized in the elementary school have determined what teachers are to teach. Certainly, reputable textbooks can make their contributions in determining what should be taught. However, should this be the sole determiner?

Individual differences would not be provided for adequately if elementary school textbooks largely determine learning activities for pupils. Selected elementary school pupils do not like reading activities for a variety of reasons and thus may not value this approach to learning as highly as other approaches, such as the use of audio-visual aids, for example. The content in elementary school textbooks should always be compared with other reference sources as to accuracy, thoroughness, and completeness. It is difficult for pupils to engage in critical thinking if comparisons are not made among different reference sources. Thus, the question arises as to possible sources for content and objectives in the elementary school curriculum. A study of learners in the elementary school, as was noticed previously, can and should provide valuable information in determining educational objectives in the elementary school.

Societal trends should also guide in determining educational objectives for the elementary school curriculum. Selected societal trends will now be discussed.

More Leisure Time Available

More leisure time is available for individuals in the United States than ever before. The use of machines has reduced the need for individuals to spend long hours in heavy manual labour. The sweatshops in the early history of manufacturing in the United States presented situations where human beings worked from sunrise to sunset with little money to show for their effects. Comfortable, attractive surroundings in these factories were certainly not in evidence. With better working conditions and a forty hour or less work week for many workers in the United States, wise use of leisure time becomes very important.

In the elementary school, teachers need to stress the importance of pupils presently developing worthwhile leisure time activities. Units of study pertaining to hobbies should be emphasized adequately in the elementary school curriculum. Pupils can bring their hobbies to school when a unit on hobbies is being pursued. These hobbies may include the collecting of stamps, rocks, and coins. These hobbies can also become a part of other ongoing units of study.

It is of utmost importance that teachers encourage and stimulate pupils to do an adequate amount of reading in their own spare time in school or outside of the school day. Special times should be set aside for learners to engage in reading trade or library books of their own choosing during the school day. The teacher could introduce selected books to pupils which would spur learners on to do more leisure time reading. Hopefully, reading then will become a good leisure time activity for pupils now as well as in future times.

Musical recordings as well as participating in a variety of activities involving music can provide situations involving the wise use of leisure time. In social studies, pupils can listen to records which relate to the unit being studied. Musical recordings can be correlated with stories that pupils read pertaining to pupil of other lands and nations. The school needs to select records carefully which pertain to music of different cultures. Pupils can listen to these recording individually at a learning centre with headphones. The recordings can also be utilized in teaching the entire class. This can provide situations where a wise use of leisure time is made presently as well as in the future. Recorded music, of course, has become quite popular in American society as far as sales are concerned.

Participating in dramatizations can be important for pupils now not only as far as revealing knowledge is concerned but also in terms of enjoying this activity. Many communities offer opportunities for individuals to take part in plays and other forms of dramatic activity. Certainly, wise use of leisure time can be made of learning activities involving dramatizations in school as well as life outside of school. Wise use of leisure time can do much to improve the quality of living of individuals.

Pollution in Its Various Forms

Air, land, water, and noise pollution is a problem in many advanced industrial countries of the world. Bodies of water have been contaminated with wastes from factories and homes. This has provided situations in which no animal life exists where water pollution is serious. No longer do those bodies of water provide beauty in the natural environment as was formerly true. Discarded bottles, cans, debris, and junk have been disposed of on banks of bodies of water as well as on land. Much land has been utilized to hold discarded items that no one wants. It is true that these waste products have been buried in many cases and the topsoil is again supporting beautiful trees, grass, flowers, and other types of vegetation. However, it is taking much farm land out of production and rendering its appearance unattractive. Too many empty containers also do not recycle the way they should for rapid disposal. In other words, it takes a very long time for tin cans to recycle in the soil where no remains of these containers ultimately exist.

Smoke from homes, factories, and other places of business has made the air much less wholesome and pure than it formerly was. Hopefully, within the next few years, a tremendous decrease in air pollution will occur due to such items as lead free gasolines and engines which will not emit wastes as presently is in evidence.

A further problem in this area deals with noise pollution. Air hammers used by workers in cities to remove unneeded sidewalks, the sound of screeching brakes, and loud noises within factories and businesses have made for situations which can be classified as noise pollution. Pollution, then, can come in several forms—air, land, water, and noise. There are important implications for the elementary school curriculum when thinking of the diverse forms of pollution in society. First of all, pupils certainly need to have ample opportunities to gain elementary school pupils should have many chances to identify problems pertaining to pollution and work toward creative solution of these problems. Third, pupils should develop those attitudes and skills which permit the use of knowledge to minimize pollution in its various forms.

Overpopulation as a Problem

Numerous countries in the world have experienced problems pertaining to overpopulation. Too many people in an area with a lack of resources can make for situations involving starvation, hunger, disease, and a lack of progress. Individuals generally need to feel well physically and mentally before they can achieve to their optimum. Children born into families or groups where overpopulation is the case generally have limited opportunities. An unwanted child even in an affluent home as many strikes against him.

Pupils need to study units pertaining to countries which have experienced major problems due to overpopulation. Ample time needs to be given in studying the consequences of these situations. Pupils must understand what it is like to live in countries where excess population is the case. Certainly, pupils should have ample time to develop understandings in depth pertaining to these consequences. Each pupil should develop attitudes which assist in developing wholesome values and ideas in wanting, not only the best for himself, but also for his classmates, friends and individuals in society.

Drug Abuse

The misuse of drugs has caused much concern in American society and the world at large. This has made for situations where users of harmful drugs have become addicts. Once an expensive need such as this has been developed, individuals have restored to crime in its various forms to support this expensive, harmful undertaking. Thus these individuals are not able to contribute positively in the world of work. Wasted lives too often have been the consequence of using harmful drugs. Suicide and mental breakdowns have occurred in cases involving drug abuse.

It is important that pupils study an adequate number of units on drug abuse. Pupils need to understand in depth the causes as well as consequences of these harmful practices. The teacher needs to accept all pupils as being important. As much information as possible should be obtained pertaining to each child's background of experiences. This information should be utilized by the teacher to do a better job of teaching. Pupils should be guided in receiving feelings of satisfaction from ongoing learning activities. Learners should b successful individuals when pursuing different learning activities. Children who are isolates or near isolates should be identified and guided in the direction of being accepted by others. Positive attitudes toward themselves as well as toward others are important for pupils. Pupils should be given enough opportunities to identify and solve problems pertaining to drug abuse.

Racial Discrimination

In society, minority groups such as the Black American, the American Indian, and the Mexican-American have not had the educational opportunities that many other Americans have received. Job opportunities and good housing have not been in their favour as compared to most people in the United States. To make for a stronger, democratic United States, it is important that minority groups have equal opportunities in obtaining the good things in life as do other more affluent Americans.

Pupils, of course, should study an ample number of units on minority groups in the United States. They should develop understandings in depth pertaining to the causes and consequences of racial discrimination. Adequate opportunities need to be given where pupils can interact with others, regardless of face and creed. These interactions should provide for satisfying learning experiences for pupils. Thus, improved attitudes of pupils should develop toward others. Pupils should also study the contributions that minority groups have made in the United States in various fields such as art, music, agriculture, education, government, religion, business, and labour.

Tension in World Affairs

Tension and wars on the international scene have taken their toll of property and lives. Southeast Asia, the Middle East, India and Pakistan, and East versus West, among other areas, involve situations where tension and war have existed. Powerful nations on the face of the earth watch carefully in these various critical areas to notice the outcomes. With rapid, accurate and efficient means of transportation and communication, these nations can intervene in a very short time with men and equipment. No nation can live unto themselves only. Countries interact with goods and services that are exchanged as well as competition with ideas.

Elementary schools need to select units of study whereby pupils can achieve needed objectives pertaining to countries which face situations involving war and tension. Textbooks alone, of course, should not determine units of study. These units should be selected carefully by teachers, supervisors, and administrators. Pupils should have a voice in determining what is taught through teacher-pupil planning. Cause and effect thinking should definitely be a skill that must be emphasized in teaching these units. Thus, pupils would be developing understandings in depth pertaining to causes for the effects noticed today on the international scene where tension is involved. It is of utmost importance that pupils understand the causes of tension and war. Solutions should be sought to minimize or eliminate situations such as these. Thus, problem solving must be emphasized. Problem areas should be identified and delimited. Needed information from various reference sources should be utilized to collect information in answer to these questions. Pupils can then develop a hypothesis of hypotheses. Further thought and study would revise the hypothesis or hypothesis if warranted. Creative thinking is involved in developing unique solutions to problems. Critical thinking is involved when information or data is evaluated as to accuracy, objectivity, and thoroughness. Favourable attitudes should be developed by learners toward themselves, classmates, and others in society so that tension may be minimized.

Change in Society

Change certainly has been a key word in American society. Rapid changes are continually occurring in ideas, knowledge, and inventions. On the American education scene, educators are aware of continual changes pertaining to the following rather recent innovations such as team teaching, the nongraded school, programmed learning, the dual progress plan, behaviourally stated objectives, performance contracting, affective education, and others.

Selected individuals in the United States can still remember when the automobile was just arriving on the scheme in the area of transportation. They also recall when seeing an airplane was something to behold due to its rarity. Some farmers remember when horses and mules were used in farming instead of a tractor. Framers did heavy manual labour on farms as late as 1940 by shoveling wheat by hand and shocking oats and wheat bundles by hand. It was necessary to haul these bundles to a central place for threshing to separate the grain from the chaff. It wasn't long until the self propelled combine came along, with its present day air-conditioned cab and power-steering, which separates the grain from the chaff with no other manual labour involved other than driving the machine and doing repair work when needed. From this combine, the grain is augered on to a large truck. The hydraulic lift with a light pull of a handle lifts the truck box and the grain runs into a small box and is augered into a grain bin for storage with little muscle activity involved. Inventions have changed farming from the heavy use of muscles to the use of machines in a comparatively short period of time.

From the first short successful flight of an airplane by the Wright Brothers at Kitty Hawk, North Carolina in 1903, one can now fly from New York to the Middle East in ten and one-half hours approximately. The flight generally is pleasant with the roughest part of the trip being smoother than boat travel on a very peaceful ocean. These planes are very compact; however, the food and the conveniences are basically good. One then can travel in a very short period of time from one area to another where cultural differences can be very great.

Pupils growing up in American or Indian society need an ample number of historical units pertaining to the various facets of change that have come about. This should guide learners in understanding the cause or causes for change. The consequences of change should also be emphasized in these units of study. Numerous opportunities for critical thinking can be given when evaluating change as it takes place. Pupils should be given ample time to predict further changes that could come about; thus, creative thinking is being emphasized. It is important that pupils adopt positive attitudes toward change when situations and conditions demand and require change. Pupils should evaluate their own ideals, values, and beliefs. Thus, important understandings, skills, and attitudes should be developed by learners which will guide them in decision-making pertaining to change in society.

Explosion of Knowledge

Content in different curriculum or academic areas is increasing at a very rapid rate of speed. Estimates differ as to how often knowledge doubles. This, no doubt, will depend upon the curriculum or academic area since knowledge is increasing more rapidly in some areas as compared to others. However, with a conservative estimate, one can say that knowledge generally doubles in ten years. There certainly is much for individuals to learn. No doubt, in future years, knowledge will increase at an even faster rate.

It behooves teachers, principals, and supervisors to select carefully what pupils are to learn in the different curriculum areas of the elementary school. If too many isolated facts are learned, much forgetting will, no doubt, soon occur. What is selected to be learned should be important at the present time. Ideally, it should be important also for future times; it is necessary to attempt to predict what will be important in the future. Thus, pupils should develop important generalizations which will make for fewer facts to be learned in isolation. Facts should support the generalizations and not be taught in isolation. Thus the relationship exists between the facts and the generalizations.

There is too much knowledge for pupils to learn when teachers emphasize the survey approach in teaching. Learnings that pupils are to develop should be attained in depth rather than using the survey approach to learning. The survey approach would indicate that pupils would cover many units in a given school year such as fifteen to twenty on each of the grade levels in the elementary school. Teaching a unit in depth would demand that six to seven social studies units be taught in a school year, for example, on the intermediate grade levels.

Poverty in Society

Many areas in the world experience extreme poverty due to overpopulation, disaster, unstable political situations, poor natural environments, and governments not concerned with the needs of people. A high standard of living in the world has been realized by individuals in American society. However, pockets of poverty exist in an affluent American society. This has important implications in American education.

Teachers need to understand the home background of disadvantaged pupils. These pupils may not speak standard English. They may also have very limited background experiences.

The teacher and pupils need to respect those learners who do not speak standard English. These pupils can learn to speak acceptable English without using force or ridicule. The use of force or ridicule may indicate to the child that his home and community was inferior since non-standard English is not respected in school. Thus, children must be respected who speak non-standard English. They can listen to models in standard English as found in the teacher's voice when speaking or reading orally, in listening to the spoken voice on tape recordings and films, by reading silently, and by listening to the spoken voice of other pupils who use standard English.

Pupils who come from poverty areas may lack necessary background experiences to benefit from a given ongoing unit of instruction. The teacher needs to utilize an appropriate sequence of experiences which are adjusted to the present achievement level of pupils. From that point, new learnings can be developed to achieve objectives which pupils can attain. Learning activities need to be selected which are beneficial to pupils in achieving important objectives. Respect for individual differences in teaching is important in a democratic society.

Mobility in School Population

Each year, many pupils change from attending one elementary school to a different school. Parents get transferred from one city to another as far as jobs are concerned. Or, parents move from one area to another area within that same city. They may also move to another state for job promotion. Sometimes, these individuals live abroad for a year or more. Thus, the child may move from one school to another. He leaves friends behind and may make new ones in the process. He begins a unit of study in the sending school and moves to a new school where an entirely different unit is being ended. Poor sequence in learning activities is then in evidence. He may study the same unit at different times in two schools (with variations, of course) in a given school year due to mobility and lose out on other important units of study. For some pupils it is difficult to adjust to a new school with its many strange faces. Other pupils make new friends rapidly in the process.

The teacher should preassess the incoming pupil's achievement to notice present achievement levels. Learning activities can then be provided in proper sequence. The new pupil can then benefit to his optimum from ongoing learning activities. The teacher needs to guide new pupils to readily become acquainted with other learners and participate actively with them in group activities Teachers need to be very accepting of new pupils arriving in an elementary school so that an effective learning environment may thus result. Teachers should also evaluate what important units of study have not become a part of the new pupil. Important, previously omitted units then can be studied by these children. Above all, new learners arriving in a particular school should be happy and successful individuals who are achieving to their optimum. They should attach meaning to what is being learned and sense purpose in ongoing learning activities. Fear of the unknown and fear of failure should be minimized as much as possible on the part of these and all learners in a classroom setting as well as in a general school setting.

In Summary

There are important criteria that should be followed by teachers when providing learning activities for pupils. Pupils should sense a purpose or purposes for learning. Thus, learners would feel that a reason or reasons exist for participating in specific learning activities. Teachers need to select those learning activities which would capture pupil interest. It is of utmost importance that learners understand what is being taught so that meaningful learning occurs. If pupils lack motivation, a lower energy level will be available for ongoing learning activities. Teachers should work in the direction of stimulating pupils so that an inward desire to learn will result. Pupils achieve at different rates of speed and at different achievement levels thus making it necessary to provide adequately for each child in the classroom. Intellectual development on the part of learners is important but is not the only category of objectives that should be emphasized when teaching pupils. There needs to be some kind of balance based on rational thought among the following categories of objectives—understandings, skills, and attitudes. Attitudes affect the degree to which a pupil will develop to his optimum in understanding and skills objectives. Attitudes are changed in some cases by obtaining more information. Developing appropriate attitudes can help in realizing understanding and skills. Each category of objectives affects other categories such as positive attitudes toward learning affect achievement in objectives which pertain to understandings. Learners need to be successful in learning and be respected by others.

Societal trends assist in determining units of instruction for pupils as well as objectives which learners should achieve. Workers in American society have more leisure time available than ever before. This societal trend states that pupils should develop worthwhile leisure type activities. Overpopulation, misuse of drugs, racial discrimination, tension in the world, change in society, situations involving the explosion of knowledge, poverty, and mobility of population state important units of study that must be emphasized in teaching-learning situations. General and specific objectives can then be derived for these units.

REFERENCES

Berman, Louise M. *New Priorities in the Curriculum*. Columbus: Charles E. Merrill Publishing Company, 1968. Chapter One.

Doll, Ronald C. *Curriculum Improvement: Decision-Making and Process*. Boston: Allyn and Bacon, Inc., 1970. Chapter Two.

Frost, Joe L., and Thomas Rowland. *Curricula for the Seventies, Early Childhood Through Early Adolescence*. Boston: Houghton Mifflin Company, 1969, Chapter Two.

Goodland, John I. *School, Curriculum and the Individual*. Waltham, Massachusetts: Blaisdell Publishing Company, 1966. Chapter Six.

Hyman, Ronand T. (Ed.). *Teaching: Vantage Points for Study*. Second Edition. Philadelphia: J.B. Lippincott Company, 1974. Section Two.

Joyce, William W., Robert G. Oana, and W. Robert Houston. *Elementary Education in the Seventies*. New York: Holt, Rinehart and Winston, Inc., 1970. Section Three.

Joyce, Bruce R., and Berj Harrotunian. *The Structure of Teaching*. Chicago: Science Research Associates, 1967. Chapter Four.

Michaelis, John U., Ruth Grossman, and Lloyd F. Scott. *New Designs for the Elementary School Curriculum*. New York: McGraw Hill Book Company, 1967. Chapter One.

Nerbovig, Marcella H., and Hebrert J. Klausmeier. *Teaching in the Elementary School*. Third Edition. New York: Harper and Row, 1969. Chapter Two.

Palardy, J. Michael (Ed.). *Elementary School Curriculum, An Anthology of Trends and Challenges*. New York: The Macmillan Company, 1971, Part One.

Wilson, L. Craig. *The Open Access Curriculum*. Boston: Allyn and Bacon, Inc., 1971. Chapter One.

Wright, Betty Atwell and others. *Elementary School Curriculum, Better Teaching Now*. New York: The Macmillan Company, 1971. Chapter One.

Objectives and the Curriculum

A vast amount of knowledge is available for consumption in American society. It is important to select carefully what should be taught in terms of understandings. The teacher definitely does not want to clutter the mind of the child with many unrelated, irrelevant facts. Nor does the teacher want to emphasize only one facet of the child's development. Children need to develop well intellectually, as well as physically, socially and emotionally. One facet of development is not adequate when teaching pupils. For example, if the teacher only emphasizes the importance of pupils developing well intellectually, then the child will suffer in other areas of growth. A child who does not achieve well socially, of course, can become an isolate. A school is a social situation with many people; an individual does not live unto himself only. Pupils who do well in intellectual development only, may find school life to be unenjoyable due to lacking in social development. A pupil who lacks in positive attitudes or emotional development may dislike various curriculum areas in the elementary school thus hindering his total development. Thus, it behooves the teacher to emphasize all facets of a child's development.

General Objectives

General objectives help teachers in directing learner achievement over long periods of time. What kind of individuals are we attempting to develop ultimately? What understandings, skills, and attitudes do pupils need to become effective participators in a democracy? There will not be perfect agreement among educators to be sure when answering these questions.

Teachers, principals, supervisors, and others in the field of education should continually attempt to define the kinds of individuals that need to be developed to strengthen concepts of democratic living in the United States.

It is important to have some kind of defensible scheme of classifying general objectives. Many educators classify these objectives in terms of understandings, skills, and attitudes. This can give the teacher an approach to use in categorizing objectives so that some kind of balance can exist in terms of different facets of pupil growth. A teacher should not emphasize understandings objectives only, when teaching pupils. Skills and attitudinal objectives are also important when working in the direction of emphasizing the total development of each child.

For each unit that is taught, careful identification of objectives pertaining to understandings is important. Much time is wasted in teaching when pupils achieve understandings which are important and irrelevant. Too frequently, the teacher has spent much time in having pupils learn many isolated facts which soon will be forgotten. Cooperatively, teachers, supervisors, and administrators should evaluate if pupils presently are gaining important understandings. Supposing that a first grade teacher is teaching a unit on "The School", what understandings should pupils realize during the time the unit is taught? There should be a carry-over of these learnings to other units of study so that transfer of learning is in evidence. As an example, the following understandings may have been identified cooperatively by those involved directly in determining resource units for a particular school:

To develop within the child an understanding that

(a) workers have different responsibilities to perform in the school;

(b) schools have an important purpose in educating the young;

(c) respect toward others is important in an elementary school;

(d) taxes are needed to provide for the costs of operating schools;

(e) school property should be properly cared for.

In terms of skills, the following, among others, would be important for pupils to realize:

(a) participating effectively in discussions;

(b) presenting ideas clearly and effectively for their stage of development;

(c) listening carefully to stories read by the teacher;

(d) listening carefully to the contributions of others;

(e) viewing audio-visual materials carefully;

(f) reading content accurately.

Attitudes that can be emphasized when teaching this unit may include the following:

(a) respecting others in a class setting and in the general environment;

(b) wanting to participate in discussions;

(c) desiring to listen carefully to the thinking of others;

(d) wanting to view audio-visual presentations thoroughly;

(e) wanting to gain much information pertaining to the topic or area being studied.

These objectives are stated broadly; learners would realize them over a period of time, such as for an entire unit or longer. Again, it is important for objectives to be selected carefully by those involved in teaching pupils. It is very important to have some kind of balance among objectives based on rational thinking, which pertain to understandings, skills, and attitudes.

Specific Objectives

Many educators believe that objectives should be stated precisely so there will be little or no interpretation as to what will be taught. These objectives would be stated in terms of what the pupil will do as a result of teaching. Pupil achievement can then be measured if the objectives have been achieved. Learners would reveal to the teacher if the objective(s) has been achieved. Thus, the teacher can observe if pupils have realized the objectives.

Examples of Specific Objectives. Students of education should study and practice the writing of behaviourally stated objectives.

These objectives should be precise and leave as little room, as possible, for interpretation. Generally, these objectives are stated in terms of what the learner should do and not what the teacher is to do. Precise objectives are measurable in terms of learner behaviour.

In teaching a social studies unit on the Middle East, the teacher may list the following specific objectives, among others, which pupils are to achieve:

1. The pupil will list in writing three causes of the Middle East conflict.
2. The pupil will voluntarily read one library book on the Middle East and report the contents to a committee of five pupils.
3. The pupil will write a paragraph of forty words on four of the following leaders, past and present, of Isreal: King David, King Solomon, Moses, Nehemiah, Ezra, David Ben Gurion, Moshe Dayan, and Golda Meir.
4. The pupil will write a paragraph of forty words on four of the following leaders, past and present, of the Arab world: Mohammed, Omar, Abu, Bakir, Uthman, Mohammed Ali, King Hussein, Gamal Abdul Nasir, and Anwar Sadat.
5. The pupil within a committee of three will make a model relief map of the Middle East.

When teaching a science unit on animal life in prehistoric times, the teacher may write the following specific objectives:

1. Given ten models of animals of prehistoric days, the pupil will correctly identify nine.
2. The pupil will select three animals of prehistoric days and write a fifty word paragraph for each.
3. Pupils in committees of three will make dioramas pertaining to a three dimensional scene of life in prehistoric days.
4. Eighty per cent of the pupils will bring a model animal of prehistoric days to class and in a report tell about the animal. (Some pupils may not have pictures or models

of prehistoric animals in the home. In an atmosphere of respect, they can enter into the discussion pertaining to animal life before history was recorded.)

If a teacher is teaching a selected unit in reading, he may, for example, have written the following objectives, among others:

1. The pupil will pronounce correctly 95 out of 100 running words when reading orally.
2. The pupil will answer correctly three out of four questions.
3. The pupil when reading a given selection of 100 words will select two facts and two opinions.
4. When given a paragraph of sixty words, the pupil will give a needed solution to the problem stated in the writing.
5. The pupil will give correct definitions to ninety per cent of the new words covered in the unit.
6. The pupil will use correctly ninety per cent of the new words in sentences.

Further examples can be given of specific objectives in other curriculum areas than those stated previously. In teaching a unit pertaining to spelling, the teacher could write the following objectives:

1. The pupil will spell correctly ninety-five per cent of the new words in the unit.
2. The pupil will pronounce correctly all words in the unit.
3. The pupil will use correctly in sentences ninety per cent of the new words.
4. Pupils will present orally or in writing at least one definition for each new word in the unit.
5. Ninety per cent of the pupils will write a cross word puzzle pertaining to spelling words in the new unit.

A mathematics teacher may write the following objectives, among others, in a specific unit of study:

1. Pupils will respond correctly to nine out of ten problems with each problem having four sets of two digit addends.
2. Pupils will add correctly nine out of ten problems in addition by using two procedures to solve each problem.

Learning Activities and Behavioural Objectives

In some of the written behavioural objectives, learning activities are stated within the objectives. For example, a social studies teacher may have the following stated objective: The pupil will write the Gettysburgh Address. Thus, pupils would engage in practicing the writing of the Gettysburgh Address as a learning activity until it is mastered. One would, of course, in units of study thoroughly emphasize critical thinking, creative thinking, as well as problem solving. Recall of knowledge and information alone would not be adequate to equip a pupil to become a contributing member of a democracy. Ample learning activities need to be provided which will assist learners to develop skills in various types and kinds of thinking. The following behaviourally stated objective would assist learners in developing skills pertaining to critical thinking: Given a paragraph of seventy-five words, the pupil will record two accurate statements and two inaccurate statements. Here, the pupil would need to contrast and compare information in terms of substantiating statements of accuracy and refuting statements which cannot be justified when using reliable reference sources. The paragraph given to pupils had not been viewed by them previously; otherwise, recall of information may be involved when recalling accurate and inaccurate statements in a given selection. Notice in the latter objective pertaining to critical thinking, the terminal behaviour does not state specifically the kind of learning activity for pupils to realize the stated objective. Indirectly, of course, the kind of learning activity is implied. In the first objective pertaining to pupils writing the Gettysburgh Address, basically a clear statement exists within the objective itself as to the kind of learning activity which will be provided for learners.

Consider the following objectives: Given ten pictures pertaining to vertebrates, pupils will classify each in terms of fish, amphibians, reptiles, birds, or mammals. This objective would mean that pupils become thoroughly acquainted with standards or criteria that pertain to each classification of animals with backbones. Learners, then, would ultimately classify each of the animals in the pictures into the appropriate category or classification. In the objective it is clearly stated that learners would need to go much beyond recall of knowledge to achieve the terminal behaviour. They would need to understand and then recall the different criteria pertaining to each classification of vertebrates. Pupils would then need to consider each animal contained in the pictures and determine their classification through evaluation.

In Summary

Objectives which pupils are to achieve should be selected carefully since there is much to learn due to the tremendous amount of information available with the explosion of knowledge as a societal trend. General objectives pertain to long range goals which pupils should achieve, whereas precise, specific objectives can be achieved by pupils in a short period of time such as in one lesson, or in lessons covering several days. Objectives can be classified in terms of understandings, skills, and attitudes, or in terms of cognitive, psychomotor, and affective domains. One category of objectives affects the other categories, such as guiding pupils to develop more positive attitudes should assist learners to achieve at a more optimum rate in understandings and skills.

REFERENCES

Collier, Calhoun C., and others. *Teaching in the Modern Elementary School*. New York: The Macmillan Company, 1967. Chapter One.

Crosby, Muriel. *Curriculum Development for Elementary Schools in a Changing Society*. Boston: D.C. Heath and Company, 1964.

Funk, Hal D. and Robert T. Olberg (Eds.). *Learning to Teach in the Elementary School*. New York: Dodd Mead and Company, 1971. Chapter Two.

Joyce, Bruce R. *Alternative Models of Elementary Education*. Waltham, Massachusetts: Blaisdell Publishing Company, 1969, Chapter Two.

Hass, Glen and others (Eds.) *Readings in Elementary Teaching*. Boston: Allyn and Bacon, 1971. Chapter Two.

Howes, Virgil. *Informal Teaching in the Open Classroom*. New York: Macmillan Publishing Company, Inc., 1974.

Keith, Lowell, and others. *Contemporary Curriculum in the Elementary School*. New York: Harper and Row, 1968. Chapter Three.

Manning, Duane. *Toward A Humanistic Curriculum*. New York: Harper and Row, 1971. Chapter Six.

Mehl, Marie A., and others. *Teaching in Elementary School*. Third Edition. New York: The Ronald Press Company, 1965. Chapters Two and Three.

Saylor, J. Galen, and William M. Alexander *Curriculum Planning for Modern Schools*. New York: Holt, Rinehart and Winston, Inc., Chapter Three.

Taba, Hilda. *Curriculum Development, Theory and Practice*. New York' Harcourt, Brace and World, 1962. Chapter Three.

3

Issues in the Curriculum

Faculty members in an elementary school must study issues thoroughly pertaining to the elementary school curriculum. There are no easy answers to certain problems in the elementary school curriculum. It would be easier to make curricular decisions if clear cut answers could be found in selected problems areas. Thus, the teacher, principal, and supervisor must gather much information pertaining to both or several sides of an issue. Educational literature, such as periodicals, pamphlets, professional textbooks, and other reference sources should be used in gathering the needed information. Faculty members must take time to talk to other professionals in the field in discussing issues relating to developing the elementary school curriculum. Information that is obtained should be evaluated thoroughly in order to make the best decision or decisions possible in improving the elementary school curriculum.

Behaviourally Stated Objectives as an Issue

In the past few years much emphasis has been placed on writing behaviourally stated objectives. Objectives that are behaviourally stated generally follow the following criteria:

1. These objectives are stated precisely as to what learners will be achieving as a result of teaching.
2. These objectives are generally stated in terms of what learners are to achieve and not what the teacher will be doing to teach pupils.

3. Words which lack clarity are omitted in writing behaviourally stated objectives; the omitted words include the following: to enjoy, to appreciate, to know, to understand, to get insight, to believe, to have skill in, and others.
4. Pupil achievement can be measured if the objectives have been achieved.
5. Teachers can observe if learners have achieved the behaviourally stated objectives.

There certainly are advantages as well as disadvantages in writing objectives behaviourally. One must first realize that not all advocates of behaviourally stated objectives would agree as to the degree of precision that these objectives should be written. Then, too, some objectives can be written more precisely as compared to other objectives:

1. The pupil will write the names of four farm animals.
2. The pupil will perform a folk dance of France.
3. The student will write a paragraph of sixty words on urban life in Great Britain.

In the first objective, there perhaps, is very little interpretation as to the content pupils will be learning. There may be some disagreement in terms of a few animals. For example, would "rabbit" be considered a farm animal that would fit into the category of being domesticated? The answer, no doubt, lies in the kind of rabbit that is being considered—wild or tame. Secondly, is a rabbit considered to be a farm animal? Or, are rabbits considered to be more of animals that live in woodlands, as well as in some areas of a large or small city.

The second objective is more general than the first objective. However, it also is behaviourally stated. One can observe if pupils can perform a folk dance of France. Thus, one can measure if learners can do the folk dance as a result of learning experience. Vagueness exists in the objective in that some pupils will perform the folk dance better as compared to other learners in the class setting. There will be degrees of "good", "better" and "best" in pupils ultimately performing the desired dance.

The third objective is also behaviourally stated. There are many questions one can ask about the final product that pupils will have completed.

1. Does the evaluator count correct spelling in evaluating the final product?
2. How much attention should be given to good handwriting in the written work?
3. What constitutes good content when writing the sixty word paragraph on urban life in Great Britain? Is one sixty word paragraph equal or equivalent to another sixty word paragraph as long as it deals with urban life in Great Britain?
4. Would all evaluators of the written product agree as to it having or not having met the behaviourally stated objective?

The writer is pointing out the fact that many objectives classified as behaviourally stated objectives are general in nature thus leaving room for interpretation as to what pupils are to learn or achieve. The following objective also meets standards pertaining to precise, specific objectives:

The pupil will answer nine out of ten true-false items correctly.

In this objective much leeway, of course, exists as to what pupils will be learning. The true-false items could be as simple as the following:

Paris is the capital city of France.

2 + 3 = 5

Or, they could be of the following difficulty:

Turkey is considered as a part of the Middle East.

213 × 95 = 18,005

Thus, many behaviourally stated objectives are very broad or general and leave much room for interpretation as to what pupils will be learning.

A further question that can be raised about behaviourally stated objectives pertains to how many sets of objectives should be written for a specific class of learners. For example, should the teacher write one set of objectives for each unit taught in social studies, science, mathematics, language arts, and the other curriculum areas in the elementary school? Or, should a separate set of objectives be written for fast learners, for average achievers, and still a different set of objectives for the slow learner? The number of objectives then that would need to be written would be endless. Advocates of behaviourally stated objectives emphasize that main focus in teaching should pertain to the stated objectives or ends and not the means to an end. Learning activities pertain to means toward an end or approaches in guiding pupils in realizing desirable objectives. If a teacher has written many behaviourally stated objectives, he still doesn't have any learning activities to use in teaching. In many cases it will be difficult to select learning activities which help pupils directly to realize a specific objective or many specific objectives. For example, the teacher has written the following objective for pupils to achieve in a unit pertaining to "Living in the Middle East."

The pupil will list in writing six agricultural products produced in the Middle East.

The following could be some of the materials used as learning activities in helping pupils achieve this objective:

reading from the textbook or textbooks

reading information from encyclopaedias

gathering data from reputable almanacs

viewing and discussing slides, filmstrips, and films

interviewing a resource person

reading pamphlets and newspaper articles

reading newsmagazines

The chances are that pupils will be gaining much additional information other than that contained in the objective. Writers of behaviourally stated objectives advocate that objectives be stated in advance prior to teaching pupils in a specific class. Then, the teacher should select learning activities which will assist learners in realizing the desired objectives. This leaves little or no room for pupils to learn other things than what is stated in the objective. Pupils have important questions that wish to have answered. New objectives should arise in the class as units of study progress, as well as when these units come to an end. Can the teacher state all objectives for learners to achieve prior to teaching? As teaching-learning situations progress in a class setting new objectives arise on the part of learners as well as the teacher. Predetermined objectives would need to be revised as the teacher continues teaching a unit or a specific lesson. The teacher may think of better objectives than those stated prior to teaching a unit or even a lesson for a particular day. The teacher may also feel and think that selected objectives should be omitted or revised as pupils are engaging in difficult learning activities.

A further question pertaining to behavioural objectives arises as the teacher attempts to sequence learnings for pupils. Can the teacher predetermine prior to teaching proper sequence of learnings for pupils? Or, do pupils sequence many of their own learnings with questions that are identified and problems that are solved by learners? The issue would pertain to who should do the sequencing of pupil learnings—the teacher, or children, or cooperative efforts by the teacher and learners.

Selecting Learning Activities as an Issue

Educators, of course, agree that a variety of learning activities should be provided for pupils to provide for individual differences. In actual practice, there still are teachers that cling to the use of textbooks basically in teaching of pupils.

The issue involved in the selection of a variety of learning activities is centered on the problem of who should do the selecting. The teacher could engage in selecting all of the learning activities to provide for individual differences in a class. The assumption here is that the teacher can do the best job of selecting these activities. A further assumption is that it is up to the teacher to know individual pupils in terms of capacity, achievement, interests, and motivation and thus select learning activities which can help each child develop to the highest possible in all facets of development. The question arises as to the teacher alone being able to determine what is best for learners. Can the teacher have the understandings, skills and attitudes to do this? At the other end of the continuum, one can think of good learning activities where pupils do much of the selecting of activities for learning with the assistance of the teacher. Thus, pupils can identify important problem areas and select necessary resources to solve these problems. Also, pupils can evaluate their achievement in having arrived at satisfactory solutions toward these problems. The teacher would serve as a consultant and guide rather than as a lecturer or explainer of facts, concepts, and generalizations.

A further problem arises as to the sequencing of these activities. Should these learning activities be sequenced as advocates of programmed learning would emphasize? The programmer would then sequence learnings so that pupils progress in very small steps and basically are continuously successful in each step of learning. Toward the other end of the continuum, pupils with teacher guidance could do much of their own sequencing with self-selection of learning activities used in the solving of problem areas. Learners should select activities which would be meaningful, interesting, purposeful, and provide for individual differences within a class. These learning activities, of course, could help learners achieve objectives which they had previously identified. New objectives can also be identified as the unit progresses with related learning activities selected by pupils with teacher guidance.

Structure of Knowledge as an Issue

In the 1960's much emphasis was placed upon specialists in a given academic area identifying key ideas or generalizations for students to realize. The thinking was that college and university professors specializing in a particular discipline would have much to offer pupils in terms of gaining important ideas. The advantages given for emphasizing the structure of knowledge, among others, were the following:

1. Irrelevant learnings would have a tendency to be weeded out.
2. Pupils would learn and approach a discipline as specialists in the field would select, evaluate, and gather data or information.
3. Learners would utilize methods or approaches in gathering data that specialists in a specific discipline use.
4. Important concepts and generalizations would then be developed by pupils.

Many educators today question the values of having pupils work only as specialists in a given discipline would work. After all, when pupils are curious, they identify their own questions and problem areas. They may also wish to read content if it is or is not related to key ideas recommended by a specialist in a specific academic area. Thus, what specialists in a given discipline hold to be important, learners may not have the same perception. Elementary school pupils, of course, are much younger than college and university professors who specialize in a given academic discipline. Interests change within individuals as they progress through the different levels of schooling and on toward a particular vocation or profession.

A further question which can be discussed pertains to academicians being able to agree on key ideas or generalizations within a discipline. For example, could economists agree as to which generalizations would be important for pupils to achieve? Or, could historians agree as to which ideas could be considered to represent the "structure of history?" To be sure, academicians can and have made a tremendous contribution in identifying important concepts and generalizations that learners should achieve. They have also contributed much in stating methods or approaches to gaining and testing knowledge within a specific discipline. Certainly, elementary school pupils too frequently have learned that which is irrelevant and unimportant.

There needs to be some kind of rational balance between what academicians emphasize as being important for learners to achieve and what curious pupils feel is important to learn. There also must be balance in methods that specialists in a given academic discipline use and methods that the pupils develop creatively in the solving of problems.

Handwriting as an Issue

Many teachers in elementary schools of the United States use handwriting booklets to teach handwriting to pupils. These textbooks used in teaching handwriting attempt to provide sequential learnings for pupils. Many teachers have pupils follow the pages through in sequence as written in these textbooks in formal periods of time devoted to the teaching of handwriting.

In some elementary schools of the United States no textbooks for pupils are used in the teaching of handwriting. The thinking here is that pupils can be assisted in developing legible handwriting when the need arises. The emphasis is not upon pupils completing the different exercises in a specific textbook in the order presented to achieve sequential learnings. For example, if individual pupils have difficulties in forming specific upper or lower case letters, the teacher then would assist learners in remedying the difficulty experienced in handwriting. The same would be true of the following kinds of specific errors that pupils would be experiencing.

1. proper and uniformity of slant of letters;
2. proper proportion of individual letters;
3. good alignment of letters and words;
4. appropriate spacing between words and between letters.

Thus, the issue in the teaching of handwriting pertains to the use or non-use of handwriting textbooks to be used in teaching pupils. These two points of view could be represented by points at either end of a continuum. In between these two points of view, one can think of various alternatives. For example, the handwriting textbook could be used in teaching pupils when learners have a need to see models which would improve legibility in handwriting in this facet of the language arts curriculum. If a pupil has difficulty in forming the letter "b", he can use the handwriting textbook to notice a model "b" and thus practice the writing of this particular letter of the alphabet until it is legible. As a further example, if a pupil cannot write the cursive letters "e" and "I" in proper proportion, the handwriting textbook could serve as a model for pupils in providing practice so that proper proportion of letters is the end result or objective in teaching. Thus, some kind of balance based on critical thinking should be in evidence between heavy emphasis and non-use of textbooks pertaining to the teaching of handwriting to elementary school pupils.

Advantages given for the use of handwriting textbooks in teaching pupils could include the following:

1. They give teachers security in the teaching of handwriting.

2. The writers of these textbooks have attempted to provide sequential learnings for pupils.
3. Specific methodology is given to assist teachers in the teaching of handwriting.
4. Experts in the field have given their time and attention to helping pupils achieve legibility in handwriting.
5. Research findings have been utilized in writing handwriting textbooks for pupils.
6. Handwriting textbooks provide models for pupils to utilize in developing legible handwriting.

Disadvantages which can be given for the use of handwriting textbooks could be the following:

1. Sequence in learning may not be sequential from the child's own perception.
2. Pupils too frequently practice that which they already can do well.
3. Textbooks are not the most interesting materials for pupils to utilize when teachers provide learning activities for children.
4. Teachers may rely too heavily upon these textbooks thus resulting in a lack of creative teaching.
5. Pupils may and do become bored with "routiness" in learning activities and teaching procedures.

Teachers need to think of creative approaches to the teaching of handwriting. These new approaches should provide for individual differences and continuous achievement on the part of each pupil.

Teaching of Spelling as an Issue

Most elementary schools in the United States utilize textbooks in the teaching of spelling in the elementary school. These textbooks generally contain on a weekly basis a list of spelling words for pupils to master on the different grade levels of the elementary school. Various learning activities for pupils are contained in these textbooks to assist learners in mastering the spelling of words. Questions that can be asked pertaining to the use of spelling textbooks could be the following:

1. Are these words commonly used by pupils in writing business letters, friendly letters, stories, summaries, and in other functional writing activities?
2. Do pupils sense purpose in learning to spell these words?
3. Are adequate provisions made for individual differences within a class?
4. Do learners have ample opportunities to use these words in new situations that arise?
5. Are the learning activities based on important principles of learning such as learner interests, needs and abilities?
6. Do the learning activities in the spelling textbook assist in developing motivated pupils?
7. Do these textbooks provide for gifted pupils as well as the slow learner?
8. Do teachers become rigid and formal in their teaching due to the use of these textbooks?

Much can be said in favour of using textbooks in teaching elementary spelling. The following would be strong points in using these textbooks:

1. Generally, the lists of words in spelling textbooks have been selected on the basis of research studies pertaining to words most commonly used in writing by pupils in the elementary grades.
2. Lists of words for pupils to master in spelling and various learning activities to assist learners in learning to spell these words are contained in the spelling textbooks to give teachers security in teaching.
3. Writers of spelling textbooks attempt to provide sequential learnings for pupils.
4. Teachers generally would not have time to develop an entirely creative spelling curriculum without the use of textbooks.
5. Attempts are made to provide for slow, average, and fast learners within the framework of utilizing spelling textbooks.

6. There are varied learning activities that pupils can pursue in a spelling textbook.
7. Teachers can evaluate how well each pupil has mastered a given list of words that come from a spelling textbook.

In appears that a middle ground position can be taken pertaining to the use of spelling textbooks. Recommendations that can be made relating to a spelling programme which would provide for individual differences in terms of needs, interests, and abilities could be the following:

1. Pretest pupils on a list of spelling words for a particular week; thus learners would not need to study the spelling of words which have already been mastered.
2. Adjust the number of words each child is to learn to spell in a week according to the present achievement level of the learner; each pupil must feel successful in the spelling curriculum.
3. Utilize words from social studies, science, and other units of study to provide spelling words for gifted and talented pupils, as well as those who are highly motivated in wanting to learn to spell words.
4. Use other learning activities than those contained in the textbook to stimulate pupils in wanting to learn to spell.
5. Develop a weekly list for each pupil according to those words which are misspelled in everyday functional writing; adjust the number of words for each child so that success on the part of each learner will be an inherent part of the spelling programme.
6. Praise pupils for doing better work in spelling; all learners desired praise for improved performance!

Basal Readers as an Issue

Basal readers are used quite commonly in many elementary schools of the United States. Generally, a basal reader series published by one of the leading textbook companies in the United States is used in an elementary school. A supplementary basal reader may be used as additional reading materials to complement or follow the main series of readers being utilized. Writers of basal readers attempt to control the number of new words added for each page of content, especially for the early primary years. Thus, young readers don't have too many new words to identify on any one page. With a carefully controlled vocabulary, learners learn to read a few new words each day. Basal readers as a whole have well developed teacher's manuals which provide the classroom teacher many ideas and approaches to utilize in teaching a given set of pupils. For example, in providing readiness for reading a given selection, the teacher's manual may have suggestions such as the following for teaching pupils:

1. Different approaches will be mentioned in having pupils develop background information for reading content. With teacher guidance, pupils can discuss the pictures related to the content learners will be reading. This helps pupils understand the content better that will be read later either silently or orally. The teacher could also use pictures from her own file, a film or filmstrip, slides, or an excursion to develop background information that would relate to the story that pupils will be reading.
2. As background ideas are being discussed with pupils, the new words that will be met in print can be printed in neat manuscript letters on the chalkboard. (Approaches and methods in teaching should always be varied). Pupils thus see the new words in print on the chalkboard before reading the new selection silently or orally.
3. Meanings of the new words written on the chalkboard should be discussed with pupils. It is important that students obtain the meaning of these words as they are used in context in the selection to be read.
4. Pupils should also sense purpose in reading. Thus, learners should, prior to this time, have raised a question for which they would want information. The information ideally would then come from silent or oral reading using the basal reader. The teacher can also state the purpose or question(s) for which learners would read to get information.

Following the reading, the teacher would discuss answers to the established purpose or purposes. This would assist the teacher in evaluating comprehension in reading. The teacher can emphasize the following purposes in reading: reading for facts; critical reading; reading to follow directions; creative reading; reading for the main idea; and reading for a sequence of ideas.

Enrichment activities can also become a part of the related learning activities when reading from the basal reader. Here, pupils could read related stories and library books. Or, children could read stories and library books written by the same author who wrote the selection in the basal reader. Related records, poems, and audio-visual materials could be utilized as enrichment activities along with the basal reader.

There are, of course, many advantages in using basal readers.

1. The manuals are well developed generally and provide the teacher with many suggestions for teaching.
2. The controlled vocabulary is an attempt to sequence new words that pupils meet in print.
3. Beginning teachers have much security in the teaching of reading with a teacher's manual that can be relied upon to guide in the teaching of reading.
4. Stories contained in basal readers are written to develop and maintain pupil interest in reading.
5. Much attention generally is paid to sequential learnings on the part of pupils pertaining to word attack skills.

Disadvantages in using basal readers in the elementary school could be the following:

1. The controlled vocabulary may destroy pupil interest in reading since the wording becomes rather repetitious on the early primary grade levels.
2. Pupils' interests differ from each other; it is very difficult to have learners in a class or even in a small group be interested in the same story contained in a basal reader.
3. Teachers may become rather formal and rigid in their teaching if the teacher's manual is followed thoroughly when teaching reading.
4. Each pupil is at a different achievement level in reading from other learners; a basal reader cannot provide for

individual differences within a class in reading achievement.

5. The basal reader limits the scope of content which pupils may otherwise be reading.
6. Sequence in learning must be perceived from the pupil's point of view.

A possible compromise solution could exist pertaining to the use of basal readers and other approaches to reading, such as the individualized reading programme. In the individualized reading programme, each child basically would select his own library book to read on his own interest and difficulty level. The pupil ideally would read at his own optimum rate of speed. The book to be read should be on the child's reading level and not the frustrational level. A conference in a one to one relationship between teacher and pupil could follow after the learner has completed reading a library book. The teacher then could also use the basal reader approach in addition to the individualized reading programme. The use of the basal reader would have its many strengths in the following specific areas:

1. Guiding learners in word attack skills such as phonetic analysis, use of picture clues structural analysis, use of context clues, and use of configuration clues.
2. Helping learners in comprehension pertaining to a variety of purposes in reading, such as reading for facts, main ideas, directions, sequence of ideas, and generalizations. Critical and creative reading also should be emphasized.
3. In general, basal readers would be utilized to assist learners in developing sequential skills and abilities in reading.

The Initial Teaching Alphabet as an Issue

The Initial Teaching Alphabet, hereafter called the ITA, has much to recommend itself in introductory programmes of reading for elementary school pupils. It, no doubt, is true that many pupils are hindered in reading achievement due to irregular spelling of words. In traditional ways of spelling English words, phonetic analysis can help much in writing words where there is consistency between symbol and sound as is true of words such as the following: man, end, sand, bet, bin, hen, and others. In the first word "man", the beginning consonant can be changed to form many new words in this family or pattern such as "can", Dan", "Nan", "pan", "ran", "tan", and "van". The final consonant in the word "man" can be changed so that the following new words arise: "mad", "map", "mat", "mam", and "Max." Changing the letter "n" to a "y" in the word "man" brings on an inconsistency between symbol and sound (such as "y" being silent).

There are many words which have inconsistencies in spelling between symbol and sound. In the following words the vowel sound is the same; however, the spelling of the sound differs from word to word: blue, too, to, two, moon, tune, rheumatism, and new. With ITA symbols, the same symbol would be utilized for the vowel sound.

With the use of ITA symbols, learners are to gain security pertaining to consistency between symbol and sound in the language arts areas of reading and spelling. Pupils have experienced difficulty in reading and spelling when inconsistencies exist, and when silent letters are an inherent part of certain words.

A major problem exists in using ITA symbols when pupils engage in making the transition to traditional ways of reading and spelling words. To be sure, certain words are spelled the same way using ITA and traditional letters of the alphabet. This can be illustrated, for example, with the following words: man, bat, set, map, tot, flop, and many other words.

A National Curriculum as an Issue

Selected educators in the United States advocate the implementation of a national curriculum. It is pointed out that high mobility of population in the United States makes it a necessity to provide better sequence of learnings for pupils than what commonly is the case today. A child in the fifth grade, for example, may be beginning a unit on Canada. He moves to a different school, city or state, and the receiving school, for example, may be ending a unit on Brazil. There is little relationship between the two units being studied. Or, a pupil in the second grade is in the middle of a science unit on "Magnetism and Electricity." He moves to a different area and the receiving school is in the middle of a unit on "Rocks and Minerals." In the receiving school, in many cases, the new child will lack background learnings for the ongoing unit entitled "Rocks and Minerals." Thus, poor sequence in learning is a part of the child's experiences when moving to a new area. It takes a conscientious teacher to provide a variety of rich learning activities which are sequential from the newly arrived child's point of view.

Advocates of a national curriculum would say that problems in pupil mobility and proper sequence in learning could be harmonized with some kind of agreement as to which units should be taught in the different curriculum areas of the elementary school. It, of course, would not be as rigid as in some foreign countries where a member of the Ministry of Education could look at his watch and state somewhat accurately what fourth graders (or its equivalent) would be studying.

In the United States, there is a decentralized system of education. Local boards of education and faculty members have considerable freedom in determining which units of study should be taught and when the units of study should be taught. Thus local school districts have had much freedom in determining scope and sequence in different curriculum areas in the elementary school. The rationale back of this would be generalizations such as the following:

1. At the local level, there can be heavy involvement at the grassroots level in improving each curriculum area of the elementary school.
2. Faculty members can actually implement those methods and approaches to teaching which they have considered as following good criteria, standards, or guidelines.
3. Local interest, motivation, and initiative would be hindered with a national curriculum.
4. Purpose in improving the curriculum is highest when faculty members can sense a need for making selected changes.
5. At the local level, major provisions can be made to provide for individual differences within a class.

Advantages which can be driven for a national curriculum could be the following:

1. Pupils would in most cases experience better sequence in learning.
2. More uniformity would exist in terms of what pupils would learning thus making it necessary to identify important understandings, skills, and attitudes that pupils should develop.
3. Specialists in different academic disciplines as well as specialists in education on the national level could be heavily involved in helping to determine which learnings are important for pupils to obtain.
4. Flexibility could still be an important concept when thinking of a national curriculum.

Students of education need to study thoroughly the arguments for and against a national curriculum. One's own conclusions should be based upon understanding through much study and critical evaluation of what has been read. In teaching pupils research results must be utilized to help each pupil achieve to the optimum.

The Teaching of Grammar as an Issue

Much time has been spent by the teacher in teaching grammar in the elementary school. Learners have been involved in much drill pertaining to learning the different parts of speech and being able to identify them in sentences. Pupils in many cases have experienced much difficulty in learning what a noun is, what a verb is, what adjectives and adverbs are, as well as the other parts of speech. Traditional grammar has emphasized that the definition of a noun is that it refers to a person, place or thing, while linguists may state that nouns are words which can be changed from singular to plural or plural to singular. Thus in proper context boy, man, woman, and toy would be nouns since these words which are singular can be changed to plural: boys, men, women, and toys. There, of course, has been confusion in traditional grammar as to selected words pertaining to nouns referring to the broad category of things. These is further confusion in traditional grammar when verbs are referred to as action words. The following sentences would indicate the problem that is involved: Singing is my favourite leisure time activity. "Singing" is the only word in the sentence that could be called an action word and yet it is the subject of the sentence. Thus, traditional grammar would have its weakness here in saying that verbs pertain to action words. It is also confusing in this sentence when thinking of a noun being a word that can be changed from singular to plural using the linguistic frame of reference. The word "singing" requires a verb which is singular. It would be incorrect to say "Singing are my favourite leisure time activity." Thus, it is difficult for learners to conceive of singing as being a word that can be changed from singular to plural and vice versa. The word "singing" is a verb and, of course, in traditional grammar would be called a gerund. Among other ways, gerunds can be used as subjects of sentences. Verbals seemingly do not fit the classification scheme of either traditional grammar or the linguistic approach.

Many elementary school pupils today study traditional grammar. No doubt, teachers in these schools feel more comfortable using this approach. Inservice education programmes provided by the various public schools have also been lacking when thinking of implementing the linguistic approach to the teaching of grammar.

A further problem pertaining to the teaching of grammar pertains to values obtained by learners. Questions that can be asked about the teaching of grammar could be the following.

1. Does a study of grammar assist pupils in communicating ideas well orally?
2. Are pupils improving in the area of written communication due to a study of grammar?
3. Do learners enjoy studying grammar in the language arts curriculum?
4. Is interest in learning being developed when pupils study grammar?
5. Do the study of grammar make sense to learners?
6. Do learners sense reasons for the study of grammar?
7. Do pupils understand how the English language operates through the study of grammar?

8. Can individual differences in achievement be provided for?
9. Are desirable attitudes developed within learners?
10. Are learnings that pupils have developed transferable to new situations in life?
11. Are higher levels of thinking being emphasized other than rote learning and drill?
12. Can a variety of meaningful learning activities be provided for pupils in the teaching of grammar?
13. Is time wasted in the teaching of grammar whereby pupils could develop other learnings which would be more useful?

There are kindergarten and first grade pupils who, of course, have basically no knowledge of grammar, and yet they speak standard English well. Some educators have wondered how effective the teaching of grammar has been to assist learners in using the English language more effectively. A study of grammar must make its positive contributions to the language arts curriculum and the broad, general objectives of elementary education.

Balance in the Mathematics Curriculum as an Issue

With the advancement of modern mathematics, pupils have studied much more geometry as compared to the decade of the 1950's. On the primary grade levels, learners in many cases, have developed complex learnings pertaining to such concepts as lines, rays, line segments, points, simple and non-simple curves, and open and closed curves. Prior to the 1960's, these and other concepts generally were taught at the intermediate and upper grade levels. It, no doubt, is true that teachers of elementary school children are better educated than ever before. They should possess much knowledge pertaining to teaching-learning situations. There are more research results which educators can lean upon in the teaching of children than ever before. More professional textbooks are available pertaining to the teaching of children than ever before. More and better teaching aids are available in the teaching of elementary school mathematics than ever before.

Prior to the 1960's, heavy emphasis was placed upon the teaching of arithmetic to elementary school pupils; this was followed by an increased emphasis upon pupils developing more learnings in the areas of geometry as well as algebra. All educators would realize the importance of geometry as well as algebra in the mathematics curriculum. There definitely needs to be balance based on critical thought among arithmetic, algebra, and geometry in the curriculum area of mathematics. There are certain questions which can be asked pertaining to implementing the concept of balance in the mathematics curriculum:

1. Can the learner use in functional every day life situations that which has been learned in mathematics?
2. Do pupils feel that reasons exist for studying each of the separate areas that make up the mathematics curriculum?
3. Are child growth and development characteristics adequately considered when developing the mathematics curriculum?
4. Is critical thinking, creativity, and probiem solving encouraged in mathematics rather than drill on definitions and giving correct answers to basic addition, subtraction, multiplication, and division facts?
5. Has a rational balance, based on criteria, been established within an elementary school among arithmetic, algebra, and geometry?

It is important that pupils be able to utilize learnings obtained from school in actual life situations outside of the class setting.

Inductive vs. Deductive Learning as an Issue

Many new programmes and materials pertaining to teaching the different curriculum areas in the elementary school emphasize the inductive approach to learning. Educators, generally, also emphasize the importance of pupils learning by discovery. The following reasons, among others, are generally given for having pupils learn inductively as compared to the deductive approach:

1. Pupils are more thoroughly involved in the ongoing learning activity.
2. It keeps learners "on their toes" when responding to questions asked by the teacher and other pupils

pertaining to an audio-visual presentation as well as other materials and ideas used in teaching.

3. Pupils become more interested in learning.
4. The teacher gets more feedback on pupil achievement.
5. The teacher can adjust learning activities better to the present achievement levels of individual learners.
6. Problem solving, critical and creative thinking can be emphasized thoroughly in teaching.

Disadvantages can also be listed for using the inductive approach. Among the disadvantages are the following:

1. Inductive learning is time consuming when there is much for pupils to learn.
2. Pupils do not need to rediscover what already has been discovered by man in the past.
3. Learners learn best when gradually moving from the concrete to the abstract rather than debating the inductive versus deductive approach to teaching.
4. With the "explosion of knowledge" as a trend in American society, objectives that children are to achieve should be selected carefully with economy of time in learning being a very important factor.

Reality in the Social Studies as an Issue

A major problem that is being discussed more and more in educational literature pertains to how much of reality should pupils experience in various units of study. To be sure, almost no one would be opposed to pupils experiencing reality in the following examples:

1. Pupils visiting a modern farm when a unit on the farm is being studied.
2. Learners taking an excursion to a modern supermarket when studying a unit on "Visiting the Supermarket".
3. Pupils actually seeing an assembly line at work when studying a unit on "Manufacturing in the United States."

There are numerous other examples, of course, that can be given in having learners develop positive understandings, skills, and attitudes in various social studies units as a result of experiencing reality.

There are selected questions which can be raised pertaining to other facets of living where it is an issue as to how much experience with reality pupils should have.

1. How much knowledge, for example, should pupils gain about violence in society?
2. If it is agreeable that pupils should develop these understandings as completely as possible, how can they develop feelings, that individuals have, representing these diverse points of view?
3. Would understandings such as these hinder in social and, particularly, emotional development of learners?
4. Should pupils develop learnings pertaining to both the positive and negative sides of American foreign policy? (There would be balance here based on rational thinking.)
5. Would learners then become democratic individuals, as well as good citizens, in their dealings with others?

These are questions that cannot be brushed aside lightly. In a democracy, it is necessary to have much information to use in decision-making processes. The issue arises as to how much experience learners should have with reality. The thinking of educators differs much in this problem area. The thinking of the lay public also differs much from person to person. One only needs to observe parents who carefully control which programmes on television their children can observe. Other parents leave it entirely up to the child to select programmes for observation on television.

Individual Versus Group Work as an Issue

Numerous programmes in education are available for the elementary school years whereby pupils generally work on an individual basis. Some of these programmes are the following:

1. Individual reading.
2. Programmed learning.
3. Individualized spelling (without the use of textbooks).

Textbooks can also be utilized on an individual basis entirely. For example, learners could complete a spelling textbook at their own individual maximum rate of speed. The pupils, of course, would learn to spell words correctly with an agreed upon per cent of accuracy.

Reasons generally given for a totally individualized programme of study for each learner are the following:

1. Each pupil has a different intelligence and achievement level as compared to other pupils in a class setting.
2. Learner's interests vary from each other.
3. Each child works at a different rate of speed.
4. No two individuals are motivated equally or in the same way.

It is a fact that all curriculum areas in the elementary school could be individualized to the point where each pupil would be working on something different from other children in the class. Each pupil would then be working at a different rate of speed on the learning activity. It is only sound educational thinking to provide for individual differences in a class. It is detrimental to a child generally to be working on a task which is uninteresting, too difficult or too easy, and lacks purpose.

Pupils also need to have opportunities to work in group situations. Social development of the learner is of utmost importance. Thus learners must have opportunities to work in committees. The following learning activities in different curriculum areas of the elementary school lend themselves well to having pupils work on committees:

1. making maps in social studies;
2. doing research on a particular problem area;
3. being on a panel or a member of a buzz group;
4. solving problems through a discussion;
5. interviewing resource personnel;
6. conducting experiments in science;
7. arriving at main ideas and generalizations inductively;
8. developing an experience chart cooperatively;

9. making dioramas, friezes, and murals;
10. constructing models and replicas;
11. engaging in choral reading;
12. participating in a dramatic activity;
13. singing together with others;
14. participating in games and physical education in general;
15. discussing continent after having viewed a film, filmstrip, a set of slides, or a series of pictures.

The programmes previously mentioned for elementary school pupils such as individualized reading are important in terms of providing for individual differences. Teachers must provide for all pupils in a class. The classroom teacher should also assist pupils to do well in social adjustment and development.

There is a delicate balance between helping pupils to achieve to their optimum on an individual basis and guiding learners to develop well socially. Thus, teachers, administrators, and supervisors need to think of balance in the curriculum between individual needs and social needs.

Using Standard Versus Nonstandard English as an Issue

There are, of course, learners who come from homes where non-standard English is spoken. These pupils may even speak the English language where it sounds somewhat foreign to a person accustomed to hearing standard English spoken continually. These pupils may use words such as the following:

"dust" meaning money

"hog" meaning an expensive car

"tote" meaning to carry

"flat" meaning house

"crib" meaning house also

"taters" or "spuds" meaning potatoes.

Selected pupils may also use sentences where the subject and predicate do not agree. "Ain't" may also be a common word in their speaking vocabulary. The "ing" ending words may be pronounced in the following ways: runnin, jumpin, singin, swimmin, and doin. To be sure a child does express himself clearly using the following choice of words: I ain't got no money nohow. No doubt, the following choice of words using standard English does not express thoughts any clearer: I have no money. Effective communication of ideas is important. Thus, individuals can communicate ideas clearly and effectively in standard as well as nonstandard English. In American society, of course, a premium is placed upon speaking standard English. In most cases, to get better paying positions in desired environments, communicating ideas using standard English is rewarded as compared to nonstandard English, all things otherwise being equal.

The child coming from a home where nonstandard English is spoken will also speak nonstandard English. The language that is spoken is learned. Thus, pupils growing up in a home where the German language is spoken largely or only, will generally become quite proficient in speaking the German language. Thus, teachers must consider the speaking of standard or nonstandard English as learned behaviour. The home may reward individuals who speak nonstandard English only, when communicating ideas. Thus, in home situations such as these, speaking standard English may not sound right and may be frowned upon. The child then is caught in a dilemma where the home emphasizes and rewards the speaking of nonstandard English. Teachers in an elementary school may reward the speaking of standard English only. They may actually call down students who choose words in speaking which do not follow the criteria of standard English. Or, pupils may be corrected so frequently in speaking that little desire is left to communicate ideas orally in front of the classroom teacher. Certainly, all pupils need to feel good about themselves. They need to feel free to participate in ongoing learning activities involving oral communication. "Calling pupils down" or minimizing their approaches to speaking will be detrimental to learners when developing an adequate self-concept or being creative in the area of oral communication of ideas. There must be better approaches in bridging the gap between standard and nonstandard English for pupils coming from homes where usage is not in harmony with middle class homes. Questions that can be asked pertaining to closing this gap are the following:

1. Could pupils speak nonstandard English at home and in the community, with standard English being emphasized in school in a non-threatening manner?
2. Could teachers be educated to accept all pupils as they are presently and help each to make continuous progress?
3. Can an adequate number of good models be provided for learners so that appropriate learnings can be developed pertaining to standard English?
4. Can pupils be assisted to feel good about themselves if standard, as well as nonstandard English, is spoken?

Foreign Language in the Elementary School as an Issue

With the passage of the National Defense Education Act of 1958 more money was spent on foreign language instruction in the elementary school as compared to earlier times. The NDEA act provided for money on a matching basis to the public schools for equipment, materials, and other needed items to organise and implement instruction in foreign languages, among other curriculum areas.

One major problem that exists for any elementary school is to determine which foreign language, if any, should be taught. Regional differences in the United States would assist in determining in some cases which foreign language should be taught. For example, in New Orleans, Louisiana, French could be important for pupils to study. In southern Texas, the Spanish language would be most functional of any foreign language to teach. In other areas of the United States, there are Graman speaking communities as well as communities where Swedish, Italian, Polish and other languages are spoken. In many areas of the United States, there, perhaps, would be little preference if any, for learning a foreign language which could be used in a functional situation. Thus, one issue inherent in the teaching of a foreign language is which language should be taught to learners.

A second issue would pertain to when pupils should be taught a foreign language. Pupils who grow up in a community where another language, in addition to English, is spoken will generally become proficient in using the second language while conversing and discussing with others in purposeful situations. Thus, all things being equal, the younger the child, the sooner he will learn to speak a foreign language. Youngsters learn a language through imitation. They repeat what older brothers and sisters, parents, and other people in the environment have said. Thus, the individual learns to speak a language which he has exposure to. One learns to speak a language; it is learned behaviour and not inherited. Infants also learn a language by experimenting with different words individually, within a phrase, or within a sentence. Thus, in trying out new words on a trial and error basis, the child makes many mistakes. He gradually learns which words are used incorrectly. Trial and error is one way of learning. Many understandings, skills, and attitudes are learned in this way. Modification of behaviour generally comes about when pupils try out new words. Feedback gives pupils responses as to words being utilized in a proper context. Thus the child must be exposed to a foreign language at a young age in order to learn the new language effectively. It takes much practice to be able to pronounce words accurately and clearly in a foreign language.

A third issue pertains to an already overcrowded elementary curriculum. Is there ample time to teach a foreign language in the elementary school when the language arts, science, mathematics, social studies, health and physical education, music, and art all need and demand their share of time in a modern elementary school? Many elementary teachers today say there is not enough time in a school day to teach the different curriculum areas of the elementary school without the inclusion of foreign language instruction. If foreign language instruction is included in the elementary school curriculum, new criteria may need to be developed in determining which curriculum area or areas need to be deemphasized in degrees in terms of allotted time.

A fourth issue pertains to the need to learn a second language in the United States. It is true that there are communities where a different language is spoken other than English. Could this other language be learned effectively in the home in functional speaking situations? There are many Americans that travel abroad, but is a second language used frequently enough by these people to warrant teaching it in the public schools? Can educators determine which foreign language pupils will need in the future? There are selected foreign languages which are more popular than others in the public schools. However, the importance of a particular foreign language can change.

Certainly, the teaching of a foreign language in the elementary school has many advantages. Among these would be the following:

1. The pupil should develop a better understanding of the problems that are involved in learning to speak a language.
2. Learners should develop appreciations pertaining to the surrounding culture of a particular language. If pupils are learning to speak the French language, they should also develop positive attitudes toward the music, art, architecture, history, geography, foods, crops, and culture in general of France.
3. Pupils can have opportunities to converse with others who have grown up speaking the foreign language being studied in the elementary school.
4. Learners should develop an attitude of appreciation in learning to speak a foreign language.
5. The child will have a better chance to communicate with others in a foreign language when situations in life demand this.

The Criterion Referenced Supervisor as an Issue

Educators continually advocate that the elementary school curriculum, as well as other levels of schooling, be improved. Each curriculum area needs to be kept up-to-date. Thus, trends in each curriculum area should be studied thoroughly. In light of these recommended trends, the elementary school curriculum should be changed from where it is presently to the recommended level. Teachers, principals, supervisors, and the lay public should be thoroughly knowledgeable and accepting of the trends before they are implemented.

One approach to improving the elementary school curriculum would be to conduct observational visits to observe classroom teaching. The purpose of the observational visit would be to focus upon improved objectives, learning activities, and evaluation techniques in each curriculum area of the elementary school. In the observational visit, the supervisor could focus upon objectives as compared to learning activities. Or, the supervisor could place major emphasis upon the quality of learning activities provided for pupils rather than the stated objectives. Following the observational visit the supervisor and teacher could have a conference to evaluate the quality of teaching. Agreed upon ways of improving the quality of teaching could be recorded and filed for future reference by the supervisor. In future observational visits, the supervisor can first study the filed observational notes to notice improvement in the quality of teaching from one time to the next.

A relatively new approach to making observational visits has been developed by advocates of behavioural objectives. The criterion-referenced supervisor goes by specific guidelines when making observational visits. The very first task of the criterion-referenced supervisor would be to look at the stated objectives written by the classroom teacher where the observational visit is being made. The supervisor has an important responsibility in making recommendations for revising, modifying, or eliminating selected objectives. Once the objectives are accepted by both teacher and supervisor, the latter observes the quality of teaching to determine if pupils are achieving the objectives. If the behavioural objectives an achieved, the teacher has fulfilled her responsibilities providing that this was not done under negative conditions. Guidelines recommended by educational psychologists must be followed when teaching pupils. Pupils must be interested in the ongoing learning activity. They must also attach meaning to what is being learned. Certainly, pupil purpose in learning is also important.

If pupils did not achieve the stated objectives, the teacher and supervisor must notice if the goals were too difficult to achieve. Evaluation must also be done of the learning activities to determine if they hindered learners in realizing the desired goals.

In the criterion-referenced approach to supervision, it is quite obvious that major emphasis is placed upon behaviourally stated objectives rather than the learning activities which are provided for pupils. Focus is placed upon the learning activities if learners do not achieve the objectives. The criterion-referenced approach to supervision emphasizes objectivity. It emphasizes that pupil achievement can be measured. Learners then demonstrate if they have or have not achieved an objective. Thus, the criterion-referenced supervisor can notice the amount of learning that has taken place. With this approach, the success or lack of success of the teacher in teaching can be observed. Evaluation of teaching success is objective when viewing if from the point of view emphasized by the criterion-referenced approach to supervision of instruction.

Advantages in using the criterion-reference strategy in supervising instruction would be the following:

1. It has a tendency to be more objective than other approaches since success in teaching in measured in terms of pupils having achieved behavioural objectives.
2. Teachers have more security in being evaluated since effectiveness in teaching is measured against the criteria or stated behavioural objectives.
3. The teacher can gather data pertaining to pupil success in learning by noticing if learners have achieved objectives.
4. The supervisor has security in evaluating teacher effectiveness by assessing learner achievement in terms of stated specific objectives.
5. The supervisor has opportunities to modify and/or suggest other behavioural objectives than those written by the teacher.
6. The effectiveness of materials and learning activities used in teaching can be evaluated in terms of the teacher's written behavioural objectives.

Disadvantages that can be listed for the criterion-referenced strategy pertaining to supervising instruction could be the following:

1. The supervisor may have little time to evaluate the relevancy of the teacher's behaviourally stated objectives prior to observing classroom teaching.
2. It is difficult to determine if the behavioural objectives which learners are to achieve could be classified as being relevant.
3. Some of the better quality objectives that learners are to achieve take much time in writing and may be difficult to state as behavioural objectives.

4. Subjectivity is involved in determining which objectives pupils are to achieve.
5. Learners may not always reveal in the supervisor's presence which objectives have been achieved.
6. It is difficult to write behavioural objectives which are attainable for pupils.
7. The teacher may feel pressure in having learners achieve the behaviourally stated objectives.
8. Other important objectives can arise in the teaching-learning situation than what is stated in the behavioural objectives. This would be true when pupils identify important questions when pursuing ongoing learning activities.

Thus, the criterion-referenced strategy pertaining to the supervision of instruction has its strengths as well as weaknesses. If elementary schools adopt this procedure, teachers, principals, and supervisors must be knowledgeable of its philosophy and accept this approach as being worthwhile. Approach used to improve the elementary school curriculum must be based on sound educational thinking.

The Tuition Voucher as an Issue

Literature on the tuition voucher has become more frequent in educational journals. The tuition voucher system is used in a very few schools in the United States. It is an experimental stage where the federal government is aiding these efforts. The tuition voucher plan has as a central idea the giving of tuition money to parents to send their child or children to a school of their own choosing. With parents is selected situations being displeased with their pupils' performance, a teacher can be selected from another school who it is believed can do a better job of providing for individual differences among learners.

Advantages of this plan in aiding learners to obtain a better education could be the following:

1. There is an attempt here in helping children get the best education possible by having parents select the best teacher who can help their offspring realize optimum achievement.

2. This would cause teachers to be selected on a competitive basis and, perhaps, aid them to develop more proficiency in teaching.
3. If there is a personality clash between teacher and pupil, parents could send their children to a different school.
4. Undesirable teachers could be weeded out when parents have a larger voice in who will teach their children.
5. Teachers would feel more accountable for their teaching. Less security may then be placed on tenure.
6. Administrators and supervisors would pay more attention to updating the curriculum as well as methods of teaching used by teachers. They would be keenly aware, no doubt, of a possible drop in enrollment due to parents sending their children to other schools.
7. Parents would become more sensitive in trying to locate the best teachers for their children.

Questions that can be raised about the tuition voucher would be the following:

1. Can parents know which teacher would do the best job of teaching their children?
2. Would some teachers then have an excessively large number of children to teach while others have very small classes?
3. Would teachers be selected in terms of competency in teaching or would hear-say by the determining factor in selecting appropriate teachers?
4. How can parents really be informed about good teachers in selected schools?
5. Is there adequate agreement as to who the good teachers really are?
6. How can teachers who are not selected as good teachers best improve their teaching skills? Should these teachers automatically be dropped from the teaching profession if they are not selected by parents under the tuition voucher system?
7. How should teachers be paid under the tuition-voucher system?

There are no easy answers to many important problems in education. Concerned parents will want the best teachers for their children. The teaching profession itself should desire to encourage and retain good teachers for the high calling of teaching pupils. Individuals who would not develop into becoming good teachers should be channeled into other kinds and types of work. Thus, the strengths of the teaching profession rest upon having high quality teachers as well as professional administrators and supervisors who assist in improving the curriculum for all pupils in the elementary school.

Accountability as an Issue

In recent years accountability has been an important topic to write about in educational literature. It is important that teachers be able to account for what pupils under their jurisdiction have learned. Educational literature generally will state the following, among other things, when expressing ideas pertaining to accountability:

1. The teacher needs to write specific behaviourally stated objectives for each child to achieve.
2. This teacher then is responsible for the strengths of these objectives as well as for pupils achieving them.
3. It is possible to measure if pupils have achieved the objectives.
4. The teacher must select learning activities to help learners realize these precise objectives in an economical way.
5. Parents, boards of education, administrators, and supervisors must have knowledge if pupils have achieved these objectives.

It sounds excellent to speak of teachers being accountable for teaching pupils. Concerned individuals will desire that all pupils develop needed understandings, skills, and attitudes. Developing individuals to their optimum is definitely in harmony with basic generalizations pertaining to democratic living.

There certainly are advantages in emphasizing teacher accountability.

1. Each teacher should help pupils achieve to the highest degree possible in intellectual, emotional, social and physical development.

2. There should be ways of determining if this is actually being done by teachers.
3. Parents should be satisfied that their offspring is receiving a quality education.
4. Supervisors, administrators, and school board members should definitely have much information as to the quality of teaching that each teacher does.
5. Poor teachers should be weeded out of the teaching profession.
6. Objectives for pupils to achieve should be assessed in terms of strengths and weaknesses.
7. Learning activities should be evaluated in terms of guiding pupils to achieve objectives.

One also needs to study the weaknesses of basic ideas expressed about teacher accountability. There are numerous questions that can be raised about this plan pertaining to quality teaching.

1. Can educators determine which objectives are good and relevant for learners to achieve?
2. Can all good objectives be stated with such precision that it can be measured if these have been achieved by learners?
3. Can it be determined if pupils have achieved these objectives?
4. What if learners have forgotten what was taught to them shortly after these learnings were achieved?
5. Can teachers be held accountable for circumstances beyond their control such as having overcrowded classrooms, emotionally disturbed pupils, inflexible supervision and administration, and an inadequate amount of teaching materials?
6. Should teachers alone be held accountable for their learner's achievement? What about supervisors and administrators being held accountable for their stated objectives and means of achieving these ends?

7. Boards of education are in an appropriate setting in most cases in influence desirable changes in education. Their deeds can hinder or help quality programmes in education. Should boards of education state their objectives behaviourally also as well as ways to achieve these stated aims?

8. Should adequate aid be provided for teachers in terms of secretarial help? Should teacher aids also be held accountable for their work? In what ways?

There are numerous factors which influence the duties and responsibilities of classroom teachers. The teacher cannot be taken in isolation and held accountable for what happens to pupils in the teaching-learning situation. Perhaps, all individuals involved directly and indirectly in the teaching of pupils should be held responsible for learner achievement. Thus, the problem of teacher accountability becomes complex indeed!

Open-space Education as an Issue

Many modern elementary schools are emphasizing the open-space concept in teaching. Advocates of this approach feel that many classroom situations are too rigid and formal.

Learning centres have become very important in open-space education. Thus, pupils have a considerable amount of freedom in selecting a learning centre from which to learn. The materials used by pupils at these different centres must be changed frequently to develop and maintain pupil interest as well as provide for individual differences. Let us view a class situation where learning centres are being utilized. In this description, the language arts programme is being stressed.

Pupils can select, from among others, the writing centre. The teacher has placed diverse pictures at this centre. A child can select a picture and write about his observations. If he has not developed a writing vocabulary, ideas can be dictated to the teacher who then does the writing. Pupils can notice that talk can be written down. The teacher together with the child may evaluate the finished product.

A second centre which pupils can select to work in could be the puzzle centre. Here learners would complete crossword puzzles as well as picture puzzles. At a third learning centre, pupils could work with puppets. Two or three children can cooperatively develop a presentation which then is presented to other pupils in the class. The puppets can be purchased commercially or they can be made such as would be true of stick and sack puppets.

At a fourth learning centre, pupils individually could select a library book of their own choosing to read. Following the reading of the book, learners with teacher guidance could determine how comprehension should be evaluated. Some of these ways could include the following: making dioramas, friezes, and murals; drawing a picture; writing a report; giving the report orally to classmates; dramatizing selected incidences; advertising the book to interested consumers; and having a conference with the teacher.

At a fifth learning centre, pupils could be engaged in the playing of games, such as seeing how many "peanuts" can be fed to an elephant. The child, for example, could write homonyms on a slip of paper shaped like a peanut. If he can do this, he can feed the "peanut" to a large attractive elephant made by the teacher or purchased commercially. The learner can then count the number of peanuts fed to the elephant. Synonyms, antonyms, and heteronyms could also be fed to the elephant.

A sixth learning centre could contain a listening centre. Here pupils could listen to stories being told. These tapes could be developed by teachers individually, as well as in committees. They can also be purchased commercially. The tape recorder would have headphones so as not to disrupt learners at other learning centres. Periodically, pupils could be evaluated on listening comprehension. Questions would need to be answered by pupils. These questions should encourage interest in listening to stories. This could spur pupils on in the direction of wanting to read the stories they have listened to. Creative approaches need to be developed to guide learners in wanting to read books of fiction and nonfiction. Too frequently, pupil interest in reading has been destroyed due to poor reading materials as well as inappropriate methods of teaching. Reading instruction must provide for the needs, interest, and abilities of each child.

A seventh learning centre could contain materials to help each pupil achieve optimum development in spelling. If a spelling textbook is used, each pupil could work at his own optimum rate of speed. Separate word lists could also be developed for each child based on individual needs. For example, if a pupil misspells the following words in a functional writing situation, an appropriate set of spelling words can be developed for pupils to study to remedy the situation: although, driver, automobile, urban, rural, neighbourhood, ocean, vacation, recreation, gasoline, mileage, and texas. The number of words each pupil is to learn to spell per week would depend upon his interest, motivation and abilities.

Thus in open-space education, the child can select which learning centre he wishes to work from. The materials on the different centres would need to be selected carefully by pupils and the teacher. They should provide for different achievement levels in a class. The interests, needs, and abilities would be very important to consider when making selections of materials for the various centres where pupil will be working. To make the open-space concept in education more flexible, it is important that pupils have ample experiences in life beyond the confines of the class and school. Field trips and excursions into the community would definitely be an inherent part of the openness in open-space education.

It is quite obvious that there are pros and cons pertaining to open-space education. The strength of the programme could pertain to the following:

1. Pupils can engage in decision making when selecting a learning centre to participate in. The centre of interest selected must contain materials which make provision for individual differences.
2. A relaxed, permissive environment is necessary in open-space education in order that learners can freely select a centre which is stimulating and contains purposeful learning activities.
3. Learning activities go on beyond the confines of the class and school. The community is very important in providing learning activities for pupil.
4. Open-space education is based upon excellent criteria in educational psychology such as providing for the interests, needs, and abilities of individual pupils.

5. Pupils can interact with other children in small groups in diverse learning activities.
6. Learners can have the opportunity of experiencing different teachers and at occasions interacting with learners who are older as well as younger.
7. Teachers serve as guides and stimulators of pupils. They definitely are not lecturers of content.
8. The feelings or attitudes of pupils is held to be very important since learners can make choices in terms of what they like to learn.
9. Good mental health becomes an important concept in open-space education. Learners are not forced in learning a specific number of facts. Neither do pupils by any means all learn the same thing.
10. Mutual respect for each other is important when stressing open space education.
11. Traditional emphasis upon the teacher being a policeman or disciplinarian basically has no value in modern methods of teaching pupils.

There are disadvantages in having pupils participate in learning activities where open-space education is emphasized.

1. Selected learners may not be responsible enough to participate in learning activities in a highly permissive environment.
2. Emotionally disturbed pupils present problems where open-space education is in evidence.
3. Teachers may not have the temperament to work with pupils in a permissive learning environment.
4. It is difficult for many teachers to do away with traditional approaches to teaching.
5. Principals and supervisors have felt that the quiet classroom is where pupils learn best in. Thus, teachers in open spaces may not get needed support.
6. A less skillful teacher may have difficulty in guiding, learner achievement where considerable freedom of choice is involved on the part of pupils in selecting learning activities.

7. Parents may be hard to convince that open-space education will help their offspring to achieve at a higher rate as compared to more traditional approaches in the teaching of children.
8. It is difficult to convert selected older buildings to a type of architecture which is in harmony with more flexible approaches in the grouping of pupils.

Teachers, principals, and supervisors must study different points of view pertaining to teaching-learning situations. Certainly, open-space education has its many strong points and would guide many learners in achieving to their highest potential.

In Summary

There are many issues in education which need to be resolved. At the present time there are no clear-cut easy answers to these problems. Some questions could be raised pertaining to issues in the curriculum which would summarize ideas well, contained in this chapter.

1. How precise should all desirable objectives be stated?
2. Who should be involved in selecting learning activities for pupils?
3. Who should be involved in selecting content for pupils?
4. What emphasis should handwriting receive in the total elementary school curriculum?
5. What role should spelling textbooks play in the language arts programme of the elementary school?
6. How should basal readers be utilized in the curriculum area of reading?
7. What are the advantages and disadvantages of using the Initial Teaching Alphabet?
8. Should there be a national curriculum in the United States? Why?
9. How much emphasis should be placed upon the teaching of grammar in the elementary school?
10. What kind of a balance should there be between inductive and deductive approaches to teaching pupils in the elementary school?

11. How can balance be developed and/or maintained among arithmetic, geometry, and algebra in a modern programme of elementary school mathematics?
12. How much reality should pupils experience in elementary school social studies?
13. How can balance be maintained between individual and group work in the elementary school curriculum?
14. How important is to for all pupils to speak standard English when communication of ideas becomes the major objective?
15. What role should foreign language in the elementary school have?
16. How does the criterion-referenced supervisor assist in improving the curriculum as compared to more traditional approaches?
17. Will the tuition voucher plan improve the quality of teaching that exists in today's public schools?
18. How can teachers be held accountable for learner achievement?
19. Can the open-space concept in education help pupils achieve their highest potential?

REFERENCES

Alcorn, Marvin D., and James M. Linley (eds.). *Issues in Curriculum Development, A Book of Readings*. Yonkers-on-Hudson, New York: World Book Company, 1959.

Alpren, Morton (Ed.). *The Subject Curriculum: Grades K-12*, Columbus, Ohio: Charles E. Merrill Books, Inc., 1967. Chapter Two.

Beauchamp, George A. *Planning the Elementary School Curriculum*. Boston: Allyn and Bacon, Inc., 1956, Chapter 12.

Berman, Louise M. *New Priorities in the Curriculum*. Columbus, Ohio: Charles E. Merrill Publishing Company, 1968, Chapter 11.

Collier, Calhoun C., and others. *Teaching in the Modern Elementary School*. New York: The Macmillan Company, 1967, Chapter 16.

Frost Joe L., and G. Thomas Rowland (Ed.) *The Elementary School, Principles and Problems*. Boston: Houghton Mifflin Company, 1969. Chapter 19.

Frost Joe L., and G. Thomas Rowland. *Curricula for the Seventies*. Boston: Houghton Mifflin Company, 1969, pp. 431-440.

Hyman, Ronald T. (Ed.). *Teaching: Vantage Points for Study*. Second Edition, Philadelphia: J.B. Lippincott Company, 1974. Sections 3, 4 and 5.

Keith, Lowell, and others. *Contemporary Curriculum in the Elementary School*. New York: Harper and Row, Publishers, 1968. Chapter 6.

Johnston, A. Montgomery, and Paul C. Burns (Ed.). *Research in Elementary School Curriculum*. Boston: Allyn and Bacon, Inc., Chapter 2.

Popham, James W., and Eva L. Baker. *Establishing Instructional Goals*. Englewood Cliffs, New Jersey: Prentice-Hall, Inc., 1970.

Ragan, William B., and Gene D. Shepherd. *Modern Elementary Curriculum*. Fourth Edition. New York: Holt, Rinehart and Winston, Inc., 1971. Chapter 17.

Oral Communication and the Curriculum

A basic, in addition to the three r's (reading, writing, and arithmetic), is oral communication. Much of subject matter and opinions communicated is done orally. Within the framework of the three r's, oral communication is continually in evidence and necessary. Thus, in reading, writing, and arithmetic, ideas are discussed, problems are identified, and conclusions are emphasized orally. In society, opinions, facts, concepts, generalizations, and main ideas are elaborated upon. It almost appears as if oral communication permeates whatever transpires between and among persons in school and in society.

Since oral communication is a basic in the curriculum, which objectives, learning experiences, and appraisal procedures are worthwhile to emphasize?

Objectives in Oral Communication

To develop student proficiency in oral communication, objectives need to be carefully identified. Each end must be relevant, significant, and useful to the learner. Trivia needs to be weeded out of the curriculum. Individual differences among slow, average, and fast achievers must be respected. No two students should be held to the same level of attainment. Each student has utmost value and needs assistance to achieve as much as possible. Objectives should be stated at an optimal level at which a student can be successful in learning. The ends then should not stress goals whereby students attain failure in oral communication. Nor should the objectives be so relaxed in that a lack of challenge in learning is in evidence. The language arts teacher needs to preassess and appraise where each student is presently achieving in oral communication. Once the ends have been stated, a stimulating learning environment needs to be in evidence so that each student can achieve ongoing objectives.

Objectives also need to emphasize meaningful content. A learner then must attach meaning to goals being achieved. Rote learning or memorization make for lower cognitive levels of objectives. Facts are the building blocks for students to move on to higher levels of thinking. Students need to comprehend and attach meaning to facts inherent in oral communication. From the cognitive level of comprehension, students need to use what has been learned. Applying what has been acquired is then significant. What is learned in oral communication has utilitarian values in society. School and society should not be separated, but be integrated entities. It is important also for students to be able to analyze or think critically about subject matter in oral communication. Critical thinking involves separating facts from opinions, fantasy from reality, accurate from inaccurate statements, and to make contrasts and comparisons. Creative thinking is a further significant goal in emphasizing meaningful learnings. Novel, unique ideas are significant in creative thinking. New ideas are needed in society to change, modify, and improve the societal arena. Objectives in problem solving truly stress integrating school and society. In society, problems abound. The problems need solutions. Evaluating the quality of each solution is necessary. Objectives then should emphasize what is meaningful to the learner. Content becomes personally relevant and understandable when it possesses the quality of meaning.

Thirdly, objectives should stress securing the interests of students in oral communication. Interest of students is a powerful factor in learning. With interest, the student and the subject matter to be learned become integrated, and not separate entities. Interest tends to provide its very own effort in learning. Interest within learners is established to achieve worthwhile learnings and attain desired objectives. Interest is not trivia or random, but focuses upon goal attainment. Relevant subject matter to be acquired is emphasized when interest becomes a dominant criterion in having students learn and achieve. A very excellent guideline, among others, for the teacher to utilize is to encourage student interest in learning. Objectives in oral communication must reflect the concept of learner interest in the curriculum.

Objectives in oral communication need to emphasize purpose in learning. Reasons then exist for having students achieve objectives. The student tends to accept what is purposeful. A lack of purpose means energy levels are low for learning. Increased purpose for learning emphasizes the student perceiving more reasons for participating in ongoing units of study. Purposes established in oral communication should be clear and attainable for each student. The purposes must be acceptable. Hopefully, from within or intrinsically, the student will perceive reasons to achieve worthwhile goals of instruction.

Fifthly, goals in oral communication should reflect affective ends. Positive attitudes then need to be developed by students. These feelings assist students to acquire subject matter learnings. Quality attitudes toward the self and others are vital. Greater achievement in oral communication is possible if students feel competent and have a desire to learn. Vital affective goals in speaking need identification. Learning activities for students to attain the chosen ends should be in evidence and implemented. Validity in evaluation procedures should follow. The language arts teacher needs to know how well students are achieving in oral communication. It is essential for the teacher to know sequential progress of each student. Only then can ordered objectives be stressed in ongoing lessons and units.

Philosophy of Teaching Oral Communication

Philosophy provides guidance and direction in teachers selecting objectives, learning activities, and appraisal procedures. Diverse philosophies will now be discussed to assist teachers in oral communication curriculum development.

The experimentalist believes that one can know experiences only in life. One then cannot know the real world as it truly is. Nor, can one know ideas alone, of what actually is and exists. Since in experimentalism the person can only know experiences, change in school and in society is in emphasis. With change, problems come into existence. These problems need clarity and identification. After the problem is adequately delimited, data or information may be gathered to secure answers to the problem. The data provides a hypothesis in answer to the problem. The hypothesis is tentative and subject to testing. The hypothesis is then subject to revision. The flexible steps of problem solving involve much oral communication, especially since committee endeavours are recommended by experimentalists. Why? In society, committees are at work to solve problems. All in society are involved in working on diverse committees at different times. Group decision making is at the heart of experimentalism, as a philosophy of education and of life. Within committees, diverse kinds of speaking activities are in evidence. Experimentalists have much to offer in guiding students to develop proficiently in interacting well orally with others. School and society must not be separate, but integrated entities. Problems can be identified by any student in each of the different curriculum areas. Solutions to each problem must be in the offing.

As a second philosophy of education, realism has much to offer to the language arts teacher. The realist tends to believe in whole or part that one can know the real world as it truly is. The real world is there independent of the observer. Since the real world can be known as it truly is, the specific of knowledge is knowable. Precise, measurable stated objectives should be utilized in teaching and learning. After instruction, it can be determined if a student has or has not attained the precise end. Independent of any observer and in measurable terms, one can know if a student has or has not attained the precise end. It is measurable to determine the number of ends achieved by any one learner if the objectives are stated with precision and in observable terms.

Speaking activities for students may emphasize precise objectives to attain. These measurable ends may be written prior to instruction. The objectives should then be announced to students prior to teaching-learning situations being implemented involving oral communication. Diverse kinds of oral expression experiences may be practiced by students such as making of introductions, impromptu speeches, discussions, after-dinner speeches, and advertising a product. After the learning opportunities have been completed, the language arts teacher measures if a student has or has not attained the precise end. The objectives must be clearly stated. After instruction, according to realists, it must be possible to determine if the ends have been attained by students. Guesswork must be eliminated in ascertaining if a student has been successful in goal attainment.

A third philosophy, namely idealism, has much to recommend itself in terms of developing teaching strategies in oral communication. Idealism emphasizes that one can only know ideas about phenomena. One then cannot know in and of themselves how objects truly are in their natural environment. The idea centred idealist stresses a subject centred curriculum. Subject matter, not an activity centred method of teaching, is important to emphasize in ongoing learning situations.

Subject matter, in all its significance and vitality, can be stressed in oral communication. Each student then must be assisted to possess accurate, comprehensive subject matter content in speaking activities in the language arts. Idealists tend to emphasize that students achieve generalizations based on facts. However, the generalizations are more salient than the facts. Therefore, idealists would recommend that students be guided to achieve broad generalizations. These broad ideas can be checked in terms of accuracy. They must be comprehensive to include specific facts.

Idealists also tend to stress ideals. Immanuel Kant (1724-1804) emphasized the Categorical Imperative. The Categorical Imperative, as emphasized by Kant, an idealist, states that one should act and behave in a way that those deeds become universal for all to live by and accept. Certainly, speaking activities can emphasize in discussion settings how to react in order that universal principles would be achieved.

Existentialism, as a fourth philosophy in the oral communications curriculum, stresses the individual in the making of choices and decisions. Life consists then of making awesome choices in an absurd environment. The social and natural environment represents anything but a rational way of life. To be human means to make choices and decisions. If others are permitted to choose for the self, the latter no longer is human. The chooser accepts the consequences of each decision made. Others are not blamed for the results of a choice. The chooser then cannot blame others for decisions made.

In oral communication, discussions, oral reports, debates, and dramatic activities, existentialism can be emphasized. Content in the speaking activities may well emphasize paradoxes in life. Clearcut answers do not exist in terms of resolving dilemmas. One must still choose and make decisions within the absurdity of life's situations. Thus, the subject matter of oral communication can definitely emphasize existential thinking.

What is to be learned by the student can also stress existentialism. Thus, students may select sequential tasks to complete and omit in the use of learning centres. Teacher-student planning of what the latter is to learn can also be stressed, outside the framework of learning centres. However, adequate input in the curriculum must be in the offing from students. Otherwise, learners cannot be involved in the making of choices and decisions, as advocated by existentialists. Content in the curriculum should emphasize values and the clarification of values. To an existentialist, knowledge is subjective, not objective, to the individual making the choices and decisions. Each initiative by the involved person must have a moral basis.

In Closing

The writers have discussed a psychological and philosophical basis to utilize in selecting objectives for students to achieve in oral communication. Criteria to use in selecting objectives would be the following:

1. individual differences need adequate provision;
2. content should make sense and be meaningful;
3. the interests of learners need to be secured for satisfaction to occur in learning;
4. students need to perceive purpose in learning;
5. quality attitudes need to be developed within students.

The above are excellent criteria for language arts teachers to emphasize in selecting goals for student attainment.

The writers also discussed a philosophical basis for making decisions pertaining to oral communication objectives. These include experimentalism, realism, idealism, and existentialism. From a study of philosophy of education, the writers recommend using the following philosophical strands:

1. problem solving approaches to acquire vital subject matter and methods to increase student skills in oral communication;
2. precise objectives and observable results from student achievement. Creative and critical thinking must be hindered in the process;
3. academic content stressing universal knowledge, as advocated by idealists;
4. students learning to make choices and decisions, as recommend by existentialism.

REFERENCES

Cruickshank, Donald R. *Teaching is Tough*. Englewood Cliffs, New Jersey: Prentice-Hall., Inc., 1980.

Henson, Kenneth T. *Secondary Teaching Methods*. Lexington, Massachusetts: D.C. Heath and Company, 1981.

Joyce, Bruce, and Marsha Weil. *Models of Teaching*. Third edition. Englewood Cliffs, New Jersey: Prentice-Hall, Inc., 1986.

Joyce, Bruce, *et al*. *The Structure of School Improvement*. New York: Longmans, 1983.

National Society for the Study of Education. *Staff Development*, Part II. Chicago, Illinois: The Society, 1983.

National Society for the Study of Education. *The Humanities in Precollegiate Education*, Part II. Chicago, Illinois: The Society, 1984.

National Society for the Study of Education. *Education in School and Non-school Setting*, Part I. Chicago, Illinois: The Society, 1985.

National Society for the Study of Education. *The Ecology of School Renewal*, Part I. Chicago, Illinois: The Society, 1987.

National Society for the Study of Education. *Society as Education in an Age of Transition*, Part II. Chicago, Illinois: The Society, 1987.

Phi Delta Kappan. *The Forgotten Half: Non-College Bound Youth in America*. Bloomington, Indiana: Phi Delta Kappa, February, 1988, pp. 404-414.

Grouping Pupils in the Elementary School

Numerous approaches have been recommended by educators in grouping pupils for instruction. Certainty does not exist as to which plan of grouping is best. Each recommended approach of grouping pupils seemingly contains strengths as well as weaknesses. Teachers, principals, supervisors, and parents must consider and assess each of these approaches in grouping pupils for instruction. The psychology of learning is important as well as child growth and development characteristics when making a final decision pertaining to grouping pupils for instruction.

Faculty members of an elementary school need to become thoroughly knowledgeable as to the various possibilities that exist in grouping pupils for instruction. Each plan should be evaluated in terms of acceptable criteria or standards. No thinking person would advocate new approaches to grouping without being fully knowledgeable about their strengths and weaknesses. It is important that there be widespread acceptance of a new plan for grouping before it is implemented. Teachers, principals, supervisors, and parents should be in much agreement about a new plan for grouping before it is implemented. Each elementary school should also study thoroughly the present plan being used for grouping pupils for instruction. Thus, a gap may be noticed between where the school is presently in the area of grouping pupils for instruction as compared to where it should be.

One of the most difficult tasks involved in implementing a new plan for grouping pupils may well be to get parental acceptance. Parents can be satisfied with the most traditional plan of grouping available. The lay public then must reach a stage of disequilibrium whereby they no longer are satisfied with the status quo. The following approaches may be utilized to develop this state of disequilibrium within the lay public:

1. Talks given at Parent-Teacher Association meetings pertaining to new plans of grouping pupils for instruction.
2. Ideas about new plans for grouping being injected when parent-teacher conferences are held.
3. Newspaper articles bringing in items pertaining to new approaches in grouping pupils for instructional purposes.
4. The possibilities of presenting concepts and generalization pertaining to grouping pupils on a local television or radio station should be explored.
5. Talking informally to parents at open house and on other occasions about grouping pupils for instruction.
6. Faculty members of an elementary school should discuss creative approaches in informing the lay public relating to proposed innovations in the schools.

Any plan for grouping pupils is not a panacea. It is a means to an end but not an end in and of itself. The new plan of grouping pupils for instruction should aid in improving the curriculum. It should guide in improving teaching-learning situations in the elementary school. Too frequently faculty members have felt that a new plan for grouping pupils should solve all ills in an elementary school. A newly implemented plan for grouping pupils could present many new problems to the involved school. If a team of teachers cannot work together cooperatively, the innovation may cause more grief than improvement over previous plans of grouping. As another example, in a departmentalized plan for grouping pupils, learners may not develop well emotionally and socially if the teacher goes overboard for teaching subject matter only. Intellectual development of pupils to be sure is important; however equally important is physical, social and emotional development.

Plans for grouping pupils have been misunderstood by teachers, principals, and supervisors. For example, there are elementary schools which are called "nongraded schools" by name only. Teachers by example in their teaching may be emphasizing the use of fifth grade materials, for example, in teaching all fifth graders regardless of capacity and achievement levels. The nongraded philosophy is definitely not being implemented in cases such as these. "Turn teaching" has been confused with team teaching. In turn teaching, each teacher does his or her own preparing for teaching with no cooperative endeavours involved in planning together with other team members in terms of objectives, learning activities, and evaluation techniques. Each teacher then takes his turn in teaching in large group sessions as well as working with smaller groups, and individual pupils. As will be discussed later, team teaching emphasizes that members of a team plan together teaching strategies for a given set of learners. It is important that teachers, principals and supervisors understand the basic underlying principles that each plan emphasizes in grouping pupils for instruction.

There will, no doubt, be different interpretations for the philosophy or rationale behind each plan for placing pupils into groups; however, there will be considerable agreement also in interpretation of the underlying principles pertaining to each plan of grouping. For example, the nongraded elementary school states the importance of pupils experiencing continuous progress. Hardly could pupils experience continuous progress if all pupils in a class are on the same page at the same time when utilizing the basal reader, for example, as a learning activity. The only exception to this case could pertain to a class of pupils which are highly homogeneous in terms of reading achievement. This would indeed be rare, however, when thirty pupils, for example, would make up the total number in a class setting. Even then there would be individual differences that need to be provided for.

The Nongraded School

The nongraded elementary school has much to offer in terms of helping learners to be successful. As was stated previously, a basic principle underlying this approach to grouping is that pupils should experience continuous progress. Teachers can be "overly ambitious" in wanting learners to achieve thus causing pupils to lose out in the ongoing activities. It is no wonder then that pupils experience failure and eventually develop or maintain feelings of inadequacy. Pupils should feel that they are achieving to their optimum thus feelings of success become a part of the child.

In the nongraded elementary school, it is important that teachers attempt to determine reading levels of pupils as early as possible. Pupils are generally grouped homogeneously based on reading achievement. It is good if an elementary school has at least three roomfuls of pupils of a given chronological age. If there were only two roomfuls of eight year olds, for example, it would be difficult to group them homogeneously. The range of achievement in reading in each room would be great indeed. With three roomfuls of pupils of a given chronological age, the chances are fairly good of achieving some degree of homogeneity in grouping pupils for instruction within each classroom. More homogeneity would be possible in grouping if there were more than three roomfuls of pupils on a given age level. Within each classroom pupils could be further grouped into three different achievement levels in reading. Pupils should be placed in the reading group which is in a harmony with their level of achievement. Flexible grouping is important. It is important to put pupils in another group if they demonstrate that the original group they were placed in was not in harmony with their present achievement level. Teachers must evaluate pupil achievement continuously to determine the group that each child would benefit most from. At the end of a specific school year, the teacher should record where learners left off in terms of materials used and skills mastered. This would be important so that pupils do not repeat unnecessarily previous materials read and skills mastered. With the beginning of a new school year, the teacher would need to do some reviewing of what learners had learned previously since some forgetting, of course, will have occurred of previously developed learnings. The teacher would also need to engage in reteaching that which necessitates doing this.

The sky is the limit in pupil achievement in the nongraded school as long as there is continuous progress for learners and success is in evidence. Thus, for example, pupils who would be in the sixth year beyond kindergarten of the nongraded schools could be reading from and using seventh and eighth grade materials providing this harmonizes with their capabilities presently in reading. A slower group of pupils in the same age group may be reading from and using fourth grade reading materials since this harmonizes with their present achievement level. The teacher would accept pupils where they are presently in reading achievement and help them to progress continuously.

Ideally, there should be no failures in the nongraded school. No one, of course, basically likes to be a failure or have feelings of failure. In the graded school concept, some pupils have repeated a grade since they did not achieve up to grade level in reading achievement or did not realize standards set by the teacher. Some cannot achieve up to grade level standards since they lack the necessary capacity, interest, motivation, or home background. For others, it is not challenging enough to realize fifth grade standards in reading, for example, if they are in the fifth grade. Their capacities, interests, and motivation would demand realizing a higher level of achievement than the grade level they are in presently. The nongraded school emphasizes the importance of providing for individual differences. If pupils fail in the graded school, they may use the same materials over again for the next school year. Certainly, this does not help learners to achieve continuous progress. He may even have the same teacher again which constantly can remind him of failure! These examples do not exemplify basic underlying principles of the nongraded school.

There are, of course, some weaknesses of the nongraded school. If pupils would be grouped homogeneously continuously, there would be no opportunities within the school setting for pupils to interact with other children of different capacity and achievement levels. Certainly life in society does not operate that way. Individuals intract with others of different capacities, interests, achievement levels, and background knowledge.

There are teachers who may not wish to teach the slowest group of pupils. They may not have the knowledge, patience, interest, and poise to work with the slowest group of achievers. The attitudes and feelings of the teacher, no doubt, will be reflected within learners. To make matters worse, parents may not have the necessary positive attitudes to accept the fact that their child is in the slowest group. Certainly parental attitudes will also be reflected within their children. Parents in the home reveal their feelings toward school to their children. Sometimes, parents speak openly about their feelings toward school in front of their children. And even if words are not used in communicating feelings and attitudes, the child in the home or school generally is able to understand nonverbal communication.

It should also be pointed out that pupils grouped among the top achievers could develop negative attitudes toward those who achieve less well and have less capacity. In the class setting, teachers need to guide pupils in accepting and respecting others. Respect for others is the heart of democratic thinking.

The Self-Contained Class

Too often, educators have been prone to criticize heavily the more traditional approaches to grouping pupils for instruction, such as the self-contained classroom. Tradition does not in and of itself make a concept or idea bad. There are many traditions in life, which, no doubt, will remain with us forever. However, many customs, beliefs, values, and ideals change due to living in a changing society. Respecting others in the home, school and community will always be an important ideal to strive toward. Critical thinking, creative thinking and problem solving, no doubt, also will always remain important skills for individuals to develop.

The self-contained classroom concept is based on the idea that a teacher can get to know pupils well by teaching them for the major part of the school day. Music, art and physical education could be taught by special teachers. By knowing children well, the teacher should be able to do a good job of providing for individual differences. The teacher can get to know well the child's interests, needs, and abilities in a self-contained class. Teachers have numerous opportunities to become thoroughly familiar with the home background of each child in a self-contained classroom.

A further advantage of the self-contained class is that teachers can help pupils sense the relationship of knowledge. The teacher, for example, can guide learners to sense that social studies and science are related. In units on air, land, noise, and water pollution, the teacher can guide learners in understanding basic scientific principles and generalizations pertaining to this problem in society. Children could also study the effect that pollution has on man. Thus science and social studies would be emphasized as being related. When a committee of pupils reports findings to the class pertaining to research conducted on pollution, the language arts area of speaking is involved. Thus, a teacher in a self-contained class has many opportunities to guide learners in relating knowledge so that it is not conceived to be in isolation. Too frequently, pupils have felt and thought that knowledge is compartmentalized and cannot be related. In problem solving, knowledge which is related will be used in arriving at solutions. In daily living it is important to be able to solve problems. Solutions to these problems generally require content which is related. Too often, individuals who compartmentalize knowledge have a difficult time in using what has been learned in the process of problem solving.

Disadvantages of the self-contained classroom can also be listed. A teacher may find it difficult to teach the different curriculum areas well in a self-contained classroom. Can a teacher do justice in teaching reading and the language arts, social studies, science, mathematics, and perhaps, art and physical education? It certainly does require keeping up with the many separate areas that make up the elementary school curriculum. Sometimes a teacher will say that he does not like to teach science or he does not feel competent in teaching science. That curriculum area then may be slighted and minimized by the teacher. There has been a trend in some elementary schools to departmentalize selected curriculum areas on the intermediate grade level. A teacher who has a strong background of course work in science and elementary education could then teach science to several classrooms of pupils. Other teachers could then select curriculum areas to teach in which they have a strong background of course work on the college and/ or university level. Teachers should teach the curriculum area or areas in which they have the strongest background knowledge in content as well as in methodology. Elementary school pupils in many cases are aware of strengths and weaknesses that teachers have. It takes good teachers to help pupils achieve to their optimum. Subject matter knowledge of teachers, of course, is not the only important consideration or important factor in teaching. The teacher must like children and have an inward desire in wanting them to achieve to their optimum. The good teacher is respectful of children and shows the necessary patience in working with all learners so they can feel successful in learning.

The self-contained classroom then has its strengths and weaknesses as do all plans in grouping pupils for instruction. Since the self-contained room is a traditional plan for grouping, it has become under considerable criticism. However, one must realize that this plan emphasizes that the teacher should know pupils well by being with a given class for a major part of a school day. Pupils in this plan for grouping can be assisted in relating knowledge. The time allotted to each curriculum area in the self-contained room can be flexible. If the teacher needs more time for teaching mathematics in a given school day, perhaps it is feasible to shorten the time devoted to teaching social studies. On a different day, needed additional time can be given for the teaching of elementary school social studies. In other words, in the self-contained classroom, flexibility in scheduling different curriculum areas of the elementary school is possible.

Departmentalization

Departmentalization emphasizes the importance of teachers being well prepared to teach in their area, or areas of speciality. Thus, an elementary school teacher, for example, may teach only mathematics or only reading. The teacher in a departmentalized elementary school generally has a strong background of course work in the area he is teaching. For example, a social studies teacher will have much course work in the social sciences together with ample course work in elementary education. The student may have a double major in the two areas previously mentioned, or have a major in elementary education with a minor or an area of concentration in the social sciences. Thus, the teacher should be well prepared in terms of credit hours in a given academic area on the college and/or university level to teach in a departmentalized school. This teacher would generally have fewer daily preparations to make in a departmentalized plan as compared to the self-contained classroom. The teacher in a departmentalized school may teach social studies, for example, to five, fifth or sixth grade classes.

Not many elementary schools emphasize departmentalization on the primary grade levels. The subject matter knowledge needed on these grade levels is generally not a major problem; however, it is very important for these teachers to be warm, friendly, understanding, and help each child realize his optimum potential.

It becomes difficult to correlate or integrate different curriculum areas in the elementary school when departmentalization is emphasized strongly. Each curriculum area may become an isolated domain upto itself. Various curriculum areas can be correlated or integrated in a departmentalized plan of grouping if teachers teaching the separate academic areas plan together. They could plan together how science and social studies may be correlated so that pupils sense degrees of relationship between these two curriculum areas. For example, when fifth grade pupils would be studying a unit on the "Age of Discovery" in social studies, they could also be developing science principles and generalizations pertaining to magnetism in a unit on "Magnetism and Electricity." With the use of steel needles and a magnet, pupils could develop resultant magnets by stroking the needles in one direction on the magnet. The magnetized needle could then be placed on a cork which is floating in a pan of water. Pupils could observe the poles of the magnetized needle.. Understandings could be developed by learners pertaining to like poles of magnets repel whereas unlike poles attract. The magnetized needle would behave in a similar way in relationship to the north and south magnetic field on the surface of the earth. Compasses became important for sailors during the "Age of Discovery" when new lands and water routes were being explored and discovered.

As a further example, reading and social studies could be correlated in a departmentalized plan of grouping pupils if teachers from these two curriculum areas would plan together. If pupils are studying a unit on "Colonization in the New World" in social studies, the basal reader may have selected stories that relate to that period of time. Thus pupils would have additional opportunities to learn more about the colonists in Colonial America in the curriculum area of reading and this could be correlated with the related ongoing social studies unit. Ample time would need to be given by teachers for planning from the different curriculum areas being taught in a departmentalized plan of grouping so that subject matter areas or different academic disciples may become related in the thinking of pupils. Correlation for the sake of correlating is to be frowned upon. Correlating and integrating of content are important when it helps pupils to develop interest, purpose, and motivation for learning. Also, pupils should not think in terms of isolated, fragmented knowledge to the point of memorizing unimportant facts for test purposes or under threat from teachers and parents. An excessive number of isolated facts which are learned by pupils make retention of learning a major problem. Generally, pupils will retain learnings longer if knowledge is perceived as being related rather than as isolated, unrelated bits of information.

Homogeneous versus Heterogeneous Grouping

Educators have long debated and discussed the pros and cons of homogeneous versus heterogeneous grouping of pupils. Some have stated that homogeneous grouping is not as democratic as it could be since pupils of a similar level of achievement would be placed in a specific group. For example, the top achievers in mathematics in the sixth grade would be in one room in an elementary school followed by the second best achievers being in a different room. Other levels of mathematics achievement would be in separate rooms with the slowest learners in this curriculum area being grouped in a room by themselves. It has been felt by some educators that pupils need to interact with others regardless of achievement levels. Principals, supervisors, and teachers could provide situations whereby learners work and play together with others regardless of capacity and achievement levels even though homogeneous grouping is emphasized for several curriculum areas. For example, pupils could be grouped heterogeneously in physical education, music and art. This type of plan for grouping pupils emphasizes heterogeneity in several curriculum areas of the elementary school. For other curriculum areas, homogeneous grouping could be emphasized such as in mathematics, the language arts, social studies, and science.

Teachers may find it easier to teach a given group of learners if homogeneous grouping is in evidence as compared to heterogeneous grouping since the range of achievement will not be as great within a class. However, teachers may not like to teach a class of slow learners as well as those who achieve at a faster rate of speed. The attitude of the teacher, of course, may be reflected within learners. Since the range of achievement in a class may be very great in heterogeneous grouping, it may pose a problem for some teachers in providing for individual differences. In certain methods of teaching it may not matter much if heterogeneous or homogeneous grouping is utilized. For example, in individualized reading, each pupil basically selects his own library book to read. He generally selects a book which is on his reading level. His own reading of the library book will involve a pace which should be in harmony with being able to comprehend the contents, adequately. Each pupil in a class will read at a different rate of speed. Also, each learner will select a library book which differs in complexity from other library books selected for reading by other children in the classroom. Thus, individual differences can be provided for regardless of capacity and achievement levels of pupils in a class or group. Following the reading of a library book, the teacher may have a conference with the pupil. The teacher can then get data on the learner having comprehend the contents of the library book as well as evaluating pupil interest, enthusiasm, and purpose for reading the book. The teacher can also evaluate the quality of oral reading of the child when the latter reads a section of the library book orally. The teacher can record the results of the conference for future reference. Comparisons can be made of conferences held with each pupil from one time to the next to notice changes in behaviour.

In using individualized reading in the classroom, it is obvious that heterogeneous or homogeneous grouping would not be a major problem. It becomes more of a problem when utilizing basal readers if the teacher feels that all learners in a class or in a group should be at the same place at the same time in using a specific series of these readers. It is only common knowledge that learners in a class differ in capacity, achievement, interests and motivation. Thus, learners in a class cannot be held in the same achievement without detrimental results. For some pupils the expected uniform standards of achievement of traditional teachers will be too difficult where frustration and failure may be the end result. For other learners these standards may be excessively low resulting in boredom and a lack of enthusiasm. The teacher must provide for individual differences regardless of the plan of grouping.

Team Teaching in the Elementary School

A rather recent innovation in grouping pupils for instruction is team teaching. The term "team" implies that teachers work together cooperatively in determining objectives, learning activities, and evaluation techniques when teaching a specific set of learners. Team teaching needs to be differentiated from "turn teaching". In turn teaching, each teacher does his own planning for teaching and then takes his turn teaching pupils either in large group or small group sessions. Other teachers also take their turn teaching these learners. However, there is little or no interaction among teachers when planning the objectives, learning activities, and evaluation techniques.

Democratic planning is very important when team members work together. Team teaching emphasizes that members learn from each other in planning sessions. Thus, inservice education is an inherent part of team teaching as a plan in grouping pupils for instruction. If a leader or member of a teaching team would be very domineering or autocratic, the chances are that individuals, of course, would not learn from each other. There needs to be mutual respect of personalities and ideas presented when team members select the best objectives, the best learning activities, and the best evaluation techniques to be utilized in teaching a given set of learners.

The talents of each teacher should be utilized when providing learning activities for pupils. For example, when large group instruction is utilized in teaching ninety pupils, each team member's strengths should be analyzed to determine who should do the teaching in the large group session. If pupils are studying a unit on "New England—Past and Present," a team member may have travelled extensively in this area as well as studied its past history thoroughly. This team member may have excellent slides, pictures, filmstrips, and booklets pertaining to the New England area. Thus, large group instruction, no doubt, would heavily involve using the talents of this member of the team. At other times, different members of the team will be utilizing their talents involving large group instruction in team teaching.

After the large group session has been completed, all teachers on the team should guide learners in small group sessions. Here, learners can ask questions pertaining to the content of learning activities presented in large group instruction. Additional learning activities, carefully selected, can be provided in small group sessions. The teacher needs to select activities which are meaningful, interesting and purposeful to learners. Pupils need to be actively involved in ongoing learning activities. A variety of learning activities should be provided for learners in small group sessions. It should be pointed out that in large group instruction, the teaching team must consider and select those learning activities which capture pupil curiosity and are relevant for learners. If activities are not selected carefully, it will be difficult to hold the attention of pupils and valuable time in learning will be cost.

Ample opportunity also needs to be given to pupils to work on individual projects and activities. With the guidance of the teaching team, pupils should work on purposeful projects and activities on an individual basis which relate to the large and small group sessions.

Team teaching has long emphasized the importance of teachers using their time wisely in what they were trained and educated to do. Thus, teachers should teach and plan for teaching rather than performing routine tasks such as collecting lunch and milk money, putting overshoes on pupils, and keeping attendance records. During the school day, there should be time available for planning. Planning should not be done before the school day begins and after it ends only. In a team approach, some planning can, of course, be done, during the school day. For example, a team which teaches only social studies in a school year should have a free period each school day when planning can be done.

There are numerous plans available which emphasize basic principles related to team teaching. In the master teacher plan, a teacher would be designated as the leader of the team with status difference. This individual may also receive more salary than other team members due to having additional responsibilities. The master teacher should have demonstrated teaching proficiency in the curriculum area or areas his team is responsible for. His background of course work on the college and/or university level should be strong relating again to the curriculum area or areas his team assumes responsibility for. The master teacher would then be the leader of the team when planning sessions are conducted. He should be able to work together well with others, particularly, team members. The team approach in planning sessions involves "give" and "take" as far as verbal interaction is concerned. The group rather than the individual determines objectives, learning activities, and evaluation techniques.

Another plan for implementing ideas pertaining to team teaching would involve a team of teachers with no one individual being designated as the leader. Teacher A, for example, would present an idea. This idea could by modified by other team members. Teacher B then could modify, substantiate, or bring in new ideas in the planning session. Each teacher as he or she participates becomes the leader at the time ideas are being presented. In planning sessions, the best of thinking must be emphasized. Each idea must be assessed in terms of its worth and value rather than on who presented the idea or ideas. Selected teachers may feel uncomfortable when their ideas are being evaluated by other teachers in a planning session. A teacher may also feel uncomfortable when teaching in front of other teachers in large group sessions. In other words, team teaching may not be the best approach to use in grouping pupils for instruction as far as all elementary school teachers are concerned. Some teachers, of course, will do a better job of teaching in a self-contained classroom where there is little interaction with other teachers in the school pertaining to actual teaching-learning situations. Team teaching, however, can be very beneficial to many classroom teachers. Team members can learn much from each other in planning sessions if a democratic atmosphere exists. Some teachers are motivated to do a better job of teaching if other teachers are observing them in large group or small group sessions as well as when helping pupils in individual projects. Teachers on teams need to be flexible in their thinking so that ideas can be modified and the best of thinking is then in evidence pertaining to teaching-learning situations. When ideas are constructively criticized in planning sessions, teachers should not be offended at these suggestions. Rather, teachers should perceive this situation as occasions to improve the quality of teaching. Inservice education then becomes a part of the planning sessions.

Grouping Within a Class

To provide for individual differences, pupils should have ample opportunities to work in groups. There should be ample times when pupils may select the group they wish to work in. For example, pupils in a class are studying a unit pertaining to Australia. A committee of pupils could be making a relief map of the country. A second committee may be developing a model sheep and cattle station, while a third committee is gathering information from several sources for a report on manufacturing in Australia.

Perhaps, a fourth committee would be involved in dramatizing situations relating to wheat farming in Australia. In teacher-pupil planning sessions, cooperative decisions can be made pertaining to the goals each committee is to realize. Ultimately, each pupil can select the committee he would want to participate in.

There will be times when the teacher may appoint individual pupils to work on different committees. In the example given previously pertaining to committee work in a unit on Australia, the teacher could select pupils to work on each of the committees. For example, pupils who do well in reading content may be placed on the committee doing research on manufacturing in Australia. Other pupils having good eye-hand coordination may be appointed to serve on the committee making the relief map on Australia. In other words, the teacher is placing pupils in committees based on learner capacity, achievement, and interest. All pupils should achieve relevant understandings, skills, and attitudes.

The teacher could use the sociometric device to determine committee members. In using this device to evaluate social and personal growth, the teacher could ask questions of pupils pertaining to the following two areas:

1. If you were doing research on Australia, who would be your first, second, and third choice in selecting committee members to work with you.
2. If you were making a relief map or dramatizing a scene relating to Australia, who would be your first choice, second choice, and third choice, in terms of committee members?

The questions need to be worded on the understanding level of pupils. Pupils must feel confident that the teacher will keep the information obtained strictly confidential. The teacher can use the data to determine committee members. Certainly, pupils will do better work in committees if they can get along well with each other as compared to having a lack of harmony. To be sure, a few learners may feel that being on a committee with friends provides situations where "goofing-off" or "having a picnic" is in order. The teacher needs to develop standards or criteria with pupils when emphasizing committee work so that optimum achievement for all will be in evidence.

It can be excellent if interage grouping is emphasized in the elementary school. In society people of different ages interact with others regardless of age levels. Thus, pupils in an elementary school should have ample opportunities to play and work together regardless of age levels.

Having completed the relief map, the research, the model sheep and cattle station, and having practiced dramatizations pertaining to Australia, pupils from other classes of different age levels can be invited to the classroom to observe the ending or culminating of the social studies unit "Living in Australia." In situations such as these, pupils who are visiting the class which is ending a unit on Australia can learn much content as well as methodology in teaching. Perhaps, the visitors may wish to have similar learning activities in their own classroom. When teachers have ample opportunities to view the teaching procedures used by other professionals, the quality of teaching in many cases should improve.

Criteria for Grouping Pupils

Each elementary school should critically evaluate and develop criteria pertaining to grouping pupils for instruction. Criteria that are developed should harmonize with research findings on child growth and development characteristics. The type or plan of grouping that is implemented in the elementary school should help pupils to achieve to their optimum in intellectual, physical, social and emotional development. The following questions should be considered when evaluating different plans in grouping pupils for instruction:

1. Does the plan of grouping pupils aid in providing for individual differences within a specific class?
2. Does the plan provide ample opportunities for pupils to engage in committee work?
3. Would pupils achieve agreed upon objectives most effectively when this plan of grouping is used?
4. Do teachers think and feel that the plan for grouping being considered would assist them in doing the best job of teaching?
5. Does the plan for grouping pupils for instruction harmonize with the architecture of the school?

6. Does the elementary school have ample audio-visual aids and other materials for teaching which would harmonize with the plan being considered in grouping pupils for instruction?
7. Do parents and the lay public adequately understand and accept the new plan for grouping before it is implemented?
8. Would the plan harmonize with revised, up-to-date educational objectives of the local elementary school?
9. Would the plan in grouping pupils for instruction harmonize with what is known about child growth and development characteristics?
10. Would the plan harmonize with the concepts and generalizations of a democracy?
11. Could a teacher learn from other professionals in the elementary school when a specific plan of grouping pupils for instruction is utilized?
12. Do pupils have ample opportunities to interact with learners of different capacity and achievement levels as well as with those of similar capacity and achievement?
13. Would pupils have occasions to work with learners of a younger age level as well as with older children?
14. Would plan of grouping pupils for instruction provide the child with needed security and status?

Numerous plans exist in grouping pupils for instruction. Each plan has its strengths and weaknesses. Thus, careful evaluation of each plan is important before it is implemented. The nongraded elementary school places primary emphasis upon continuous progress of learners. The self-contained classroom stresses the importance of teachers getting to know pupils well so that this information can be used to do a better job of teaching. Relating of different curriculum areas is also emphasized as being important in the self-contained classroom. The departmentalized elementary school emphasizes the importance of using the strengths of teachers in teaching a specific curriculum area such as mathematics, social studies, science, or reading. Thus, the teacher can become specialized and highly proficient in teaching a specific curriculum area. Homogeneous grouping stresses the importance of having pupils in a class who are as alike as possible in capacity and achievement. Heterogeneous grouping emphasizes the importance of learners having a variety of capacity and achievement levels within a specific class. In team teaching, teacher strengths must be utilized in teaching a specific curriculum area, such as social studies, science, mathematics, or reading. This would be true of large group and small group sessions as well as in aiding learners in individual study. In a term approach, members have ample opportunities to learn from each other when planning sessions are in operation to determine objectives, learning activities, and evaluation techniques for a given set of learners. Teaching in a team approach have occasions to observe each other in teaching-learning situations. Within a class setting, the teacher must use a variety of acceptable criteria in grouping pupils for instruction in order to provide for individual differences.

REFERENCES

Blitz, Barbara. *The Open Classroom, Making it Work*. Boston: Allyn and Bacon, Inc, 1973.

Collier, Calhoun C., and others. *Teaching in the Modern Elementary School*. New York: The Macmillan Company, 1967. Chapter Four.

Ediger, Marlow. *Social Studies Curriculum in the Elementary School*. Kirksville, Missouri: Simpson Publishing Company, 1971. Chapter Six.

Goodland, John I. *School, Curriculum, and the Individual*. Waltham, Massachusetts: Blaisdell Publishing Company, 1966. Chapter Four.

Hilson, Maurice (Ed.). *Elementary Education, Current Issues and Research*. New York: Free Press, 1967. Part X.

Jarvis, Oscar T., and Lutian R. Wootton. *The Transitional Elementary School and Its Curriculum*. Dubuque: William C. Brown Company, 1966. Chapter Five.

Lee, J. Murray, and Doris May Lee. *The Child and His Curriculum*. New York: Appleton-Century-Crofts, Inc., 1960. Chapter Five.

Lee, J. Murray. *Elementary Education Today and Tomorrow*. Boston: Allyn and Bacon, Inc. 1969. Chapter Seven.

—*Foundations of Elementary Education*. Boston: Allyn and Bacon, Inc., 1969. Chapter Seven.

Wolf William C., and Bradley M. Loomer. *The Elementary School, A Perspective*. Chicago: Rand McNally and Company, 1966. Chapter Nine.

Discipline in the Elementary School

Not much is written about the problem of discipline in the elementary school. One reason for this, perhaps, deals with the fact that children differ from each other in many ways and approaches to disciplining one child may, of course, not work with another child. Another reason may be that the word "discipline" has a negative connotation. Also teachers perceive things differently when identifying a child as being a discipline problem. Thus, teachers disagree with each other as to which child or children are discipline problems.

Approaches of the Past Used in Disciplining Learners

In Colonial America, Purtians in New England felt that pupils were born in sin. Since Adam in the Garden of Eden had eaten fruit from the forbidden tree, Puritans thought that each human being was thus born in sin. The thinking then was that evilness or sin was inherited since each person was born in sin. It was of utmost importance to Puritans that teachers had correct beliefs pertaining to the Bible and the Puritan religion. Thus teachers would know what was correct for children to believe. Many teachers generally could then drive the evilness or sin out of pupils through the use of physical punishment, according to beliefs of the Puritans. Not all teachers in Colonial days, of course, believed in using physical punishment in disciplining children.

Puritans, as a whole, generally did not believe in play as being a worthy goal for children. Thus, children being born in sin needed to be corrected and learn that which adults felt was important to learn. Materials used in teaching did not emphasize that which was in harmony with pupils' interests. For example, in learning to read, the pupil would first memorize the individual letters of the alphabet. Certainly, this activity generally did not get the interests of pupils. The memorization method of learning as emphasized here stressed the importance of pupils learning that which is abstract to begin with. The horn book which was first used to teach pupils in Colonial New England had one page of content consisting of the upper and lower case letters of the alphabet plus the benediction and the Lord's Prayer. These were abstract learnings then that pupils developed through the methods of rote learning and memorization. Rote learning and memorization of content as a method of teaching, of course, generally does not capture the interests of pupils. Educators have long advocated that pupils begin with the simple and move to the more difficult gradually. Or, pupils should begin with the real or concrete and move to the semi-concrete and then to the abstract as their present achievement level will permit in developing meaningful learnings. It is small wonder that Puritan teachers used physical punishment in disciplining children if the following beliefs were adhered to:

1. Individuals were born in sin due the original sin committed by Adam in the Garden of Eden.
2. Sin had to be driven out of children.
3. Teachers could be obtained who had correct beliefs pertaining to the Bible and Puritan doctrine.
4. Individuals were predestined to be saved.

As individuals from diverse faiths entered Colonial America, religious and educational thinking was revised. The harsh treatment given by Puritans of their own children and of others who did not adhere to their doctrine would soon aid in minimizing the importance of their thinking.

After the American Revolutionary War, the thinking of Americans turned gradually away from the heavy emphasis upon religion to more secular thought in the curriculum. With more diversity in religious faiths, modification of thinking was bound to occur. People would hear of the religious thinking of others and gradually change their own thinking. The Revolutionary War emphasized that the here and now was important in wining the war with Great Britain. Increased trade within and outside the original thirteen states of the United States stressed the importance of secular facets of living such as the study of arithmetic. Records, for example, needed to be kept of goods and services bought and sold as the United States in the beginning of its history increased its efforts in trade and commerce.

With the introduction of the Lancastrian Monitorial System of Instruction from England to the United States, new approaches to teaching were emphasized. In the area of discipline, emphasis was placed upon the use of more humane approaches other than the use of physical punishment. Thus, pupils were encouraged to behave "properly" through the use of embarrassment. A child who did not behave as the monitor or master teacher wished him to behave could be paraded around the room so other pupils would clearly notice the offender. The offender then in the future would, no doubt, vow to never do the same thing again which caused this embarrassment. Children could also be punished in groups using the methods of embarrassment. They would then be seen by all other pupils in the room who could vividly observe the wrongdoers.

There are teachers today who still implement the outdated approaches of using physical punishment and/or embarrassment in disciplining pupils. In most cases, these approaches would not be used as rigidly today as compared to the days of Colonial America or the Lancastrian Monitorial System. The following reasons would be given for not using these approaches in the 1970's.

1. Pupils are not helped in emotional development since positive attitudes cannot be developed when pupils are negatively affected by physical punishment or embarrassment in classroom teaching.
2. Learners cannot develop well socially if individual pupils are isolated from other children when negative approaches to disciplining are being used. Thus pupils may not respect those who are being punished in a negative way. Good teaching would help learners to be accepted by others.
3. It is very difficult for pupils to develop adequate self concepts when being threatened by physical punishment or embarrassment.

4. Positive efforts of pupils should be rewarded; learners then will want to get rewards, such as praise, and thus put forth more effort in exhibiting positive behaviour in order to get needed recognition.
5. Some pupils may get needed recognition through negative ways of disciplining unwanted behaviour in the class. These pupils may not get recognition in any other way. Thus, the teacher is actually encouraging negative behaviour on the part of selected individuals.
6. Minimizing human beings is not in harmony with basic ideas relating to democracy as a way of life. Democratic living stresses the importance of human beings respecting each other.
7. If pupils are to become contributing members in a democratic society, they must develop positive attitudes toward others, the school, and society.
8. The teacher serves as a model to pupils in the area of democratic living. Pupils in the elementary school are always learning from their environment. The classroom teacher is a very important person in this environment.
9. Pupils should have a voice in determining standards of conduct for learners to follow. There should be frequent evaluation of pupil achievement in terms of these guidelines. Self-evaluation by pupils would be important in the evaluation process. The teacher should also continuously evaluate pupil achievement in developing self-discipline.
10. The teacher should evaluate his own teaching to determine if discipline problems arise because of faulty objectives, learning activities, or evaluation techniques.
11. Certainly, better approaches can be found to discipline pupils other than physical punishment or embarrassment.
12. The different curriculum areas of the elementary school should definitely not provide content to use when disciplining pupils.

Stimulus-Response Psychology and Discipline

Each school of thought pertaining to how pupils learn has some basic principles to suggest in disciplining pupils. The stimulus-response school of thought would emphasize reinforcement as a very important concept. A child who behaves well should be praised for his efforts in disciplining himself. Thus, the learner will do his best to exhibit proper behaviour since he generally will want recognition or reward. Most people desire praise for work well done and the child is no exception. Too frequently, teachers have hesitated in giving pupils recognition for good behaviour. The stimulus-response school of thought pertaining to how pupils learn emphasizes that undesirable behaviour will have a tendency to lose its power if the teacher and pupils do not pay attention to it. In some cases, this is very difficult to do. If the child continues to disrupt the class, certainly the teacher needs to approach this problem from the point of view that other children cannot realize their highest achievement in situations such as these.

Reinforcement of positive behaviour of learners has long been recognized as an important way of dealing with behavioural problems in school. The law of recency would also be important here in that, all things being equal, the more recent reinforcement has been used in praising positive behaviour, the more effective this approach will be. This would also mean that continuous reinforcement of desired behaviour from pupils would have positive results. The law of effect would pertain to the more favourable the child responds to what is being learned, the sooner the learning will be achieved. This would be true if all other factors or variables cold be kept constant. Thus, rewarding good behaviour should have positive effects upon pupils.

The gastalt school of thought in terms of how pupils learn emphasizes the total child in a given situation. The child who is scolded in front of the class for a misdeed generally will not feel positive over the incident. Continuous experiences such as these would make for poor emotional development. The child then will not like school as well as he should. The feelings, a child has toward school will affect the total child. These feelings, positive or negative, will have their influence in how well a child achieves intellectually. If a child has a negative attitude toward school and himself, he will not do well in realizing understandings objectives. He will also lack in achievement in the area of skills development. If a child is reprimanded in front of others for misbehaviour, he may not be able to make the friends he would desire to make. His friends may minimize or desert him. Or, he may join others who feel rejected and left out of the mainstream of affairs. Thus, social development is being hindered in situations such as these. If learners feel negatively toward themselves and others, together with underachievement intellectually, the chances are the learner also will not develop as well physically as he should. Thus, gestaltists emphasize the total development of pupils. Negative approaches to disciplining a child then would have its effects upon the total development of pupils.

It is quite obvious that both the stimulus-response and gastalt schools of thought have important implications for disciplining pupils in the elementary school.

Don'ts in Disciplining Pupils

Practitioners in the field of education many times ask the question pertaining to how then should pupils be disciplined who disrupt others in the class. There is definitely no easy answer to this question. What works with one child may not work with another child with positive approaches that are utilized. Negative approaches, of course, have harmful effects upon pupils in terms of personality development. Reputable teachers, principals, supervisors, as well as writers in the field of education emphasize the following "don'ts" pertaining to disciplining children.

1. Do not use subject matter to punish children. For example, do not have a child work page 57 in his mathematics textbook for a misdeed. He may associate punishment with mathematics if this is done. Thus, he generally will learn to dislike mathematics is situations such as these.
2. Don't scold pupils for their shortcomings in front of other children. If this is done, the child being reprimanded has a tendency to be isolated from friends and peers. Children should rather be helped in the making of friends.
3. Don't have children stay in during play period for misbehaving. Pupils need variety in learning activities, and play makes for a definite change in daily routine.

Learners need ample opportunities to engage in physical exercise in addition to those learning activities which require little or no physical movement.

4. Don't use physical punishment since this is not humane and better approaches are available to change pupil behaviour.

5. Don't use approaches in disciplining pupils which tend to minimize children. Each child needs to develop an adequate self concept so he can achieve to his optimum in school work as well as in society.

In the previous discussion, many references have been made as to what not to do in attempting to change negative behaviour of pupils. There are many things the teacher can try in attempting to improve pupil behaviour in the school setting. Among these ways would be the following:

1. Learn as much as possible about the home of the child. If parents do not get along or if there is illness in the home, this will definitely affect a child's behaviour. Abnormal disagreements and rivalry among children in a home will also affect a given child's behaviour in school. A neglected or an unwanted child in a home situation can definitely not exhibit the best kind of behaviour in school. Thus, teachers need to learn much about the home situation and try to understand the child from his very own point of view.

2. The teacher should evaluate his own teaching. A textbook centred approach to teaching does not provide for enough children. For some learners, the textbook is too difficult to learn from. For others, it is too easy. In other cases, the textbook is not the most interesting material to use in teaching. All pupils crave variety when it comes to materials and methods in teaching. Discipline problems can arise when approaches to teaching children need to be modified or changed completely.

3. A few teachers expect pupils to be passive individuals. Their thinking is that children need to sit very quietly at their desks in order for learning to take place. Learning then is equated with pupils being quiet and passive.

Somehow, these teachers have not kept up with recent trends in teaching. They do not recognize that pupils should be actively involved in ongoing learning activities. When pupils in committees engage in conducting and discussing science experiments, there will be some noise in the class; however, learning in a positive direction may be taking place. Certainly, noise for the sake of having noise is a negative approach to teaching. Busy learners, however, will be making some noise. Learners in a committee sharing ideas obtained from using a variety of reference sources cannot do this in a quiet classroom environment where one could hear a pin fall to the floor.

4. The teacher should definitely not confuse creativity and misbehaviour of pupils. Some teachers have scolded pupils who ask many questions and do not like prescribed ways of doing things. These learners may also have been scolded for not giving exact answers to questions in words that the teacher wants the responses to be in. Perhaps, the teacher has only asked questions where one word or several words are needed as answers. These are pat answers to questions. Creative children like questions where diversity of ideas can be discussed. Thus, unique answers to problems can be discussed. This gives opportunities for creative children to be playful with ideas. Teachers need to study characteristics of creative children and provide for these learners in the elementary school.

5. The teacher should use praise freely for those who are meeting proper standards of behaviour pertaining to a good learning environment. There are teachers who are afraid to praise positive behaviour. Perhaps, they feel that pupils will then misbehave as a result of having received praise. Other teachers have never engaged in the practice of rewarding learners for good behaviour. Teachers need practice in giving praise to pupils for better behaviour. They can tape-record their own teaching and notice if adequate rewards are given. In the analysis of the tape-recording, the teacher can notice if the verbal reward is

varied or if it is the same. It gets rather monotonous for pupils unless there is variation not only of learning activities, but also of verbal rewards. The teacher can use the words "that's good!" to praise learners. Other varied expressions should also be used such as following" "excellent!" "tremendous!" "very good!" "that's dandy!"

Nonverbal communication can also be used effectively in praising pupils for improved behaviour. The following, among others, can be used to reward pupils using nonverbal communication:

(a) a smile by the teacher;

(b) a positive nod of the head by the teacher.

6. Reasonable criteria or standards of conduct should be developed cooperatively between the teacher or teachers and learners. Pupils entering a new class for the first time, in many cases, do not know what is expected of them in terms of standards of conduct. There are first grade teachers, for example, who have a permissive learning environment. They permit pupils to talk freely with each other during the school day pertaining to different learning activities. Learners here can get materials from different places in the classroom whenever the need arises. Also, pupils can move sequentially from one centre of learning in the class to another centre of their own choosing. The teacher serves as a consultant or helper to pupils but not as a lecturer or an explainer of knowledge. He is a friendly, secure person in dealing informally with pupils. Pupils learning this class setting and moving to a second grade room for the next school year could experience the following as the year progresses:

(a) Pupils sit in straight rows.

(b) No one can get up from their desks without permission from the teacher.

(c) There is no committee work.

(d) Pupils are learning largely from the use of textbooks, workbooks, and duplicated materials.

(e) The teacher does much lecturing and explaining.

(f) There is basically no noise in the room.

(g) A rigid time schedule is followed in teaching pupils.

(h) Pupils line up to come into the room and to leave the classroom.

(i) Exact one, two or three word answers are given to questions asked by the teacher.

(j) The teacher is very formal in teaching much subject matter to pupils.

(k) Children basically are not praised for improved efforts and work.

(l) The teacher is a very rigid individual expecting learners to complete all textbooks, workbooks, and duplicated materials in the allotted time he feels is just for the class as a whole.

It is no wonder that pupils having been in the previously described first grade room and now being members of this second grade class find it difficult to determine as to what makes for good behaviour. It certainly is necessary that all educators keep up-to-date pertaining to modern trends in the teaching of elementary school children. It is also necessary to discuss with pupils standards of conduct that will permit a good learning environment. Democratic living emphasizes that pupils be actively involved in developing these standards with teacher guidance. Pupils need to know what criteria to follow in terms of standards of conduct in the class setting. The teacher, as well as pupils, needs to evaluate these criteria frequently to determine if they stand in the way of each child realizing his optimum achievement. Quality standards of conduct in the class and in the general school environment should help each child achieve to his highest potential. The teacher should guide learners frequently to assess their behaviour in terms of these standards.

7. A common cause of misbehaviour in the class occurs when the teacher uses too much lecture. It is easy for pupils to refrain from listening in situations such as these.

During the time the lecture is in operation, it is difficult for the teacher to actually know if learners are comprehending. The child may even look at the teacher making it appear as if he is listening when this is not actually the case. Carefully selected questions should be used in teaching to determine pupils' present level of achievement as well as comprehension. The teacher must observe pupil behaviour carefully when teaching. If pupils appear to be bored or if they have turned off, the teacher then can change the kind of learning activity that is now being provided to something different thus avoiding many behavioural problems. The teacher must approach each pupil in terms of getting him involved on his present achievement level so that no time basically is available for misbehaviour.

8. The teacher can definitely not afford to have pupils lose interest in learning. If pupils are not interested in what is being taught, behavioural problems have a tendency to develop. The kinds of learning activities that generated interest in learning a generation ago are no longer suitable for today' pupils in the elementary school. Too many teachers complain about pupils not wanting to learn when actually the teacher is not carefully selecting learning activities in terms of learner interest. These teachers, no doubt, may actually feel that pupils should be interested in learning no matter what is being taught. This is impossible! A few teachers actually feel that by piling work on pupils (way beyond what his capabilities permit), a challenge exists for completing the work. These teachers then may feel that this is a good way of challenging pupils.

There are selected learning activities which are more interesting to pupils as compared to others. Among these would be the following on the appropriate achievement levels of pupils: using films, filmstrips, slides, excursions, pictures, discussions, resource personnel, tapes, replicas, and models. Thus it should encourage the teacher to assess prior to teaching, during teaching, and after teaching, as to which learning activities capture pupil interest. Too many teachers are not willing to engage in self-evaluation and ask if their own teaching is at fault when discipline problems arise. Learners definitely will engage in more misbehaviour if they are not interested as compared to being interested in an ongoing learning activity. The teacher could involve pupils in evaluating learning activities which have a tendency to interest pupils as compared to those which do not capture pupil interest.

9. Pupils will also tend to exhibit problems in behaviour if they do not understand what is being taught. Thus, there is more time available for disrupting others since the learnings presented do not make sense. The teacher must assess learner achievement to determine where they are presently in achievement. The activities must then be provided in good sequence from the child's point of view. If this were done, discipline problems in the class could be cut down considerably. It, of course, will not eliminate all discipline problems, but it will tend to cut down on many of these problems.

10. Teachers perceive their roles incorrectly. The task of the teacher is to teach all children. Too frequently, teachers have thought of their responsibilities consisting of sorting learners in terms of those who should be successful as compared to those who are to be failures in life. These teachers may even verbalize that everything possible is being done to provide for individual differences in the class setting. They may use slogans like "making learning interesting, meaningful, purposeful, and meeting the needs of learners." However, careful observation of these same classes may reveal that all pupils are at the same place at the same time with reading materials being utilized predominately. Those pupils that do not meet the arbitrary standards of the teacher are called down in front of other children and scolded in a rude manner in class. What is actually done in teaching pupils is much different from the verbal statements that are made. There are numerous causes for this situation:

   (*a*) Teachers may actually not know what it means to provide for individual children in a class.

(b) They may be biased toward pupils who are below average in capacity or who underactive in different curriculum areas of the elementary school.

(c) Selected teachers do not like pupils who come from disadvantaged homes. These pupils may not dress neatly and may not have good clothes in terms of teacher expectations.

(d) There are teachers who, unfortunately, are baised toward pupils who come from minority groups. They may even feel these pupils should be flunked rather than taught. There certainly is a big difference in attitudes between teachers who are positive and feel that all children should be taught to realize their highest potential versus teachers who are negative and have the concept of failing pupils in their minds continuously.

(e) A few teachers having taught in a specific district for some time have felt that a child cannot do well in school because one or both of the parents were failures in the different curriculum areas of the elementary school. Sometimes, the feeling exists on the part of these teachers that the father and/or mother of a pupil never "amounted to much," so how can the offspring be any different.

(f) The mental health of selected teachers certainly is not what it should be. The teacher may have a personal need to dominate children. Perhaps, the teacher has an easy way of releasing her frustrations by taking it out on children. It would be excellent if there were a test which could very accurately measure the mental health of teachers in relationship to liking all pupils and wanting to help learners realize their optimum achievement.

(g) Too many teachers after having received a baccalaureate degree in teaching do not keep up with modern trends in teaching the different curriculum areas of the elementary school. They lack information pertaining to the psychology of teaching and learning. If the teacher has this information, it may not be utilized in the teaching-learning situation. Thus teachers need to study recent trends in elementary education. The school must have a professional library for teachers to use. Good teaching must be identified and rewarded, thus spurring other teachers on in improving their own skills. Workshops should be conducted to improve the curriculum. Improving the curriculum deals with a good learning environment for pupils where all can realize their potential!

In Summary

Outdated approaches in disciplining elementary school pupils would pertain to the use of physical punishment and embarrassment of pupils. These approaches are still used by some teachers in public schools of the United States. There are many reasons which can be given for not using negative techniques in dealing with discipline problems in the public schools. Among these would be the following: *(a)* emotional and social development are not developed to their optimum; *(b)* it is difficult to develop feelings of adequacy; *(c)* it may actually give pupils needed recognition; *(d)* democratic living is then not in evidence; *(e)* teachers do not present good examples for learners to follow; *(f)* the teacher may be at fault for discipline problems existing in the class setting; and *(g)* pupils can learn to dislike the school and what it stands for.

The stimulus-response school of thought pertaining to how pupils learn emphasizes the importance of teachers reinforcing positive behaviour on the part of children. The gestalt theory of learning stresses the importance of the whole child when thinking about disciplining pupils. In other words, how a child feels toward the teacher and school will affect intellectual, social, and physical development.

Numerous "don'ts" have been given pertaining to disciplining pupils for negative behaviour. Among these "don'ts" would be the following: *(a)* subject matter areas should not be used to punish children; *(b)* pupils should not be reprimanded in front of others; *(c)* play-time should not be used for changing negative behaviour; *(d)* the use of physical punishment as well as embarrassment of pupils are negative approaches to changing learner behaviour.

There are many things the teacher can do to keep discipline problems from arising in the class. Among the approaches that can be utilized are the following: *(a)* know the child and his home background thoroughly; *(b)* evaluate one's own teaching to determine if this causes some of the discipline problems in the class; *(c)* the teacher should not expect pupils to be passive individuals; *(d)* teachers must keep up with modern methods of teaching; *(e)* good behaviour should be reinforced; *(f)* reasonable, consistent standards of conduct should be employed by teachers throughout the elementary school years of pupils; and *(g)* principles of learning recommended by educational psychologists should be followed when teaching pupils. Good mental health on the teacher's part is very important when teaching pupils.

REFERENCES

Clarizio, Harvey F. *Toward Positive Classroom Discipline*. New York: John Wiley and Sons, Inc., 1971.

Collier, Calhoun C., and others. *Teaching in the Modern Elementary School*. New York: The Macmillan Company, 1967, Chapter Eleven.

Crary, Ryland W. *Humanizing the School, Curriculum Development and Theory*. New York: Alfred A. Knopf, 1969. Chapter Four.

Frost, Joe L., and G. Thomas Rowland (Eds.). *The Elementary School, Principles and Problems*. Boston: Houghton-Mifflin Company, 1969. Chapter Eight.

——. *Curricula for the Seventies*. New York: Houghton-Mifflin Company, 1969. Chapter One.

Inlow, Gail M. *The Emergent in Curriculum*. New York: John Wiley and Sons, Chapter Four.

Jarvis, Oscar T., and Lutian R. Wootton. *The Transitional Elementary School and its Curriculum*. Dubuque: William C. Brown Company, 1966. Chapter Four.

Hoover, Kenneth H., and Paul M. Hollingsworth. *Learning and Teaching in the Elementary School*. Boston: Allyn and Bacon, Inc., 1970. Chapter Fourteen.

Hyman, Ronald T. (Ed.). *Teaching: Vantage Points for Study*. 2nd Edition. Philadelphia: J.B. Lippincott Company, 1974. Section 1.

Lee, J. Murray, and Doris May Lee. *The Child and His Curriculum*. New York: Appleton-Century-Crofts, Inc., 1960. Chapter Five.

MacDonald, W. Scott. *Battle in the Classroom*. Scranton: International Textbook Company, 1971.

Nerbovig, Marcella H., and Herbert J. Klausmeier. *Teaching in the Elementary School*. Third Edition. New York: Harper and Row, Publishers, 1969. Chapter Sixteen.

Smith, James A. *Setting Conditions for Creative Teaching in the Elementary School*. Boston: Allyn and Bacon, Inc., 1966.

Thomas, George I., and Joseph Crescimbeni. *Individualizing Instruction in the Elementary School*. New York: Random House, Inc., 1967. Chapter One.

Spelling in the Curriculum

Correct spelling of words needs adequate emphasis in teaching-learning situations. Why? Proficient communication is aided when written or typed content contains words which are correctly spelled. A quality language arts curriculum then must place thorough emphasis in aiding students to spell words correctly.

Criteria for a Quality Spelling Programme

Whatever decisions are made in life, standards or criteria are utilized. In teaching and learning situations, the teacher needs to:

1. Select worthwhile goals for students to attain. Trivia must be omitted in the curriculum. In spelling, the words students are to master need to be significant presently, as well as in the future. There is much for each to learn. It behooves the instructor to choose carefully those words for learners to spell correctly which are salient and relevant.

2. Smphasize the concept of balance in the curriculum. Thus, in spelling pupils need to develop vital understandings, as well as skills and attitudes. All three kinds of objectives need to be stressed. Understanding goals are not adequate in and of themselves, such as learners acquiring facts, concepts, and generalizations related directly to definitions or meanings of spelling words. Rather, skills (utilizing the newly mastered spelling words in functional writing) and attitudes (positive feelings in wanting to learn to spell words

correctly) are equally significant goals. Skills then pertain to the use of what has been achieved within the framework of understanding goals. Attitudes reveal a desire to increase the levels of understanding and skills.

3. Guide pupils to perceive purpose or reasons for mastering a given set of spelling words. When inductive methods are utilized, the teacher guides students in discovering reasons for learning to spell selected words accurately. With a deductive method, the language arts instructor explains reasons as to why students need to learn to spell words correctly within a spelling unit. In using extrinsic rewards to aid students to perceive purpose in spelling, awards are announced ahead of time as to the number of words a learner needs to spell correctly in order to receive a prize, a badge, or certificate for achievement. Exhortation may also be used by the teacher to promote perceived purpose. Thus, the teacher stresses the importance of learning to spell words correctly. However, reasons are not given. With exhortation the teacher could say, "It's very important for you to learn to spell these words correctly in unit one in our spelling textbook."

The teacher needs to utilize the four above-named means of guiding students to perceive purpose early in a spelling unit as well as frequently.

Norton wrote:

> Many current articles deal with the writing crisis in American schools. Poor spelling is often cited as a major problem with children's writing. The school programme must help students learn to spell the words they need to know; provide instruction in reliable spelling generalizations; develop an understanding of word meanings and vocabulary; equip the speller with more than one strategy for spelling-word attack; incorporate spelling into all areas of the curriculum; proceed from sound diagnostic evaluation; and provide for the development of motivation, positive student attitudes and sound habits for studying spelling and proofreading.
>
> Diagnostic approaches to spelling instructional stress the placement of students on appropriate spelling instructional levels. In addition to instructional placement, the diagnostic teacher also analyzes the

types of errors a child makes in writing. This information is used to individualize the spelling programme for each child. Informal tests for spelling placement, spelling generalizations, and error analysis can be developed by the classroom teacher.

Spelling words are selected according to several different criteria. The frequency-of-use approach stresses that spelling instruction should be based on the words that are the most frequently used. Consequently, it is believed that words most frequently used in writing should be taught first, words commonly used by children in a specific grade should be taught in that grade, and words needed in other content areas should be taught in the appropriate grade. Another quite different selection criterion emphasizes the phonic regularity of words. The words selected for this approach would follow a consistent spelling pattern. Some linguists and psycholinguists also stress the consistency of spelling patterns in words of similar meanings. Thus, spelling instruction should allow students to compare, contrast, and categorize words according to root words, word origins, and similarities in structural patterns.

Several techniques have proven valuable in a developmental approach to spelling instruction. The corrected-test method allows immediate feedback, and liberates students from the systematic study of words already mastered. The self-study method allows students to master their own individualized spelling words. An inductive approach to teaching spelling generalizations allows students to discover and use the reliable spelling generalizations.

Remedial spelling approaches have been developed for the more disabled speller. The Fernald approach has been useful with learning disabled children. In this multisensory method, the child looks at the word, traces the word, then writes the word without looking at it. Spelling games are useful for reinforcing and motivating the remedial spelling student. Spelling should not, however, be taught as an isolated subject. Students, whether remedial, regular developmental, or gifted, require many opportunities to use spelling in meaningful situations.

4. Choose a variety of interesting learning activities for students. To achieve interest within learners, diverse activities need to be in the offing. The experiences may include:

   (a) activities contained in spelling textbooks, workbooks, and worksheets;

   (b) commercial and teacher developed games;

(c) crossword puzzles in which the list being studied in spelling provides answers for the vertical and horizontal lines;

(d) computerized drill, practice, and games;

(e) spelling bees where competition is wholesome and educational;

(f) purposeful, practical experiences including writing friendly and business letters, announcements, plays, poems, stories, and skits;

(g) patomimes, creative dramatics, and formal dramatizations.

5. Evaluate student achievement comprehensively. Diverse procedures need to be utilized to appraise learner progress. The evaluation procedures may include

(a) teacher developed tests;

(b) standardized tests;

(c) learner abilities to spell words correctly within the framework of functional writing situations;

(d) weekly results from students being tested on lists of words contained in spelling textbooks being utilized in the classroom.

6. Assist students to utilize correct spelling of words. Students who utilize what has been learned are less likely to forget subject matter acquired. The teacher needs to provide situations in which pupils may use that which has been learned.

Retention in learning is a perennial problem. Human beings feel and believe that an inadequate amount of content has been retained. Retaining the correct spelling of words is no exception. Teachers need to think of means and methods of helping students remember understandings and skills achieved.

Utilitarian theorists believe that useful spelling words need to be mastered by students. If students learn to spell words correctly which have been identified as being functional, errors in spelling would decline greatly. With utilitarian words mastered by students in spelling, learners might then study what is useful. What is useful will be utilized frequently. That which is used tends not to be forgotten.

Burns and Broman wrote:

> Some spelling programmes are based on the theory of social utility; that is, words are selected on the basis of their importance in the different spelling activities of life. There are a number of investigations about spelling vocabulary, but perhaps the most important one is by Ernest Horn. He studied letters of bankers, excuses written to teachers by parents, minutes of organisations and committee reports, letters of application and recommendation, the works of well-known authors, letters written in magazines and newspapers, personal letters, business letters—a total million words and 36,000 different words. From this, the most important 10,000 words were selected as basic words, according to these criteria:
>
> 1. The total frequency with which the word was used in writing.
> 2. The commonness with which the word was used by everyone, regardless of sex, vocation, geographical location, educational level, or economic status.
> 3. The spread of the word's use in different kinds of writing.
> 4. The cruciality of the word as evidenced by the severity of the penalty attached to its misspelling.
> 5. The probable permanency of the word's use.
> 6. The desirability of the word as determined by the quality of the writing in which it was used.

Horn suggested three criteria for introducing these basic words in the spelling programme:

> The most important words should be introduced in the beginning grades and those of lesser importance in the later grades.
>
> The simplest words should be introduced in the beginning grades and the more difficult words in the later grades. Those words that are used often or needed in the curriculum activities of children should be introduced when appropriate.

7. Guide students to perceive patterns in the correct spelling of words. There are numerous sets or word families which follow a pattern. For example, first grade pupils need to learn to spell correctly the following: ban, can, fan, man, pan, van, tan, and ran. With a change in the initial consonant of each of the above-named words, a new word emerges. Another pattern of words for young

learners to master in spelling include bat, cat, hat, mat, pat, rat, and sat. Inductively (by discovery) and deductively (through meaningful explanations) pupils need to observe that selected English words form a pattern in spelling. Even the following irregularly spelled words—rough, cough, through, and thought follow a pattern emphasized in the "ough" letters. Linguists are strong advocates of students noticing pattern which assists in spelling words correctly. Young pupils should study words which pattern in phoneme (sound—grapheme (symbol) relationships contained in a family such as bet, met, set, let, yet, and get. In sequence, as learners progress through the diverse grade levels, words containing less of consistency between phonemes and graphemes can be emphasized such as bake, cake, fake, make, rake, and sake. Each of these words contain a silent "e" ending and might well be appropriate, as an example, for second graders. On the third grade, students might learn to spell words which gradually contain less relationship between phonemes and graphemes. These include my, pie, sigh, island, aisle, rye, and ride. Each of the above-named words contains a long ī sound as a linguistic element. As a final example, sixth grades might well learn to spell words which pattern with the vowel sound as in the word blue. The letters "ue" in sound pattern with to, too, two, rheumetism, flu, new, and soon. There are seventeen diverse ways to spell the same sound as represented by the letters "ue" in the word blue.

Stewig wrote:

Having children experience patterns in spelling is not the complete task, however, As they progress through the spelling programme, they must be exposed to the idea that in addition to patterns, there are exceptions. The danger in any generalization is that the pattern may be over-extended or applied to words for which it is inappropriate. Much inaccurate spelling results from overzealous application of generalizations. The child who spells bizzy (for busy), honer (for honor), and ankshus (for anxious) is only trying to apply what he or she has learned.

Trying to explain the logic behind some of these exceptions is largely futile; many exceptions must simply be learned on a rote basis. For example, children are often taught the pattern: when words begin with an initial /k/ sound, they are spelled with the letter K when the letters i or e follow, and are spelled with the letter C in all other cases. The alert child will soon notice, however, that there are exceptions. In such words as chaos, character, and chorus, the initial ch spelling is necessary to represent the initial /k/ sound. This is because such words are borrowings from the original Greek spelling, with the ch- retained, instead of modified to fit the more general English system (Corcoran, 1970). Does this make sense? Of course not, if one is searching for logic is a system that developed in piecemeal fashion. The child simply has to learn that there are exceptions to the system. While it would be more convenient for everyone concerned if some of these obscure borrowings were changed in written form to conform to the system, this is unlikely. Therefore, the onus of learning not only the system but also the exceptions falls on the child. An unfair requirement? Probably, but one which is unlikely to be changed! The teacher's job is, therefore, to make the learning of the system as palatable as possible.

8. Assist students to develop effective ways in learning to spell words correctly.

Petty, et. al. wrote·

The basic goal in spelling instruction is to teach children to spell the words they use in their writing. This means the writing they do in school and the writing they will do after their school years. Of course it is impossible to determine all of the words any person may need to spell in a lifetime, but everyone should learn to spell the words that are most frequently written. It is also important to encourage children's increasing awareness of the structure of their language and how aspects of this structure relate to spelling specific words. Finally, a positive attitude toward spelling correctly and habits which support this attitude need to be developed.

Since spelling requires putting into written form words that are familiar from speaking, reading, and listening, two important abilities are needed. One of these is the ability to recall how words look—the words that the child has studied and those that have frequently appeared in his or her reading. The other basic ability is that of associating letters and patterns of letters with specific sounds. These two abilities become closely allied in the spelling efforts of most children, and both are influenced by the children's understanding of syntactic and morphemic aspects of the language.

A good speller naturally must know the letters of the alphabet and how to write them in both lowercase and uppercase forms. He or she should know how to alphabetize words and how to use this knowledge to find the spelling of words in dictionaries and glossaries. He or she should be able to pronounce words clearly and accurately and to use a dictionary, including its diacritical markings and key words, as well as phonetic and structural aids to help with pronunciations.

Good spellers, no doubt, have developed quality methods in learning to spell words accurately. Those students doing poorly in spelling may need to develop methodologies which work in spelling words correctly. Which methodology might the teacher assist students in acquiring?

(a) Each student needs to look at a word carefully prior to studying its spelling. The sense of sight must be emphasized so that configuration clues might be utilized by the learner. A student cannot master a set of words in spelling unless he/she attends carefully to each new word. Some words are longer than others. Selected words are taller or shorter as far as individual letters within a word are concerned. Thus, distinguishing features must be observed prior to learning to spell that word.

(b) Students individually need to be able to pronounce each word correctly. Incorrect pronunciation of words can well make for spelling errors. Also students need to listen to the sounds within a word to associate sounds with symbols. Irregularities in spelling need to be noticed by the student. A learner can over generalize on the use of phonics. Phonetic analysis may also not be utilized adequately by the student in learning accurate word spellings.

(c) The involved student may now close his/her eyes and attempt to see the new word being studied. The mental image is then checked against the correct spelling of the word in print.

(d) Students individually may now write the new spelling word from memory. The written word needs to be checked against the accurately printed word being studied.

(e) The student should now write the new word in isolation as well as within sentences to show mastery.

9. Provide a quality learning environment to develop positive attitudes within students. Quality feelings toward any curriculum area, including spelling, assists learners to achieve more optimally. Pupils need to feel that spelling words correctly is important in communication ideas in writing. Appropriate courtesy and manners are also expressed when words are accurately spelled. The receiver of written content develops certain impressions of a writer if words are spelled correctly or incorrectly. When letters of application for a position or job application forms are completed by an applicant, certainly, words that are misspelled will influence an employer.

How can a teacher then assist students to feel that spelling words correctly in writing is important?

(a) Pupils need to look at written products in which words are spelled incorrectly. Here non-examples are used in teaching-learning situations. Students might then notice how effective communication is hindered through incorrect spelling of words.

(b) Learners need to receive responses to business and friendly letters written. Reasons exist for writing business or friendly letters. These reasons might include to order free or inexpensive materials for an ongoing unit being studied in the classroom A business letter then needs to be written. Correct spelling of words in the letter assists in communicating ideas. To correspond with friends, relatives, and acquaintances, friendly letters need composing by students. Politeness in writing and effective communication demands that words be accurately spelled.

Microcomputer Use in the Spelling Curriculum

With an increased number of microcomputers and software available in spelling, students might experience a relatively new kind of experience. There are selected philosophies that may be emphasized in microcomputer instruction.

Tutorial programmes provide opportunities for pupils to experience new learnings in spelling. With proper debugging of the software, students may experience sequential learnings in spelling. Adequate opportunities in the programme should be given to pupils to interact or respond to questions or multiple choice items contained in a programme. A reward system must be in evidence which reinforces correct answers given by learners.

Kemp and Dayton wrote:

> Tutorials attempt to emulate a human tutor. Instruction is provide via text or graphics on the screen. At appropriate points a question or problem is posed. If the student's response is correct, the computer moves on to the next block of instruction. If the response is incorrect the computer may recycle to the previous instruction or move to one of several sets of remedial instruction, depending upon the nature of the error.

Diagnostic and remediation programmes are significant for selected pupils. The concept of diagnosis emphasizes the need to determine specifically which problems pupils experience in spelling. The following may cause difficulties for students in learning to spell words accurately:

1. Words that do not follow a grapheme-phoneme relationship, e.g. one, two, rough, and high.
2. Words that represent spelling demons, e.g. always (allways), occur (ocur), running (runing), and rabbit (rabit). Words in parenthesis stress incorrect spellings.
3. Words that are easily mispronounced.
4. Words that are homonyms, e.g. hear-here; their, there, they're; bear, bare; and wait, weight.
5. Words that are heteronyms, e.g. subject (My favourite *subject* is geometry) and (Don't *subject* the child to hard work).

Quality software needs to pinpoint specific errors in spelling of a student. Remediation efforts must then follow.

Di Stefano, Dole, and Marzano wrote:

> Hagerty (1981) found that the majority of words third graders and fifth graders misspelled in writing were high frequency words that had little phoneme-grapheme representation, like "sed" for "said"

and "becuz" for "because". Using the words that students misspell in writing, you can have students develop a student dictionary based on each individual's misspelled words.

Drill and practice are vital in spelling. Otherwise pupils may not retain the correct spelling of words. Forgetting can be quite rapid for many students. It behooves the teacher to assist pupils to remember that which has been learned by students. Transfer of learning is also important. If students, for example, have mastered the spelling of a list of words, they must reveal increasingly that the new words can be spelled correctly in functional, utilitarian writing situations.

Software emphasizing drill and practice must

1. relate to those words students need more help in to retain/remember their correct spelling;
2. emphasize relevance or usefulness in everyday writing situations;
3. provide for success in achievement;
4. indicate a need for reviewing the correct spelling of selected words;
5. reflect student interests and purposes.

Too frequently, drill and practice activities are boring to learners. A lack of challenge is involved in the routine and mundane. A sheer lack of interest may then follow. A meaningless curriculum is an end result. Students fail to achieve vital goals, as a consequence. Certainly learning activities involving drill and practice should be stimulating to students so that sequential learning can follow.

Dennis and Kansky wrote:

> Associative learning, as required for success in a spelling competition, calls for the services of some kindly soul who will sit for hours pronouncing words and checking your spelling against that of the ruling lexicographer. You can claim success (learning) when spaced presentations of the pronunciation of sarcophagus (the stimulus) are met by your unerring verbal dissection s-a-r-c-o-p-h-a-g-u-s (the response). The procedure is known as drill. It's not a very exciting activity for your partner, so you might want to try shouting in order to ensure his or her consciousness.

> Textbooks and teachers are not the most effective resources for drills. Textbooks cannot respond with the flexibility needed to shape the student's learning. Teachers cannot give each individual student the time needed to fix all of the associations that are part of education. Using a teacher to carry out such a tedious, unrewarding task is as unforgivable as using a Ming vase as a paperweight.
>
> The computer has been shown to be an effective drillmaster in promoting associative learning. Students achieve mastery of such associations quickly and show high levels of retention. And for reasons that are anyone's guess, students appear to be highly motivated to engage in drill activity with a computer.

Games can be an enjoyable method of learning for students. The writer observed a teacher made game utilized in the classroom to challenge students to learn to spell words. A pupil would spin a spinner with the numerals one to five spaced congruently for the spinner to point to. For example, flipping the spinner with the finger, a student spins a value of three. Five piles of congruent cards are placed face down. Pile one has the easiest words while stack five has the most difficult words to spell. Piles one, two, and three are more complex than stack one and less complex than pile five, in a hierarchical manner. With the spinner pointed to number three, an opponent picks up a card from pile three turning it face up. The opponent pronounces the word to the involved student who must correctly spell orally or in writing the spelling word pronounced by the opponent in order to move three spaces forward on the game board. Each player takes his/her turn to cross the finish line.

There are selected excellent programmes for microcomputer utilization emphasizing the gaming approach. CompuCat Spell is a game for pupils to play in the area of spelling. The following are inherent in the game:

1. rules are presented for two players to play at a time;
2. there are three different games in the above-named software;
3. the involved students can select slow, average, or fast for the speed of the software presentation;
4. ten, twenty, thirty, or forty points can be earned for each question answered correctly;

5. the student must respond to a question on the screen before a "cat" jumps from block one to block ten. If the learner does not respond within this allotted time, he/she loses ten points;
6. extra bonus points can be earned in the game. This is indicated when a "cat" moves across the top of the screen. One extra bonus point frame has the following item:

   A pup is a:

   1. dug
   2. dig
   3. dog
   4. dag

The learner needs to type the correct numeral on the terminal to receive an extra point.

7. Each student can receive a printout of results of the game played. The printout, among other items, contains the number of questions answered correctly, questions missed, and total questions answered. The printout also contains the correct answers to items missed by the involved student.
8. Sound is available for reinforcement of correct responses given by students.
9. The manual contains a scope and sequence chart of content contained in the software, such as game one containing short and long vowel monosyllables; short and long vowels; synonyms, antonyms, and word meanings; as well as students choosing correct spelling of sound-spelled words.

Computer managed instruction (CMI) can save much time in developing the spelling curriculum. One means in utilizing CMI is to permit the microcomputer to check the results of student achievement in spelling in:

(a) pretests to ascertain where a student is presently in achievement;

(b) criterion checks to determine how well students are achieving goals as a unit progresses;

(c) post tests in measuring gains at the completion of a unit.

Test results of students may be stored and retrieved, as needed, in computer managed instruction. A printout of measurable objectives in spelling together with the related learning activities to achieve each goal may be sent home to parents. The printout would show which objectives a student has achieved and which goals need achieving. Parents' support may then be enlisted, as homework for the involved pupil, to assist their offspring in sequential goal attainment. The classroom teacher, the parents, and the pupil might then know which specific objectives in spelling the latter individually has attained and which are left to achieve.

Pertaining to storage and retrieval of information, Grossnickle, *et al*. wrote:

> The power of a computer depends largely on two factors:
>
> 1. Its ability to store and retrieve large amounts of information quickly.
> 2. Its ability to make decisions.
>
> A high level of technical programming skill is required to take full advantage of the decision-making power of the computer. However, using relatively inexpensive software and with the basic technical knowledge, it is possible for a beginner to store and retrieve information.
>
> Information fed into a computer is usually lost when the computer is turned off, but with proper peripheral equipment, information can be stored on cassette or disk. Although a disk drive costs almost half as much as computer, it is almost essential for efficient school use. Storage and retrieval are nearly instantaneous with a disk drive, and are far more time consuming with cassette.

In Conclusion

There are selected criteria which teachers need to utilize in selecting objectives and learning activities in spelling. These include:

1. significant objectives need to be selected for pupils to achieve;
2. understandings, skills, and attitudinal goals need to be stressed in goal attainment for learners. Emphasizing

only one of the above categories in teaching deemphasizes the concept of balance in the curriculum;

3. perceived purpose needs to be developed for learning;
4. a variety of activities and experiences must be in the offing in the spelling curriculum;
5. diverse procedures need to be utilized to assess learner progress;
6. students need to use the correct spelling of new words in functional writing situations;
7. patterns and irregularities need to be observed by students in spelling;
8. appropriate methodologies should be used by pupils in learning to spell words accurately;
9. positive attitudes toward spelling, as a curriculum area, need to be developed and maintained.

Microcomputer utilization has numerous objectives for pupils to attain. Thus, microcomputers may be used for

1. tutorial instruction;
2. diagnosis and remediation;
3. drill and practice;
4. the playing of games;
5. computer managed instruction purposes.

The spelling curriculum must reflect the interests, needs, and purposes of students. Each learner needs guidance to attain optimally in spelling.

REFERENCES

Burns, Paul C. and Broman, Betty L. *The Language Arts in Childhood Education*. fifth edition. Boston: Houghton Mifflin Co., 1983.

CompuCat Spell. New York: McGraw Hill Book Company, 1985.

Dennis, J. Richard and Kansay, Robert J. *Instructional Computing*. Glenview, Illinois: Scott, Foresman and Company, 1984.

Grossnickle, Foster E. *et al. Discovering Meanings in Elementary School Mathematics*, Seventh Edition. New York: Holt, Rinehart and Winston, 1983.

Kemp, Jerrold E. Dayton, Deane K. *Planning and Producing Instructional Media.* New York: Harper and Row, Publishers, 1985.

Norton, Donna E. *The Effective Teaching of Language Arts.* second edition. Columbus, Ohio: Charles E. Merrill Publishing Co., 1985.

Petty Walter T. *et al. Experiences in Language.* Fourth Edition. Newton, Massachusetts: Allyn and Bacon, Inc. 1985.

Stephano, Philip Di, Dole, Janice, and Marzano, Robert, *Elementary Language Arts.* New York: John Wiley and Sons, 1984.

Stewig, John Warren, *Exploring Language Arts in the Elementary Classroom.* New York: Holt, Rinehart and Winston, 1983.

Reading and the Language Arts

One of the most important curriculum areas in the elementary school is reading. If the teacher emphasizes much reading of content in social studies, science, mathematics and the other curriculum areas of the elementary school, then reading in the elementary school curriculum becomes very important. Not being able to read well may then mean that pupils do rather poorly in all curriculum areas of the elementary school. In a modern elementary school, however, a variety of learning activities is important to provide for individual learners.

Reading can well be an excellent kind or type of leisure time activity. In a student's spare time in school or in the home, reading can provide for needed information useful in solving one's problems in everyday situations in life. A student may also read content for purposes of sheer enjoyment. In either case, reading content can aid learners in enjoying life and gaining experiences vicariously. Adults should do much reading in their spare time. It can be an excellent way of enriching the perception of the adult.

It is important for kindergarten and first grade pupils to have satisfying experiences related to realizing optimum achievement in reading. Thus a good reading readiness programme is important for young children prior to engaging in a formal programme of reading. Many pupils fail in reading due to a poorly developed and conducted reading readiness programme. What can the teacher do to help kindergarten and first grade pupils in a good reading readiness programme?

Utilizing Pictures in Teaching

The teacher must develop a good file of pictures for use in classroom teaching. These pictures, among other ways, can be used in a reading readiness programme. If pupils are studying a unit on the farm in social studies, they can develop background information pertaining to the names of farm animals, machinery, and buildings through the study of related pictures. Thus, later on when pupils may be reading content from basal readers on farm life, they will understand the concepts and generalizations better than if they had not had the unit relating to the farm. Building background information is an important facet of a reading readiness programme.

Reading readiness books from a basal series contain many pictures. Here, the teacher must assist learners to develop interest in and discuss the pictures. Many valuable suggestions are given in the manual in helping teachers provide interesting, meaningful, and purposeful learning activities. The teacher must be creative in using the suggestions for teaching. In some cases, the experienced teacher may think of better methods and approaches to use in teaching than those given in the manual. The manual is a guide and is not prespective.

As a result of studying pictures from the teacher's own file and from the reading readiness series of a basal reader, the child should think in terms of pictures supplying valuable information in learning. The learner when reading in a formal reading programme can be aided in identifying and unlocking new words with the use of picture clues. For example, if a child is reading content on a specific page, he may not know the correct pronunciation of a particular word such as "lamb." He looks at a picture on the same page from which he is reading and in the illustration a lamb is pictured. This word makes sense within the sentence. Thus, the learner has used picture clues to determine the meaning of the new word. Pupils need to have ample opportunities to study pictures in a reading readiness programme to develop background information as well as to be able to use pictures later in formal reading programmes to unlock and identify new words.

Once pupils are engaged in learning activities involving reading with the use of basal readers, pictures in the series as well as related pictures from the teacher's own file can be used to develop interest in reading. If pupils are to read a story pertaining to the life and times of Benjamin Franklin, related pictures from the basal reader and from the teacher's own file can be used to arouse pupil curiosity for reading. Questions can be asked by both pupils and the teacher pertaining to the pictures. Answers to these questions can be discussed which will assist learners to understand content better when actually reading the story. The new words for the reading activity can be printed in neat manuscript letters on the chalkboard prior to reading. These words can be written on the chalkboard as they relate to the discussion of pictures in the basal reader and from the teacher's own file. In the ongoing discussion, questions raised by the teacher and pupils, pertaining to the previously mentioned pictures, can be utilized in having pupils read content with a purpose. For example, supposing that a pupil or several pupils ask the following question pertaining to a picture. "Why did noblemen in many cases live in castles during the Middle Ages?" This could then provide an excellent situation where pupils can read the needed pages from the basal reader in order to get an answer for the question.

Using Real Objects in Teaching

Pupils must experience reality in ongoing learning activities. Inaccurate concepts and generalizations may result when little attention is paid to reality.

Much background information can be developed within pupils in a reading readiness programme when real objects are used. If kindergarten and first grade pupils are studying a unit on the neighbourhood shopping centre, with teacher guidance an excursion should be planned to visit a shopping centre. Prior to the visit, questions can be identified for which information and data will be sought. During the excursion, information can be obtained in answer to the questions. Following the excursion, ample time needs to be given to discussing answers to questions as well as other observations which were made. Later on, pupils may be reading about the neighbourhood shopping centre utilizing the basal reader. Thus, the background information gained from the excursion should assist learners in developing desirable understandings, skills, and attitudes presently, as well as providing necessary information to understand content which will be read later using a series of basal readers.

Interest centres in the classroom can provide pupils with many valuable learnings. For example, during the fall months, pupils can bring leaves of many colours, caterpillars, insects, shells, an empty bird nest, and other items for an interest centre. An excellent discussion by pupils with teacher guidance can follow pertaining to the items on the centre. Later on, when pupils will be reading related content, they should understand better what is being read due to having had related background information.

Making Pictured Dictionaries

Pupils can learn to identify new words as well as build background information when making and using pictured dictionaries, also commonly called pictionaries. If pupils in a readiness programme are studying a farm unit, they could bring pictures to school of the following farm animals and machines: cows, pigs, sheep, hens, tractor, combine, harrow, plow, and disk. The pictures could be neatly arranged in a scrap book with the related abstract words printed below each picture in neat manuscript letters. Pupils can thus learn to identify abstract words by studying the related pictures. For example, the word "tractor" will be printed beneath the picture of the tractor. Some pupils may not have the needed magazines in their homes from which a good source of pictures can come. Perhaps, the teacher and/or the school has old magazines which can be utilized by these pupils in developing the pictured dictionary.

Several leading publishing companies publish pictionaries. These books can also be used by the teacher to guide learners in studying pictures to develop an adequate number of concepts and generalizations as well as recognize abstract words.

Placing Labels on Objects

The teacher needs to select some important objects in the classroom and place related labels on them written in neat manuscript letters. It is important, however, not to clutter the classroom with labels. Cluttering the classroom with labels on objects may frustrate the child rather than helping him in word recognition and identification. Labels could be placed at the proper place pertaining to the following objects neatly displayed on an interest centre: house, car, boy, girl, man, women, grass, street, and bicycle. This activity should assist learners in identifying abstract words.

The teacher could place labels on objects in the classroom, such as "table", "desk", "book", "door", and "window". The purpose of this activity would be to assist learners to develop a basic sight vocabulary which is useful for more formal reading activities at a later time.

Criteria to utilize in selecting objects which should have labels attached to them in a reading readiness activity could be the following:

1. the objects selected pertain to words commonly used by children in speaking activities;
2. the objects selected would relate to common experiences in the lives of children;
3. the objects selected would pertain to words the child will meet up with later when reading abstract words;
4. the objects are interesting to learners and meaning can be readily attached to them.

Developing Experience Charts

A very valuable approach to help pupils develop readiness for reading is the developing of experience charts. As the name indicates, learners need to have acceptable experiences from which a chart containing abstract words can be developed. At the beginning of the kindergarten or first grade year, pupils could take an excursion to various important places within the school building. They could visit the principal's office, the cafeteria, and the custodian's quarters. Each person in the above designated places could speak about his duties and responsibilities. Pupils should ask questions pertaining to comments made about duties and responsibilities as presented by the principal, cafeteria workers, and the custodian. After the excursion has been completed, an experience chart can be developed by pupils with teacher guidance. The teacher should write pupil's comments in neat manuscript letters on the chalkboard. In the time devoted to a presentation of ideas by the pupils pertaining to experiences on the excursion, learners may present comments like the following which the teacher can write on the chalkboard:

We saw the cooks preparing food.

They were very friendly.

The principal showed us his office.

He told us of his work.

The custodian helps keep our school clean.

Generally, the teacher would write ideas just as they are given by pupils. The teacher could ask for a different way to state a sentence if there is a lack of pupil clarity in expressing ideas. Pupils can notice that talk can be written down. They are presenting the ideas, and the teacher is doing the recording.

Illustrations can be drawn by pupils pertaining to the content on the experience chart. Pictures may also be collected and put next to the related ideas on the experience chart. Pupils with teacher assistance must spend an adequate amount of time reading the content on the experience chart. The teacher would point to the words as pupils read content. Soon, pupils will begin to recognize words on the chart. Thus, in the reading readiness programme, learners are beginning to develop a sight vocabulary. They will notice that some words are longer than others. Some have taller letters than others. Thus, pupils will notice likenesses and differences between and among words and letters.

The experience charts can be placed into a binder resulting in a booklet for future pupil reference and reading. Pupils can again look at these experience charts and read them on their own or with teacher leadership. The experience chart approach is excellent in a reading readiness programme when emphasizing the following criteria:

1. Pupils have had life-like concrete experiences from which ideas can come for the experience chart.
2. Learners present the content pertaining to ideas on the experience chart.
3. Pupils can see and notice that ideas which are presented can be written down.
4. Pupils under teacher guidance can read content pertaining to their very own experiences.
5. Experience charts can be filed for future reading by pupils.
6. Pupils are involved in many experiences pertaining to oral expression which is of utmost importance in communication.

7. Excursions generally provide for individual differences since learners can interpret experiences at different levels of complexity in accordance with capacity and achievement levels.
8. The experience chart concept provides experiences for pupils to develop more proficiency gradually in the reading of abstract words.
9. Since the content of the experience chart is based on experiences pupils have had personally, meaningful learnings for pupils should thus be a result.

Using a Variety of Audio-Visual Aids

To provide for individual differences in any class, a variety of learning activities must be provided. This should also assist in providing for different learning styles in a class. A variety of different learning activities involving the use of audio-visual materials can do much to develop readiness for reading within a given set of learners.

The use of transparencies and the overhead projector can provide interesting, meaningful, and purposeful learning activities for pupils in a reading readiness programme. In a unit on transportation, different forms and types of transportation such as cars, buses, taxis, trucks, and bicycles can be shown on transparencies. These different means of transportation can be discussed with pupils. Later, learners will be reading about these different types of transportation. Reading becomes easier for pupils if previously they have acquired concepts and generalizations pertaining to the abstract words which will be encountered.

Films, filmstrips, and slides can provide learning activities which will assist learners in a reading readiness programme. These audio-visual aids, as one example, may pertain to a unit on holidays; perhaps, Christmas customs in the United States as well as other countries are shown. Later on, in a more formal reading programme, pupils will be reading about Christmas customs in different lands; thus the readiness programme has played an important role in developing within pupils background information essential for reading.

The opaque projector also has an important role to play in a good reading readiness programme. Pictures from magazines, newspapers, and old textbooks can be shown on the wall or screen with the use of an opaque projector. The teacher can point out specifics pertaining to pictures shown. For example, a teacher can point out how toys differ from one nation to another with the use of the opaque projector. Pictures pertaining to toys of various countries and nations of the world should be carefully selected. It is almost a certainty that pupils will be reading about toys in a more formal reading programme.

Telling Stories

It is important that learners develop appropriate skills for story telling. The teacher should read stories to pupils on their understanding and interest levels. Pupils learn much from listening to these stories being read to them. If the stories are short, pupils can practice telling them. This requires an attention span of adequate duration to listen to the story or stories. It also requires the child being able to recall the story. Ultimately, the child needs to be able to tell the story. Proper order or sequence of events and ideas is important in this learning activity. Thus pupils are engaging in the use of oral or spoken language. They are also presenting ideas in a group situation or setting. Stories from library books or from basal readers follow a specific sequence. Thus pupils, in a reading readiness programme should have an ample number of experiences pertaining to telling a story in proper order as far as sequence of ideas is concerned. If pupils can learn to tell a short story using proper sequence of ideas in a reading readiness programme, learners will then be able to follow a story better when reading abstract words since a certain sequence of ideas will be followed when reading that story.

Stories that children tell to other learners should provide situations where success is an inherent part of the learning activity. Thus, the child will be spurred on to greater efforts in the area of reading.

Visual Discrimination

The teacher must select learning activities which will assist learners in visual discrimination. The act of reading abstract words requires that learners be able to notice likenesses and differences among and between words. For example, in the act of reading pupils must notice the length of different words. To be sure, some words are longer in length as compared to other words. Some words begin with taller letters; others begin with shorter letters. Within a word there are variations in the height of letters. Some letters, of course, go below the line.

Pupils need many experiences in a reading readiness programme to notice likenesses and differences among pictures, individual letters, and words. To begin with, the teacher would want to have pupils develop skill to notice gross differences among and between pictures. Reading readiness books contain, in many cases, learning activities such as the following pertaining to noticing likenesses and differences in pictures:

1. The pupil is to cross out the picture of a boy that looks different from the other two boys which look exactly alike.
2. Learners are to place a mark on the pail that looks different from the other two pails which are identical in appearance.

The teacher can also use pictures from her own file in guiding learners to become more proficient in noticing gross likenesses and differences such as in the following activities:

1. The pupil is to point to the apple that looks different from two other apples.
2. Pupils are to identify the cat which is different in appearance from the other two cats.

The teacher needs to think of learning activities which follow good sequence from the learner's point of view when determining sequential achievement for pupils pertaining to visual discrimination. The learner will reveal if he needs more practice in making gross discriminations between and among pictures. If the child demonstrates that he has mastered learnings related to gross discrimination among pictures, then sequential learnings can be provided whereby learners gradually differentiate between and among pictures where finer distinctions need to be made. An example can be given at this point where pupils would mark the picture that is different from the other two, such as three men looking exactly alike, however the buttons on the shirt of one man are missing. The child wouid need to utilize visual discrimination in noticing this fine difference when comparing and contrasting the three pictures.

The teacher also must provide learning activities for pupils where ample opportunities are given to notice the configuration of abstract words. For example, in introducing learning activities of this kind, the teacher could duplicate or mimeograph papers pertaining to the following exercise where pupils cross out the word that is different from the other two words:

1.	man	table	man
2.	girl	boy	boy
3.	wagon	cow	wagon
4.	lion	lion	cub
5.	run	jump	jump
6.	horse	pig	pig
7.	lamb	so	lamb

The number of examples which pupils are to work will depend upon the purpose pupils will perceive from the ongoing learning activities. Pupil interest in reading readiness activities should be developed and maintained. Having pupils work at a learning activity such as this for an excessive length of time will generally destroy learner interest in reading.

Gradually, the words selected by the teacher for pupils to notice likenesses and differences should be more nearly alike in configuration such as is evident in the following examples:

1.	man	mouse	man
2.	run	rat	rat
3.	bird	bird	boy
4.	nest	nose	nest
5.	boy	baby	baby
6.	way	wagon	way
7.	the	those	those

In the examples given above, all words start with the same letter for the set in number 1, number 2, number 3, and so on. The ending of one word is different from the other two words in each set.

The teacher can also have pupils develop skills in visual discrimination pertaining to crossing out the letter that looks different from the other two letters such as would be the case in the following examples:

1. m t m
2. b y b
3. o l l
4. p a a
5. c c b
6. d o o
7. n l n

The above examples pertain to pupils making discriminations in letters for each numbered item. The following exercise pertaining to visual discrimination would come at a later time in proper sequence from the learner's point of view:

1. c o c
2. b l l
3. f d d
4. r r s
5. m s m
6. e o e
7. i i j

It is much more difficult for pupils in a reading readiness programme in noticing which letter is different from the other two letters in the following exercise as compared to the preceding one:

1. d b d
2. n n m
3. t l t
4. g y y

5. h h k
6. v v w
7. u v u

The letter "d" and the letter "b" look very much alike. In reading readiness activities, learners may look at a letter or word moving from right to left instead of left to right. Thus it is easy to see why learners would confuse the letter "b" with the letter "d" or vice versa. Reading the letter "d" from a right to-left progression makes the same letter appear as a "b". The letters "m" and "n" look quite similar in appearance and configuration. The letters "t" and "l" are comparable in height with a slight variation in appearance. This exercise then would involve the making of fine discriminations. It would come late in a reading readiness programme involving visual discrimination.

Auditory Discrimination

To develop skill and proficiency in reading, the pupil should be guided in noticing likenesses and differences in sounds that are made by letters and within words. The teacher should select poetry carefully to be read to pupils in which cases learners could hear words which rhyme. Carefully selected poetry can capture the interests of pupils and develop proficiency in hearing words which rhyme.

The teacher, for example, could ask pupils which words rhyme with each of the following: fall, man, hill, and moon. Pupils, of course, will be at different achievement levels when giving words which rhyme with other words. For some learners, hearing likenesses and differences in sounds is extremely difficult. A few children may not be able to hear these sounds. They will benefit more from learning activities involving visual discrimination. The teacher needs to be understanding, kind, and patient in working with all learners regardless of achievement levels. Pictures can be used by the teacher to initiate a discussion pertaining to rhyming words. Pupils can give words that rhyme with an object in the picture.

The teacher can also have pictures pertaining to selected words whereby pupils are asked to give other words which have the same beginning sound. If the teacher is showing a picture of a cat, learners may volunteer words which have the same beginning sounds, such as "cow", "can", "cable", "call", and "cane". Learning activities such as these should assist learners in developing proficiency in auditory discrimination.

Giving words which have the same ending sound as a word given by the teacher is more difficult for learners as compared to giving words which rhyme or have the same beginning sound. For example, the teacher could have pupils give words that end like "pet". Pupils can give words which rhyme; however, other words should be given also, such as "hat", "bat", "hit", sit", and "pot".

When pupils look at labels on selected objects or engage in reading content under teacher guidance from the experience chart, associations will be made between symbol and sound or sounds by pupils. The same would be true of pupils reading words when studying pictures in a pictured dictionary. Pupils also learn to associate sound with symbol when studying words which follow a particular pattern such as in the following:

cat mat fat

rat bat hat

sat pat vat

In the preceding list of words, pupils can develop generalizations pertaining to what happens to a word like "cat", for example, when the initial consonant is changed. The teacher can introduce a lesson such as this by showing a picture of a cat with the abstract word "cat" below the illustration. Learners can be asked to give words which rhyme with cat. These words can be written on the chalkboard as they are given by pupils. Thus, children can see the relationship of sounds to symbols.

Determining Readiness for Reading

The teacher needs to evaluate pupil achievement continually to determine if learners are ready for a more formal programme in reading. The sequence must not be abrupt when changing from a reading readiness programme to one which is more formal. In the reading readiness programme, pupils were starting to identify words by studying experience charts, labels on objects, words in pictured dictionaries, and words which follow a pattern as far as sound-symbol relationships are concerned. In a more formal programme of reading, pupils would gradually be learning to identify more and more new words.

Numerous approaches can be utilized to determine if pupils are ready for reading. There are many standardized reading readiness tests which can be utilized to assist in assessing if pupils are ready for reading. The reader should survey, study, and analyze a variety of reading readiness tests. Certainly, schools will want to evaluate, in particular, the validity and reliability of the standardized tests currently being used in their schools.

Teacher observation can be a good procedure to use in determining if pupils are ready for reading. The teacher should consider the following questions pertaining to each child being ready for reading.

1. Does the pupil enjoy looking at illustrated library books at the reading centre?
2. Is the learner asking how to pronounce selected words being observed in library books?
3. Are learners interested in ongoing activities in the reading readiness programme?
4. Can pupils individually notice likenesses and differences between pictures, words, and letters?
5. Are learners developing proficiency in auditory discrimination?
6. Can pupils individually on their present developmental level tell a story in proper sequence?
7. Does the child generally pronounce words accurately?
8. Do learners work and play together harmoniously?
9. Does the pupil have feelings of an adequate self concept?
10. Is the child cooperative when interacting with others?
11. Does the pupil accept responsibility for his actions?
12. Is the attention span of the child adequate to benefit from a more formal reading programme?
13. Does the child exhibit characteristics in having good physical and mental health?

Assisting Pupils in Identifying Words

Pupils need to develop an ample number of techniques to identify, recognize, and unlock new words. Too, frequently, pupils have not developed an adequate number of approaches to recognize new words. Thus, they are hindered in reading achievement. It is important for the teacher to utilize a variety of approaches in guiding learners to use various techniques of word recognition and identification. If approaches are not varied, boredom and a lack of interest in reading may result. Purpose may also be lacking in learning to identify new words.

Using Configuration Clues

Pupils need to notice how words differ in form and shape. Occasionally, learners will not look at words carefully to notice how they are alike and how they are different. Some may not retain the mental image of a word. Teachers must use a variety of approaches in helping learners recognize words by sight.

In introducing a new selection to be read, the teacher could print in neat manuscript style the new words for the reading lesson. Pictures could be discussed which would directly relate to the new words so that learners attach meaning to each of the new words. Thus, the pupil would learn a definition, or definitions, for each of the new words as they will be used in context within the selection to be read. Pupils should look carefully at each new word printed in neat manuscript letters on the chalkboard. This is necessary so that pupils obtain an accurate mental image of each new word. Thus, pupils will be noticing the length of the word, the size and shape of letters within each word, and the general configuration of the new word. If the chalkboard alone is used to introduce new words, the method or approach used in teaching can become monotonous. Thus, other approaches should also be used such as the use of the overhead projector with the new words printed on transparencies. New words for a selection to be read by pupils can also be printed in neat manuscript letters on flash-cards. Pupils would have as much time as is needed to study the configuration of new words from the flash-cards.

Using Context Clues

In some situations where learners cannot determine a new word, many meaningless words are inserted which do not make sense within a sentence. The learner then is not using context clues. Consider the following sentence: The man was hunting rabbits. Supposing the child does not know the word "hunting". Let us assume he guesses what the unknown word is. The following words would be correct as far as the use of context clues is concerned: chasing, wanting some, dressing, a friend of, disliking, jumping over, shooting, petting, feeding, and washing. The following words would not fit in as far as context clues are concerned when making a substitution for the unknown word "hunting": heavy, hole, humming, hinting, and him. The child needs to be assisted in selecting words which make sense or are meaningful within a sentence. However, using context clues is not adequate when attempting to identify a new word. Many words can be substituted for an unknown word and the completed sentence is meaningful. Phonetic analysis is thus also important in identifying new words.

Using Phonetic Analysis

The child who is beginning and progressing in the area of reading must also use phonetic analysis in determining unknown words. In the following sentences, many words would make sense when the blank space is filled in: I see a——. One could respond with the following words and be correct in terms of using context clues: cat, dog, mouse, rabbit, horse, lion, lamb, cow, and zebra. The child must use context clues to identify new words. However, this is not adequate in many cases; it was noticed that many words make sense within the preceding sentence. If the child has had interesting, meaningful, and purposeful learning activities pertaining to phonics, the child should select the word "rabbit" (assuming it is the correct word) as the new word encountered in reading since the letter "r" has a completely different beginning sound as compared to other words in the list. The word "rabbit" also has a different ending sound than do other words in the list. The letter "t" is rather consistent in its relationship to a specific sound as would be true of the following words: bat, hat, cat, mat, pat, and rat.

Using Syllabication

Pupils with teacher guidance should develop skills relating to analyzing words into component parts in order that new words may be identified. For example, a pupil may think that the word "unlike" is a new word he is encountering in reading in the following sentence: Bill and John were brothers, but they were unlike in many ways. The pupil has identified other words previously which had the prefix "un" such as the following: unable and unimportant. He has also read the word "like" previously. By dividing the word "unlike" into syllables, the pupil can readily identify what was believed to be a new word. The word "unlike", however, was not a new word; it consisted of old words or parts of words rearranged into a new combination. Thus the child can unlock or recognize many "new" words when dividing these words into syllables.

The pupil may also be able to identify words which are new through the technique of syllabication and phonetic analysis combined. The pupil may be reading a sentence containing the new word "irrelevant". The word is rather lengthy and may appear to be quite difficult to the child. By analyzing the word and dividing it into parts, the pupil has a fairly good chance in determining its pronunciation. The correct way to divide the word into syllables would be the following: ir/rel/e/vant. Sound and symbol relationships are quite consistent here. The pupil will have a much easier time to identify the new word when attempting to divide it into syllables as compared to looking at the configuration of the word only.

A word of caution must be presented here. Pupils can spend an excessive amount of time in analyzing words in terms of syllabication and phonetic analysis. Analyzing words should not cut down in pupil interest in reading. Words that pupils can read as sight words should not be analyzed unless it helps pupils to identify new words. Ultimately, good readers identify words quickly by noticing the configuration of words being read.

Using Picture Clues

Pupils can identify many new words by using picture clues. For example, the pupil may be reading the following sentence and cannot identify the word "car": Billy was washing the car. By looking at the picture on that page, it may show a picture of a boy washing a car. Thus the picture could tell the child what the unknown word is. To be sure, in some situations, pictures will not give clues in helping to determine the unknown word. Or, there way be too many persons, objects, or scenes in a picture in assisting the reader to determine the unknown word through the use of picture clues. Consider the following sentence and assume that "house" is a word which the pupil cannot identify while reading: Billy was a house. In the picture on the same page where the pupil is reading content, there are many things that Billy could have seen such as a car, a man, a woman, and a dog. With knowledge of phonetic analysis, the child can associate the proper sound with the initial consonant "h" in the word "house" and thus identify the correct word. No other object, person, or place being represented in the picture has the same beginning sound.

Purpose in Reading

Not all content, of course, is read at the same rate of speed. Comprehension is the important factor in reading. Time is wasted if the reader does not understand what is being read. The purpose involved in reading, among other things, will assist in determining the rate of speed an individual reads. Too often, pupils, as well as adults, want to read all content at the same rate of speed.

Reading for Facts

If a pupil reads content to gain facts, a somewhat slow kind of reading will generally result. Each word becomes important in reading when pupils read content to comprehend facts. It is important for learners to have a purpose for reading content. Comprehension, generally, then will be at a higher rate. If other readiness activities have been provided for, the teacher can, for example, have the following purpose involved in reading whereby pupils would read to gain facts: Lets read to find out what machinery is used by farmers to seed and harvest wheat. In this example, pertaining to a unit on the Great Plains area, pupils would read factual information related to the established purpose such as a plow, harrow, disk, springtooth, grain drill, combine, truck, and tractor. The information needed to answer the question or purpose for reading was highly specific or consisted of facts.

Another example, if pupils are to read content pertaining to a unit on the Middle Ages, the teacher and/or pupils may have the following purposes which would relate to gaining facts: What kind of furniture would you find in a castle? What kind of work did serfs do? What are the different kinds of rooms used for in a castle?

Skimming

A rapid kind of reading for pupils involves skimming. Not every word cn a page needs to be read when skimming content is a goal in silent reading. If pupils are studying a unit on the city, they could skim for the name of a city such as Boston, New York, Chicago, or Cleveland. If pupils are studying a unit on the Civil War, they could skim content pertaining to the beginning or ending date of that war. Or, in studying a unit on Great Britain, pupils could skim content pertaining to famous persons in British history, such as Winston Churchill, Anthony, Eden, and Edward Heath.

When skimming content becomes an important purpose in reading bits of information such as important names, dates, places, and events should be stressed. Certainly, pupils should not skim content which is unimportant and irrelevant. There is too much content available in various academic disciplines for pupils to spend time on that which is trivial.

The names of persons and places generally start with capital letters thus giving learners a clue in how these words differ in appearance from other words. To be sure, each word that begins a sentence will also start with a capital letter. However, many words, of course, on a page do not start with capital letters. Dates are written with numerals and have a completely different appearance as compared to abstract words. Pupils can benefit much by learning to skim content for important names, dates, places, and events.

In using the index, no one would waste time in looking up an entry by starting with the first listed entry in the index and taking each listed entry after that in sequence. If a pupil is looking up information on magnets, he generally will not start with the first entry under the letter "a" and look at all the other entries under that letter before going on to the entries under letter "b" followed by other letters of the alphabet in sequence. The entry "magnets" will come somewhat in the middle of the index. Once the entries have been found under the letter "m", pupils should then locate the beginning entries under the letter "m" since the word "magnet" will come in that general area. Thus, the child is skimming content when using the index. Much time can be saved in reading when skimming becomes an important goal in gathering information at selected intervals.

When a pupil uses the table of contents in a book, skimming also becomes an important purpose. If a pupil wishes to find information on the topic of electricity, he could skim chapter headings in the table of contents of an elementary school science textbook to notice if a clue is given as to which page in the book has the needed information. If the table of contents doesn't give this information, the pupil may skim entries in the index.

Reading for Sequence in Ideas

It is very important for pupils to think in terms of sequence when reading content in many different curriculum areas. For example, if pupils are reading information on Eskimo's building sleds for use in the Arctic areas, the purpose may arise in reading as to how the sleds are built. The child would then read content pertaining to the order or sequence of steps involved in building the sled.

Historical content very frequently deals with order of happenings. Too many pupils have erroneously generalized that George Washington was the first President while Abraham Lincoln was the second President of the United States. The sequence, of course, is incorrect. A purpose in reading historical content related to the appropriate unit could be the following: Lets read to find out who the first four presidents of the United States were in order of their becoming president.

Reading to Follow Directions

Life in society demands that individuals become proficient in reading to follow directions. When frozen food packages are purchased, individuals need to be able to read directions accurately and follow them so that a good final product will result. In preparing frozen foods, one needs to know nothing whatsoever about cooking. If the directions are followed carefully, a good dish of brussel sprouts, peas, corn, okra, or other vegetable will result.

Elementary school pupils, generally, are very interested in constructing model rockets, cars, airplanes, and boats. In many cases this requires accurate reading of directions so that a good model will result.

In working exercises from worksheets and textbooks, the pupil first needs to read the directions necessary for completing the work.

Otherwise, exercises may have been worked incorrectly. In taking standardized tests, it is very important to follow directions carefully. Otherwise, money and time has been wasted in taking the tests. The results may then not have any value.

When pupils read to follow directions, each word must be identified correctly. Comprehension of content when reading to follow directions is of utmost importance. The directions cannot be followed unless the reader comprehends what has been read.

Reading for a Main Idea

Facts that are read should be related to a larger framework of thought or a main idea. Facts will generally be forgotten sooner as compared to a main idea. Thus , the teacher needs to have pupils read for main ideas. Main ideas, however, can be supported with facts.

From the reading of an entire novel, one can state in a sentence or several sentences the main idea or ideas. Pupils can state the main idea after having read a library book. They can also state the main idea or ideas from reading a story in the basal reader. A main idea can also be selected from reading a page of content pertaining to a particular story.

In the reading of social studies content, for example, pupils may have realized as one main idea pertaining to a unit of study on Great Britain that individuals, people, and nations are interdependent. To support this main idea with concrete examples, Great Britain exports manufactured products such as cars, buses, motors, tractors, furniture, and toys to other nations of the world. Great Britain imports agricultural products such as meat and grain from other nations of the world. Thus, Great Britain is independent upon other nations for an adequate food supply. Whereas, other nations of the world depend upon Great Britain for manufactured products. Interdependency between and among nations is then involved.

Main ideas that pupils develop can be utilized, in many cases, again and again. The main idea that pupils developed pertaining to individuals, people, and nations being interdependent can be used again and again as different nations and areas of the world are being studied. Areas and nations depend upon each other for peace, food, shelter, clothing, other necessities, and luxuries. Pupils should be assisted to develop important main ideas. They should check the main ideas developed with supporting facts. The accuracy of each main idea can be checked and evaluated.

Determining Reading Levels of Pupils

It is, of course, no secret that all fifth graders in an elementary school, for example, cannot benefit equally in reading from a fifth grade reader. In a heterogeneously grouped fifth grade class, the range in reading achievement may vary from the second or third grade to the sixth or seventh grade level. The range in reading achievement could be even greater than that depending upon the capacity, past achievement, interest, and motivation of pupils.

It behooves the teacher to determine reading levels of pupils at any early age and thus provide for individual differences. If a pupil is in the fifth grade, what is his reading level? What materials for the teaching of reading will be most beneficial for this child? Some third and fourth grade pupils read better than do some fifth graders. It is possible that a few second graders may read better than do some fifth grade pupils. Grade levels may mean very little in terms of pupil achievement in an elementary school.

One approach that the reader may utilize to determine reading levels of pupils is to use an informal approach which requires no standardized tests. At the beginning of a given school year, the teacher could mark off 100 running words in a beginning part of a basal reader. The pupil must have no prior practice or experience in reading the content. The pupil individually reads the content orally to the teacher. The teacher records the number of words that the child cannot identify. He also asks questions of the pupil pertaining to comprehending the contents. The child should be able to identify approximately 95 to 98 out of 100 running words read to the teacher. The pupil should be able to answer correctly, approximately, three out of four questions covering the content. These standards are approximate and not absolute. The teacher can then determine if reading materials presently being used by the child are too difficult. Additional ways should be utilized in evaluating which reading materials are most beneficial for a particular child.

Numerous standardized tests are on the market to assist in determining reading levels of pupils. Directions as given in the manual for each standardized test should be followed carefully. Test results for each pupil should be evaluated accurately and carefully. It is of utmost importance that the tests have high validity and reliability. These tests must be valid from the point of view in helping to determine reading levels of pupils. They must be reliable in that consistency of results would be in evidence if learners took the same test over again without opportunities to practice what is contained within the test. Consistency of results would also be in evidence if a given set of learners took a different form of the test for the second testing. It is highly recommended that standardized tests be evaluated in terms of what specialists in testing and measurement say about each test.

The classroom teacher of reading through careful observation of each pupil's progress can do much to evaluate if materials used in the teaching of reading are beneficial to each child. Pupils must use reading materials which are interesting and meaningful. They should find that reading is an enjoyable activity and an important curriculum area as well as being a very worthwhile leisure time activity. If pupils are to become avid readers in adult life, they must like reading in the elementary school.

Handwriting in the Elementary School

The elementary school teacher needs to think of a variety of approaches and methods to help pupils achieve to their optimum in handwriting. Pupils must write legibly so that effective communication may take place. If poor quality handwriting is in evidence, the reader must take an excess amount of time in determining what has been written.

Pupils should be assisted individually in evaluating the kinds of errors that are made in handwriting. Learners may not improve in the area of handwriting unless they have knowledge of the kinds of errors made in handwriting. Pupils may be cursively writing the letter "t" with a loop in it and not crossing the letter properly, thus making it appear as the letter "l". If the letter "e" is written too tall in cursive writing, it will look like the letter "l". Pupils need to form each letter correctly. These letters should have proper proportion.

Proper slant of letters is important if legible writing is to take place. When uniformity of slant is lacking, an excess amount of time may be spent in determining what is to be read.

One common cause of difficulty in legible handwriting is that proper alignment of letters and words is not in evidence. A pupil may try to add a word on a line in the margin resulting in letters which do not properly stay on the line. The letters ending a line may then curve either upward or downward. The reader then has difficulty in determining readily what these words are. If the letters have also been formed incorrectly, legibility of handwriting may indeed be very poor.

Pupils should also space letters and words properly. First grade teachers, for example, may have observed pupils write the following in manuscript style: The cat ran away from the dog. It is quite obvious that the reader will take more time in reading the above sentence the way it is written as compared to having proper spacing between letters and words. Some learners crowd words together thus making it difficult for the reader to comprehend the contents.

It is important for teachers to praise pupils if they are doing better now than formerly in handwriting. Then all learners can receive praise. Too often, pupils who have high quality handwriting receive praise. Thus, some pupils may receive much praise for very little effort in working toward improved performance in handwriting since this is an area they may excel in. Others may try very hard to improve in the area of handwriting, but eye-hand coordination is lacking. These learners may receive no praise if those who excel in handwriting are given praise only. The teacher should think in terms of having each pupil progress continuously in the area of handwriting. Praise given for improved performance in handwriting for each pupil will spur pupils on toward greater efforts. All learners then can receive praise since each child can improve over previous efforts. It is important for pupils to develop an adequate concept of the self. Pupils must develop feelings of an adequate self to insure optimum achievement.

The teacher must plan and provide for a variety of learning activities for pupils. "Sameness" in learning activities makes for feelings of boredom on the part of learners. A wide variety of learning activities should be provided for pupils involving handwriting. Pupils can improve the quality of their handwriting by writing business letters, friendly letters, poems, stories, invitations, and engage in other functional writing activities. Generally, pupils lose interest in improving the quality of their handwriting when drill becomes the only important kind of learning activity.

On Teaching Handwriting

To communicate ideas effectively, pupils need to become proficient in legible handwriting. Handwriting that is not legible presents problems to the reader in terms of time taken to understand ideas expressed in written communication. The teacher must provide quality learning activities involving handwriting so that each pupil can improve over his past performance in increased legibility. A variety of learning activities should be provided so that pupil achievement is in evidence. What can the teacher do to help pupils achieve at an optimum rate in handwriting?

Pupils on an individual basis should receive praise for improved performance in handwriting. Even the pupil with the poorest quality of handwriting can receive praise if he is doing better than formerly. This should spur learners on to greater efforts in this area. Praise, however, should be given only if there is evidence that improvement is taking place.

Each pupil should have knowledge of the specific kinds of errors he has exhibited in handwriting. For a pupil to improve, he must receive guidance in diagnosing weaknesses that need to be overcome in handwriting. A pupil may not cross his "t's" and leave a small loop in that same letter resulting in a final product which looks like an "l". Or a pupil may write the letter "e" excessively tall making it appear as an "l". Based upon diagnosis, the pupil can then receive practice to overcome deficiencies in handwriting.

Pupils should attach positive attitudes toward handwriting. Too often learners have been asked to practice skills that have already been mastered. Instead new learnings should be developed. Opportunities should be given to help achieve more legible handwriting rather than being drilled on handwriting skills which have already been gained. Thus each pupil should engage in practicing the following as the need exists to improve over his previous performance: *(i)* improving the slant of letters and words;

(ii) forming individual letters correctly; *(iii)* having proper alignment of letters and words; *(iv)* spacing letters and words properly; *(v)* writing letters in proper proportion.

Pupils should not engage in handwriting activities which are excessively long or too difficult. For example, first grade teachers must be careful that excess tension and anxiety do not develop in pupils due to experiences involving lengthy handwriting exercises. These pupils among others must have a variety of interesting learning activities so that learning becomes an enjoyable experience.

The teacher can group pupils for teaching handwriting. Pupils who need the most guidance and assistance should be placed in one special group in an atmosphere of respect. These learners can receive necessary help in the area of handwriting as the need arises. In the same class some pupils may need very little assistance in handwriting. They can work independently in a variety of learning activities involving handwriting such as developing a special report based on research about a specific unit of study. In today's modern elementary school, desks in a classroom can be moved quietly in a small amount of time so that pupils can be placed into two or three groups for instruction in handwriting.

Originality in handwriting should be encouraged by the teacher. Each child is different from others in capacity, achievement, height, weight, energy level, and muscular coordination. Thus all learners in a class cannot form each capital and small letter in exactly the same way; however, legibility can still be in evidence with these variations. Each pupil therefore should be guided to develop his own unique style of legible handwriting.

Pupils should be guided to exhibit their best handwriting in all curriculum areas in the elementary school. Too frequently teachers have emphasized good handwriting only during the time handwriting is actually taught. Pupils may then not transfer the skills of good handwriting to different curricular areas such as social studies, science, mathematics, and the other language arts areas. For example, a pupil may have written slovenly when writing a report in social studies, but his handwriting may have been of good quality in a formal session devoted to teaching these skills. While the pupil is writing the first draft of the social studies report, he will generally not be using his best handwriting. The pupil must think of ideas first in writing content. In the final copy of the report, however, the child can exhibit his best handwriting possible. Pupils needs to have ample opportunities to practice good handwriting in the different curricular areas of the elementary school.

Learners should sense that purpose is involved in learning activities involving handwriting. The teacher alone in too many cases has felt that pupil purpose was involved in the ongoing learning activities. Purpose needs to be developed within pupils for learning. Pupils can write business letters ordering free charts and pictures about a specific social studies or science unit. In this situation a need exists for ordering materials for a unit of study. Each pupil should be encouraged to use his best handwriting since ideas need to be communicated effectively Pupils can also write friendly letters to relatives and friends. Legible handwriting must be in evidence here so that the receiver of the letter can read the content rapidly. The child should also feel that politeness is involved when using his best possible handwriting to communicate ideas in written form.

Pupils should develop interest in handwriting. No doubt, interest in handwriting has been destroyed by emphasizing much drill on letter formation, slanting of letters, alignment, proper proportion of letters, and spacing of letters and words. When pupils practice these selected handwriting skills, an interest in the purpose needs to be felt and accepted by learners. A variety of well-chosen learning activities can help learners to develop and maintain interest in handwriting.

Unfair competition among pupils has also hindered many pupils from liking the area of handwriting. Pupils in a class exhibit different achievement levels in handwriting. The teacher needs to accept each pupil on his present achievement level and guide all learners to make continuous progress.

The teacher of handwriting must be interested in the teaching of handwriting. The attitudes of the teacher in many cases may be reflected within pupils. The classroom teacher needs to think of methods and approaches to teaching handwriting which would capture the interest of pupils.

Learning to Listen

Many opportunities for learning are lost due to poor listening habits. It is important for individuals to be good listeners so that effective communication of ideas occurs. In American society the "explosion" of knowledge will increase at a faster rate in the years to come as compared to previous times. One way to obtain knowledge is to listen carefully to the thinking of others.

There are other reasons for being a good listener. To be respectful and considerate of others, it is necessary to listen carefully. One who is a good conversationalist must react to the thinking of individuals he is conversing with. When taking part in discussions, each must contribute ideas. Problems cannot be solved unless solutions proposed are carefully evaluated. This requires careful listening. In introducing a visitor to other individuals, it is of utmost importance to listen carefully to the names and other related information of persons being introduced.

Since careful listening is an important skill to develop, what learning activities can the teacher provide?

1. Classroom teachers should evaluate their own teaching to determine if directions given to pupils are repeated too frequently. Pupils may feel directions for an assignment will be repeated if they are not grasped the first time. The teacher needs to evaluate if his directions were given accurately, concisely and clearly. If directions are lengthy, they should be written on the chalkboard for pupil referral.

   When teachers present explanations and discuss content with pupils, evaluation needs to be made of repetitious statements which encourage poor listening on the part of the listener. Pupils can come to depend upon statements being repeated excessively by the teacher and thus poor listening is encouraged.

2. Cooperatively, pupils with teacher assistance could develop standards pertaining to good listening. Following the completion of a selected learning activity, pupil achievement could be evaluated in terms of these standards. Weaknesses in listening could be identified with further practice being given to overcome these deficiencies.

3. Devote special class sessions to helping learners become better listeners. For example, tape recordings could be made of different sounds in a selected environment such as the sound of a chain saw sawing wood, a caterpillar leveling land, and carpenters building a new home. Pupils with adequate background knowledge could attempt to identify these sounds.

   The teacher could have pupils put their heads on their desks and identify sounds made in the classroom. Listeners, in this situation would not be able to see the action taking place when the sound is being made. For example, the teacher could hit a piece of wood with a hammer, pour water from a pitcher, or tap his foot on the floor. Pupils would then be asked to identify these sounds.

   When pupils are taken on an excursion, call their attention to sounds in the environment such as birds singing, squirrels chattering, and dogs barking. Ask pupils to identify different sounds made in the environment.

4. The teacher and pupils need to provide a learning environment which promotes good listening. Unnecessary noises which hinder optimum achievement in listening should be avoided. Too frequently, competing sounds in the environment hinder pupils from gaining necessary ideas.

   A pupil may pay more attention to unnecessary noises made by others rather than concentrating on ideas being presented.

5. The teacher and pupils periodically should evaluate the temperature in the classroom. A too warm temperature makes pupils drowsy. If the room temperature is cold, pupils would concentrate more on being cold than on listening to ideas being presented in various listening activities. Proper ventilation is also important.

6. A variety of learning activities involving listening should be provided for pupils. Tapes, filmstrips, films, slides, excursions, construction activities, research, art activities,

and dramatizations provide opportunities for pupils to engage in speaking and listening. Learning activities must be varied so that pupils do not become bored with "sameness." Pupils' interest must be developed and maintained so that a high degree of comprehension will result from the ongoing learning activities. It is also important to select learning activities which provide meaningful learnings for pupils. Pupils in many cases will listen carefully when they can attach meaning to what has been presented verbally.

7. The teacher should be a good example for pupils to follow in the area of listening. If the teacher is a poor listener, pupils may think and feel that careful listening is not necessary. In the classroom as well as in the school cafeteria and playground, the teacher should make a definite effort to listen carefully to the ideas of pupils.

8. In learning activities provided for pupils, purpose should exist for the listening activity. The teacher can briefly discuss with pupils why they need to listen carefully to a learning activity involving the use of oral language. Hopefully, learners will sense it is important to listen intently.

9. Stress the importance of good listening in all curriculum areas of the elementary school. There needs to be a transfer of listening from special times devoted to teaching listening skills to careful listening in the elementary school throughout the school day.

10. Pupils with hearing difficulties should be seated as close as possible to the spoken voice. In this way, they also can observe the lips and facial expressions of the speaker.

11. Pupils should receive praise for improved performance in listening. Learners like to be rewarded for doing better than formerly. Thus, praise given judiciously would spur learners on to greater efforts in listening. All pupils in a class can then receive praise for improved listening.

Linguistics in the Elementary School

Linguistics have made many contributions in improving the elementary school language arts curriculum. They place heavy emphasis upon pupils participating in various learning activities involving the spoken language. In the past, pupils have learned very little about the English language and its use when filling in blank spaces in workbooks and exercises from textbooks. Too frequently, pupils have filled in blank spaces in sentences with "is", "are", "was", or "were". They may even have completed the exercises correctly. And yet, these same pupils later when conversing with each other have used sentences where the subject and verb do not agree. Or, these learners may have written sentences using "is", "are", "was", and "were" incorrectly. The point is that filling in blanks contained in exercises within workbooks and language arts textbooks lacks reality pertaining to situations faced in life. When individuals in every day society speak or write, they generally do not fill in blank spaces.

Linguists differentiate between the concepts of "grammar" and "usage". Grammar is a description of how a language works or operates. A noun, for example, is a word that can be changed from singular to plural or from plural to singular. "Man" is a noun since it is singular and can be changed to plural as would be true of the word "men." Each of the following words is a noun since it refers to one in number (singular) and can be changed to mean more than one (plural): duck, cow, boy, girl, woman, tiger, elephant, baby, owl, turkey, dog, cat, and monkey.

Verbs are words that can be changed from present to past tense or from past to present tense. The following words are verbs since they indicate something that is happening presently and yet each word can be changed to indicate a happening which has already occurred: run, swim, sing, walk, dance, jump, hop, skip, move, and eat. The past tense of each of the above named words would be the following: ran, swam, sang, walked, danced, jumped, hopped, skipped, moved, and ate.

In traditional grammar, parts of speech were classified in terms of definitions. For example, a noun was a word which referred to a person, place, or thing. A verb was defined as a word which dealt with action or a state of being. Thus "running" was a verb in the following sentence since action was involved. The boy was running a race. Much confusion exists in the following sentence when thinking of verbs being action words: Running is my favourite exercise. The word "running" pertains to doing something or action is involved. However, "running" is the subject of the sentence and not the predicate or verb. The word "is" is a verb in the sentence and yet it does not relate to action. The word "is" however can be changed from present to past tense.

Usage can be thought of as choices that are made when words are selected to be used in sentences. When giving an oral report to a class of graduate or undergraduate students, the tendency would be to choose words and sentences which would be more formal and sophisticated as compared to conversing with a well-known friend or one's husband or wife.

No all individuals from different socio-economic levels choose the same words when speaking. The concepts of standard and non-standard English can be brought into the discussion. The individual from a very low income family might select the following words to express himself: I ain't got no money no how. Using standard English, one would use the following words to express the same idea: I have no money or I haven't got any money. When thinking of usage then, choices are made among words.

Patterns of Sentences

Pupils in the elementary schools use various patterns of sentences. The child entering kindergarten may express himself very well by using sentences containing six or more words. He can convey ideas very well to others and yet have no knowledge of grammar. Too frequently, much time has been spent in teaching grammar with very limited results in terms of improved speaking and writing. The study of grammar should help pupils improve in communicating ideas effectively to others. This objective has not been achieved in too many cases.

Generally, pupils, as they progress through the elementary school, can identify five patterns of sentences which are used frequently when communicating ideas with others.

The first sentence pattern consists of the noun-verb or subject predicate pattern. The following are examples of this pattern:

1. Dogs bark.
2. The boy swims.

In the first sentence "Dogs" is a noun and the subject of the sentence. "Dog" can be changed from singular to plural or plural to singular. "Bark" is the verb. It can be changed from present to past tense or vice versa. In the second sentence "boy" is a noun and the subject of the sentence whereas "swims" is the verb or predicate of the sentence.

A second sentence pattern used by elementary school pupils would pertain to the noun-verb-noun pattern or subject-predicate-direct object pattern. The following are examples:

1. The boy caught the ball.
2. The carpenter built the garage.

In the first sentence, "boy" is a noun and is a word which can be changed from singular to plural (boy-boys); boy's is the subject of the word "caught." "Caught" is a verb since it is a word which can be changed from past tense to present tense (caught-catch). The word "ball" is the object of "caught," such as the boy caught what? The answer, of course, is "ball."

A third sentence pattern would pertain to the noun-linking verb-predicate adjective pattern. The following sentences would illustrate this pattern:

1. The flowers were beautiful.
2. The man was tall.

In the first sentence, the word "flowers" is a noun since it can be changed from plural to singular (flowers-flower). The word "were" is a verb since it can be changed to present tense (were-are). The word "beautiful" is a predicate adjective since it tells about or describes "flowers." Linguists may think of adjectives as patterning with the word "very". The word "beautiful" would be an adjective then since it patterns with the word "very" such as "very beautiful." The word "beautiful" is not a noun since it cannot be changed from singular to plural or vice versa. It is not a verb since "beautiful" cannot be changed from present to past tense or vice versa.

A fourth sentence pattern could pertain to the noun-linking verb-predicate noun pattern as would be illustrated by the following sentences:

1. John is a boy.
2. Mr. Brown was a farmer.

In the first sentence "John" and "boy" refer to the same person. Both are nouns since each word can be changed from singular to plural. The word "is" is a verb since it can be changed from present tense to past tense. In the second sentence "Mr. Brown" and "farmer" refer to the same person and these words are joined together by the verb "was."

A fifth sentence pattern used by elementary school pupils is the noun-verb-noun-noun or subject-predicate-indirect object-direct object pattern. The following sentences are examples:

1. John gave Jim a present.
2. The girl made Sally a scarf.

In the first sentence "John" is a noun and is used as the subject of the sentence. "Gave" is a verb which can be changed to present tense when thinking of a rationale for classifying that word. John gave what? The answer is "present." The word "present" is a direct object and tells what was given. The question arises as to whom or for whom the present was intended. The answer would be "Jim." The word "Jim" then would be classified as an indirect object. Some pre-schoolers, as well as early primary grade pupils will already use sentence patterns which follow the noun-verb-noun-noun pattern. When pupils celebrate their birthdays or at Christmas time, they will be using oral expressions, such as the following:

1. I gave John a present.
2. Janica gave Sally some dishes.
3. The teacher gave each pupil some pencils.
4. Mother bought me a doll.
5. Daddy bought us some candy.

Expanding Sentences

To make sentences more descriptive and more meaningful, writers can expand each of the five sentence patterns discussed previously.

One way that sentences can be expanded is through modification. The following sentences follow the noun-verb pattern:

1. The boys walked.
2. The girls sang.

Certain questions can be asked about each of these sentences. For example, in sentence one, the following questions could be asked:

1. How many boys were there?
2. How old were these boys?
3. How did they walk?

If modifiers are added to the sentence, more clarity in writing will result. For example, the first sentence—"The boys walked"—could be expanded to read as follows:

1. The three tall boys walked slowly.
2. Two kindergarten boys walked rapidly to the playground.

A second approach used to expand sentences is through compounding words, phrases, clauses, or sentences. Notice the following sentences:

1. Jim likes to read library books.
2. John likes to read library books.

In these sentences, the subjects "Jim" and "John" can be compounded to make a meaningful sentence which would read as follows: Jim and John like to read library books. The writing also becomes less monotonous when the words "Jim and John" become compound subjects.

Other words can also be compounded in order to expand sentences. Notice the following sentences:

1. Dora sang.
2. Dora danced.

These sentences can be written in a much more interesting way through compounding the verbs as would be true of the following expanded sentence:

Dora sang and danced.

Phrases can also be compounded when expanding sentences.

1. The boy walked in the yard.
2. The boy walked around the house.

These sentences can be combined with the phrases "in the yard" and "around the house" compounded, such as in the following sentence: The boy walked in the yard and around the house.

A third way of expanding would be to use subordination. The following basic sentence would follow the noun-verb-noun or subject-predicate-direct object pattern: John made a touchdown. This sentence can be expanded by adding a subordinate clause. John, who played the entire game, made a touchdown. Additional information describing John "who played the entire game" is added to the basic sentence "John made a touchdown." A subordinate clause could also modify the verb or predicate: While he felt very tired, John made a touchdown. The subordinate clause "Write he felt very tired" modifies "made" since it tells when the touchdown was made.

A fourth way of expanding sentences is through the use of appositives. Notice the following basic sentence: Carl Jones lived on Line Street. Additional information can be added pertaining to Carl Jones such as would be true of the following sentences:

Carl Jones, an employee of the post office, lives on Line Street.

Carl Jones, a professional golfer, lives on Line Street.

In the first sentence, "Carl Jones" and "employee" refer to the same person with no verb or predicate to join the two words. In the second sentence, "Carl Jones" and "golfer" refer to the same person.

Using appositives in sentences makes for variety and interest in the kinds of sentences which are written. Monotonous writing occurs when sentences are written in the following manner:

Carl Jones lives on Line Street. Carl Jones is an employee of the post office.

The first sentence can be expanded by using an appositive thus omitting the necessity of having the second sentence:

Carl Jones, an employee of the post office, lives on Line Street.

Building New Sentences

A basic sentence, also called a kernal sentence, can be taken and changed to various other kinds of sentences with little or no change in the choice of words used.

Consider the following kernal sentence:

John plays football in the yard.

This is a declarative sentence stating a fact. Pupils with teacher guidance can change this sentence so that a question is asked:

Does John play football in the yard?

The original kernal sentence can also be used to state a negative:

John doesn't play football in the yard.

The order of words can be changed in the kernal sentence thus making a different kind of transformation.

A command or request can also be indicated by changing the original kernal sentence. The sentence when transformed may thus read:

Play football in the yard, John.

Please play football in the yard, John.

Pupils should have ample opportunities to transform kernal sentences to indicate the following:

(a) questions

(b) negatives

(c) inversions

(d) commands or requests

Stress, Pitch, and Juncture

When individuals communicate ideas orally to each other, stress, pitch and juncture are in evidence. Not all words, of course, are stressed equally much when orally communicating ideas. Consider the following sentence when thinking of one pupil asking another pupil a question:

Did you get an A in social studies?

If the pupil asking the question stresses the word "you" rather heavily in speaking, it may sound as if it were impossible for the listener to receive an A grade in social studies. It also emphasizes you as an individual being spoken to rather than someone else. If the letter grade "A" is stressed heavily by the speaker, it may indicate that it is difficult to receive such a high mark in social studies; it may also emphasize that an "A" grade has been received rather than a lower grade. If the word "social studies" is stressed heavily, the emphasis is upon social studies and not a different curriculum area. Pupils should have ample opportunities to study a particular sentence by emphasizing or stressing one word within the sentence more than the other words. Learners can then notice the effect this has on the meaning of the spoken sentence. Sentences which are spoken orally can be tape recorded in order to evaluate the degree of stress or emphasis a particular word received. Linguists recognize and identify four degrees of stress.

Pupils should also study the highness or lowness in pitch of words as they are spoken in sentences. Sentences can change in meaning depending upon the pitch of words. Notice the following sentences:

1. Tom swims.
2. Tom swims?

The same words are used in both sentences. In the first sentence, the voice is lowered at the end of this declarative sentence since a fact is stated. In the second sentence, the speaker raises the pitch of his voice at the end due to asking a question about Tom being able to swim. Not always, of course, is the ending word pitched higher than the other words in a sentence when a question is asked. With teacher guidance, pupils should have much practice in listening to selected sentences where the same word within a sentence is pitched differently. The tape-recorder should be used to assist pupils in thoroughly evaluating sentences through replays as to meanings changing when words are pitched at different levels. Linguists recognize and identify four levels of pitch.

The concept of "juncture" is also very important for pupils to understand. When sentences are written, commas, periods, question marks, and exclamation points indicate where pauses occur when reading content. When oral language is utilized, the speaker needs to pause at appropriate places in order that the listener can attach accurate meanings to ideas. If the speaker omitted all pauses in the following sentence, it would be difficult to determine the kinds of foods served at a picnic:

At the picnic, the family had ham, sandwiches, jello, salad, and milk.

If the speaker did not pause adequately after the word "ham", the listener may interpret that the family enjoyed "ham sandwiches" at the picnic rather than "ham" and "sandwiches". The same would be true if the pause would not be adequate between the words "jello" and "salad"; the listener may think that "jello salad" was served. Pupils with teacher guidance should listen to selected sentences and determine how meanings change within a sentence if pauses are not adequate at specific points.

Teach Them to Communicate

Elementary pupils need opportunities to practice speaking so that they may learn to communicate effectively.

The classroom teacher must implement certain guidelines if pupils are to experience continuous success in learning activities involving speaking. These guidelines are:

1. Learning activities involving speaking should have purpose. The teacher may ask children to select information on a topic and present their conclusions to the class. Pupils, however, may "sense" little or no purpose in this learning activity. They need to feel that purpose is involved. For example, in a social studies unit, pupils should be stimulated to ask questions. Attractive and interesting scenes on a bulletin board, a film or filmstrip will encourage this. Pupil's questions can then provide the basis for gathering information and presenting findings to the class. Oral reports based on purposes of the pupils help improve oral communication.
2. Learning activities involving speaking should be interesting. "Sameness" generally reduces pupil's interest. For example, if pupils must give an excessive number of oral book reports, interest in activities involving speaking may be lost. The classroom teacher needs to think of a variety of activities to help pupils develop speaking proficiency. In completing a science unit, for example, pupils may have developed models of volcanoes, faults and folding. They can explain these models to other pupils in the classroom. In a social studies unit, a pupil or committee could interview a person who had lived for some time in a foreign country being

studied. Interviewing the resource person for other children provides variety in activities involving speaking. Hobbies brought to class can form the basis for a speaking activity. Different learning activities should be explored as means of helping pupils develop interest in speaking.

3. Learning activities involving speaking should be meaningful. A child who has memorized content may not attach meaning to facts in situations involving verbal communication. Learning activities using films, filmstrips, excursions, reading, discussions and pictures help pupils understand and attach meaning to what has been learned. Meaningful facts, concepts, and generalizations developed by the learners should assist him in communicating effectively.

4. Learning activities involving speaking should help pupils realize objectives. Pupils differ in achievement, capacity, energy, level, motivation and coordination, among other things. The teacher needs to consider differences among pupils when determining goals for each pupil in oral communication. Each child needs to be evaluated in terms of improvement over his previous performance in speaking. The learning activity in speaking should help pupils feel successful in realizing their objectives. The teacher and pupil together should decide which objectives in oral communication the student should realize.

5. Learning activities involving speaking should evaluate pupil achievement. Tape recordings of discussions and conversations help pupils determine with teacher guidance, strengths and weaknesses in oral communication. Respect for the thinking of others is important. Strengths of pupils should be rewarded through praise. Needed areas of improvement can be cooperatively identified. Additional speaking activities should be provided to overcome these deficiencies. A variety of techniques should be used in evaluating pupil achievement in oral communication.

In Summary

Teachers in the elementary school must provide a reading readiness, programme which provides for individual differences in the class setting. A variety of learning activities must be provided for pupils in the reading readiness programme. Pupil achievement in reading should be evaluated continuously to provide for sequential achievement on the part of learners. Skills must be developed on the part of readers to identify and recognize new words. Pupils should have ample practice in reading for a variety of purposes.

Teachers must follow recommended teaching procedures in helping learners realize the objectives of legibility in handwriting.

Pupils should be guided to develop optimum proficiency in listening through carefully selected learning activities.

Linguists have made important contributions in improving the language arts curriculum. Teachers of language arts should assess and compare traditional grammar with the linguistic approach.

REFERENCES

Anderson, Paul S. *Linguistics in the Elementary School Classroom*. New York: The Macmillan Company, 1971.

Anderson, Verna Dieckman, and others (Eds.). *Readings in the Language Arts*. New York: The Macmillan Company, 1968.

Applegate, Mauree. *Essay in English*. New York: Harper and Row, 1960.

Carter, Homer L., and Dorothy J. McGinnis. *Teaching Individuals to Read*. Boston: D.C. Heath and Company, 1962.

Burns, Paul C., and Leo M. Schell (Eds.). *Elementary School Language Arts, Selected Readings*, Second Edition. New York: Rand McNally and Company, 1973.

Corcoran, Gertrude B. *Language Arts in the Elementary School*. New York: The Ronald Press Company, 1970.

Dollmann, Martha. *Teaching the Language Arts in the Elementary School*. Dubuque: Willima C. Brown Company Publishers, 1971.

Dechant, Emerald. *Linguistics, Phonics, and the Teaching of Reading*. Springfield: Charles C. Thomas, Publishers, 1969.

Donoghue, Mildred R. *The Child and the English Language Arts*. Dubuque: William C. Brown Publishers, 1971.

Harris, Albert J. *How to Increase Reading Ability*. New York: David McKay Company, Inc., 1961.

Smith, E. Brooks, and others. *Language and Thinking in the Elementary School*. New York: Holt, Rinehat and Winston, Inc., 1970

Taylor, Elvin. *A New Approach to Language Arts in the Elementary School*. West Nyack: Parker Publishing Company, Inc., 1970.

Tidyman, Willard F., and others. *Teaching the Language Arts*. New York: McGraw-Hill Book Company, 1969.

Tiedt, Iris M., and Sidney W. Tiedt. *Contemporary English in the Elementary School*. Englewood Cliffs: Prentice-Hall, Inc., 1967.

Trauger, Wilmer K. *Language Arts in Elementary Schools*. New York: McGraw-Hill Book Company, 1963.

Reading and the Elementary Curriculum

Each pupil should develop optimum proficiency in reading. Reading can be a very enjoyable leisure activity. Individuals enrich themselves by engaging in reading activities. In society, it is important for individuals to do much reading and thus remain informed about problems and issues on the local, state, national, and international levels. Each person may then have additional alternatives from which decisions can be made. A broad base of background knowledge may assist learners to increase their proficiency to make decisions.

Each pupil differs from other children in the class setting in achievement, capacity, interests, and motivation for reading. Thus, the teacher must make provision for individual differences among learners in the reading curriculum.

Experience Charts and Reading

In a reading readiness programme for early primary grade children, experience charts may be developed cooperatively by pupils with teacher guidance. The experience chart approach is sound since it is based upon personal experiences of involved pupils. Thus, pupil's experience ideas from excursions, filmstrips, films, pictures, slides, or discussions. Following the experience, pupils present content for an experience chart. The teacher in this situation prints the content using neat manuscript letters. Most pupils generally have not developed a writing vocabulary to do the actual writing. After the content has been written in large, highly legible manuscript letters, pupils read what has been written with teacher guidance. The teacher points to words and phrases as they are being read by pupils. Learners then are reading what they have experienced.

The following assumptions support utilizing experience charts:

1. Pupils are actively involved in experiences which provide content for an experience chart.
2. Learners present ideas for the experience chart.
3. Pupils with teacher help read content pertaining to their very own experiences.
4. Learners may notice how ideas are written down utilizing abstract letters in words.
5. The content in the experience chart is familiar to learners since it relates to their own personal lives.
6. The experience chart method may assist pupils to develop interest in reading.
7. Individualization is inherent in using experience charts since each child has unique experiences. Each child may then present content for a group or individual experience chart.

Learning Centres and Reading

A different approach to individualize instruction in reading pertains to the use of learning centres. One of these centres might well be a reading centre. Library books should be on diverse reading levels and on various stimulating topics. Ideally each pupil selects an interesting library book to read on the appropriate reading level. Following the reading of a library book, pupil achievement may be evaluated in several ways.

1. Task cards at the learning centre could be written with open-ended questions for pupils to respond to.
2. The teacher and pupil might discuss contents of a library book which the letter has completed reading.
3. The child may choose his/her own approach in revealing comprehension pertaining to content in a library book such as in completing a diorama, a dramatization, a frieze, or a picture.

4. The pupil might share ideas gained from reading a library book within a small group or committee.

Any approach that is used to assess pupil achievement should stimulate learners to do additional reading.

Reading Readiness and Individualized Instruction

There are numerous learning activities which assist pupils in learning to read through a quality reading readiness programme. Providing for individual differences is an important concept for teachers to follow when selecting learning activities in a reading readiness programme.

Background information must be developed within pupils in a quality reading readiness programme. Later, pupils will read much content where familiarity with ideas is important. To aid in developing background information, the following learning activities, among others, may be utilized.

1. Discuss pictures with pupils pertaining to ongoing units of study.
2. Show and discuss films, filmstrips, and slides.
3. Have pupils take an excursion and discuss observations made.
4. View and have follow-up activities pertaining to a telecast on educational television.
5. Develop learning centres with appropriate activities to help pupils achieve relevant background information.

For each of the above learning activities, purpose must be developed within pupils prior to participation. The learning activities can provide for individual differences even though learners at selected intervals may be taught in large group instruction. Pupils may then interpret content from audio-visual materials on their own individual present achievement levels. It is best if most of these activities can be used in small group or committee work. Pupils may then have increased opportunities to interact with other learners in discussing acquired facts, concepts, and generalizations. The frequency of interaction in a discussion per pupil in small group work is greater than would be true of larger groups or the class as a whole.

In a quality reading readiness programme, it is important for learners to experience hearing likenesses and differences in sounds. Thus, for example, a teacher may ask pupils to present words which have the same beginning sound as does the word "bat". Pupils may also be asked to give words which rhyme with "bat". These activities should aid learners to become increasingly proficient in phonetic analysis. Later, in more formalized programmes of reading instruction, the use of phonetic analysis will aid in unlocking new words.

In a reading readiness programme pupils begin to make associations between symbol and sound. When pupils are reading from an experience chart with teacher guidance, they may well notice specific letters in words and make the proper associations with sounds.

When selected objects are labeled in a class, pupils ultimately will also make associations between symbols and sounds. If they cannot identify the abstract word, the real object will tell its meaning, such as the labeled abstract word "chair" or a real chair. Pupils learn to identify individual words at different rates of speed. Provision may then be made for individual differences.

Pupils should have ample opportunities to browse through interesting and appealing library books containing quality pictures. Illustrated books have a tendency to provide for individual differences when chosen by pupils. Learners may then interpret illustrations on their own individual achievement level. The teacher also needs to read library books to pupils in a reading readiness programme. Thus, pupils may become motivated in wanting to learn to read.

Further learning activities in a reading readiness programme might consist of pupils advancing at individual levels of achievement in noticing configuration clues. Experiences in noticing configuration clues must be provided in proper sequence for each learner. Among others, these learning activities may include the following:

1. Pupils make a cross on which word looks different from two other words (man lonely man).
2. Learners place an "X" on which letter appears different from two other letters (h h a).

Gross discriminations need to be made by pupils followed in sequence by those involving finer discriminations. Fine discriminations are involved in which a word or letter looks different in appearance from the remaining words/letters in each of the following sets:

1. house, hen, house;
2. b, b, l;
3. horse, hill, hill;
4. a, a, b.

Basal Readers and the Pupil

Basal readers are used quite frequently in elementary school classrooms. Teachers need to utilize the manual directly related to the basal reader in a creative manner. Too frequently, the manual is utilized rigidly. Suggestions pertaining to objectives, learning activities, and assessment procedures found in manuals of basal readers should be adapted to individual differences in the class setting. The manual can give teachers many excellent suggestions to use in teaching-learning situations. The following criteria are recommended in helping pupils achieve to their optimum when basal readers are utilized:

1. Basal readers should be on the present achievement level of pupils when learning activities are provided.
2. Prior to reading a given selection, pupils should have adequate readiness activities such as:
   (a) gaining adequate background information;
   (b) seeing new words in manuscript print and attaching meaning to these words;
   (c) establishing purposes for reading. The purposes may pertain to questions which require answers from reading a given selection.
3. Following the reading activity, pupils should have appropriate follow-up activities, such as:
   (a) discussing purposes or answers to questions after reading a given selection;
   (b) writing a summary of main ideas read;

(c) developing an illustration, freize, mural, or diorma;

(d) reading additional literature related to the content read;

(e) selecting stories and books written by the same author;

(f) reading selected portions orally;

(g) writing diverse forms of poetry;

(h) dramatizing selected sections of the content;

(i) developing a related bulletin board display.

Basal readers have been misused by classroom teachers. Certainly, teachers must apply relevant principles of learning in teaching-learning situations involving the use of basal readers. These principles would include:

(a) providing for individual differences;

(b) attaching meaning to what has been learned;

(c) stimulating learners in desiring to learn;

(d) praising pupils for improved performance regardless of past achievement;

(e) diagnosing pupil difficulties and working toward remediation;

(f) having learners achieve at their own optimum unique rates of achievement;

(g) selecting interesting learning activities;

(h) having pupils sense reasons for participating in ongoing learning activities;

(i) providing sequential learnings for learners;

(j) having pupils voice their concerns and interests in selecting reading materials;

(k) maintaining balance among objectives pertaining to learning word recognition techniques, reading for a variety of purposes, and reading for enjoyment.

There are selected procedures which have been used in situations involving the use of basal readers which definitely cannot be recommended. Among others, these include the following:

1. All pupils in a class being on the same page at the same time in a basal reader.
2. Every learning activity in the manual being utilized in teaching-learning situations for all pupils in the class setting.
3. Pupils rigidly developing learnings pertaining to phonetic analysis and other word recognition techniques when they already are reading proficiently.
4. Teachers emphasizing recall of information largely, when purposes for reading are being pursued on the part of pupils. Higher levels of thinking also need adequate emphasis, e.g. critical thinking, creative thinking, and problem solving.
5. Little emphasis being placed on pupils reading for enjoyment.
6. The same or similar methodology being used rather continuously in teaching reading.
7. Content in basal readers not being correlated or integrated with other curriculum areas in the elementary school.
8. Teachers not diagnosing pupil difficulties in reading adequately and not working toward remediation of problems.
9. Pupils not being taught in terms of using child growth and development characteristics.
10. Recommended principles of learning not being utilized in teaching-learning situations.
11. A lack of teacher knowledge or enthusiasm in teaching reading.

The teacher of reading needs to engage in self-evaluation to determine which trends in a modern reading curriculum should be emphasized in teaching-learning situations in the class setting.

Linguistics and Reading

Selected specialists have emphasized the importance of linguistic approaches in guiding learners to achieve in learning.

According to one linguistic school of thought in beginning reading instruction, pupils should learn to read words which have rather through consistency between symbol and sound. Pupils may then learn to read sentences in which words follow a specific pattern in pronunciation and spelling. Thus, the teacher might guide pupils in learning to read sentences containing the following words:

man fan Dan pan tan

ban can Nan ran van

Or, pupils in beginning reading could learn to read words such as the following in sentences:

bet net pet vet

met let set wet

It is difficult, of course, to write sentences with involved words following a pattern such as in the above named "man" family or "bat" family of words. This approach in the teaching of reading has been acceptable by some teachers. However, in the curriculum area of spelling, pupils in many units of study, learn to spell words where patterns are important. Thus, pupils are learning the structure of words such as in the following set where the initial consonant can be changed and a new word results: pat, rat, fat, cat, bat, hat, Nat, and sat.

There are advantages that linguistic approaches in the teaching of reading emphasize. These implications may also hold true for spelling. Among others, the advantages include the following:

1. Pupils can be aided in reading instruction by noticing how selected words pattern rather consistently between symbol and sound.
2. Learners develop understandings pertaining to structure of related words following a general or specific pattern.
3. Pupils may learn to identify new words when thinking of related patterns.
4. Learners develop a positive approach in identifying new words when viewing structure or pattern of words.

Disadvantages in using linguistic approaches in the teaching of reading might be the following:

1. Monotonous reading activities may be experienced by pupils, especially in beginning teaching-learning situations.
2. There might be a lack of relationship in terms of how pupils speak using functional sentences as compared to reading content in beginning reading using selected linguistic approaches.
3. Many words are spelled in an irregular manner in the English language and do not pattern well, such as "my", "sigh", "I", and "lye." These words contain the long "i" sound.

In using linguistic approaches in the teaching, pupils encounter more of irregularly spelled words as they progress through the elementary school years. There also are irregularly spelled words which follow a pattern, such as "bright", "flight", "might", "plight", "sight", and "night."

Specific Objectives and Rcading

Selected teachers, supervisors, and administrators advocate the use of specific objectives in the teaching of reading. These objectives are written in a precise manner. It is possible to measure if pupils have achieved specific objectives after instruction. Through observation, as one method of appraisal, the teacher can evaluate if pupils have or have not achieved the desired ends. Specific objectives must be selected carefully, prior to instruction, by those involved in teaching pupils. Thus, relevancy is an important concept to emphasize in selecting specific objectives for pupils to achieve.

The following are examples of specific objectives which pupils may achieve on their own unique achievement level:

1. The pupil will voluntarily read a library book and be able to answer three out of four questions correctly in evaluating comprehension.
2. The learner will pronounce correctly 95 per cent of words encountered in reading a selection from the basal reader.
3. Reading a story of his/her own choosing, the pupil will state the main idea in the selection.

4. Having identified a problem in any curriculum area, the pupil will select five reference sources to gain a relevant solution.
5. The pupil will present at least three generalizations related to content read from a self-selected library book.
6. The learner will analyze a selection in reading by identifying three opinions given by the writer.
7. After completing the reading assignment, pupils will assess content in terms of presenting two accurate statements and two inaccurate statements.
8. The learner will tell a story pertaining to content read using appropriate sequence of sentences.
9. Following the reading of content in social studies, the pupil will give five facts contained in the selection.
10. Having read content pertaining to five story problems in mathematics, the pupil will tell in his/her own words information needed to provide viable solutions.

It is important for teachers to write significant objectives when specificity is important. Too frequently, specific objectives are written which can be stated quickly and may then represent irrelevant learnings. Each objective in reading must be evaluated thoroughly in terms of acceptable standards.

Determining Reading Levels

One of the most important problems facing teachers of reading is to determine levels of individual pupils. Once this has been accomplished, the teacher has a further responsibility in finding materials which are beneficial to each individual. How can the teacher determine present reading levels of each pupil in the class setting?

1. The school may use standardized achievement tests to determine reading levels of pupils. These tests need to be assessed in terms of being valid and reliable. Grade equivalent test results from standardized tests may provide guidance to teachers in determining reading levels of learners on an individual basis.
2. The teacher may mark off approximately 100 running words in a basal textbook. The content has not been read previously by the pupil. The learner orally reads the

selection to the teacher. Generally, pupils should pronounce 95 to 98 per cent of the words correctly, if the involved book has content on the instructional level of the learner. The teacher also must select, with great care, four questions covering the selection to be read by pupils. Each pupil basically should be able to answer correctly three out of the four questions to assess comprehension in reading.

The figures given pertaining to correct word pronunciation as well as reading comprehension are approximate. If pupils, for example, pronounce 75 per cent of the words correctly in a selection, comprehension will suffer. Thus, the book being considered is not on the instructional level of individual pupils. Or, if a pupil continually pronounces all words correctly without previous practice and can continually respond correctly to all relevant questions asked to assess comprehension, the book being considered will generally be too easy for the learner. The textbook might then be considered to be on the recreational level of reading. There is no room for growth in recognizing new words in reading on the part of individual pupils if, without previous practice, the child can pronounce 100 per cent of the words correctly. Thus, in a quality reading programme, there is room in each lesson for pupils to learn to identify a few new words as well as be challenged in the area of comprehension.

The teacher then has an important responsibility in determining reading levels of individual pupils. Appropriate materials must be obtained to assist each pupil in achieving optimally in reading.

Evaluating Reading Achievement

In assessing pupil achievement in reading, teachers need to ask themselves, among others, the following questions:

1. Did I guide each child in learning to read to his or her highest potential?
2. Were reading materials provided for each child's own unique level of achievement?
3. Did pupils engage in more independent reading than formerly?
4. Were pupils guided in developing proficiency in word attack skills so that comprehension of content was at an optimal level?

5. Did it appear that pupils enjoyed learning activities involving reading?
6. Were pupils developing optimal skills in reading for a variety of purposes?
7. Did learners have ample opportunities to assess their own achievement in reading?
8. Were pupils permitted to make an adequate number of choices in terms of selections to be read?
9. Did each achieve stated objectives in reading instruction?
10. Were attitudinal objectives emphasized adequately as well as skills and understandings objectives in teaching-learning situations?
11. Did pupils develop appropriate appreciations toward quality literature in the reading curriculum?
12. Were pupil difficulties in reading diagnosed adequately?
13. Was remedial reading instruction emphasized adequately for needy learners?
14. Did I attempt to determine reading levels of each pupil?
15. Were appropriate learning activities selected to provide for individual differences?
16. Did I use valid evaluation techniques in assessing learner achievement?
17. If pupils did not achieve desired objectives, did I attempt to determine cause for this happening to remedy identified deficiencies?

In Summary

There are many innovations in the teaching of reading. Teachers, principals, and supervisors must become thoroughly familiar with new methods of teaching. New approaches in teaching reading should be evaluated thoroughly before being introduced in an elementary school. Objectives in reading must be carefully selected for pupils to achieve. Learning activities to achieve desired ends, as well as appraisal procedures to evaluate achievement, need to provide for individual differences among learners.

The Integrated Reading Curriculum

Considerable debate has been in evidence pertaining to how reading should be taught. During the 1960's and 1970's, the debate centred around approaches to the teaching of reading. The approaches included the use of individualized reading, basal, readers, language experience methods, the Initial Teaching Alphabet (ITA), linguistic procedures, as well as programmed textbooks.

During the 1980's, behaviourism as a psychology of learning has been strongly advocated. With behaviourism, the following are in evidence:

1. precise, measurably stated objectives for students to achieve;
2. state mandated objectives for teachers to stress in teaching students;
3. state-wide testing to determine the extent to which students are achieving the precise goals;
4. the use of standardized tests (norm referenced) to measure learner progress in reading.
5. instructional management systems (IMS) developed on the local district level. IMS plans contain behaviourally stated objectives. After instruction, the teacher can measure if a student has/has not achieved the specific goal.

The New Debate in Reading

With IMS and state mandated testing, emphasis is placed upon students achieving precise, measurably stated objectives. The tests within the IMS or state mandated testing are to be valid. The test items then measure what has been taught by the reading teacher to assist students to attain the precise ends. If a first grade teacher has ninety objectives in reading for learners to achieve, much emphasis in ongoing lessons and units will focus on students achieving the stated objectives. Each objective is highly specific, such as the student will underline the "fr" sound correctly on a worksheet in ten words pronounced by the teacher. With ninety precise objectives for student attainment in a school year, much drill and practice can be in evidence. There may be little time left over for enjoyment of reading. The measurably stated objectives have fragmented the act of reading into developing specific skills in phonics, syllabication, and structural analysis. Reading orally and silently to comprehend worthwhile subject matter may be minimized.

The act of reading is holistic and involves acquisition of facts, concepts, and generalizations. Relationship of words, phrases, sentences, and paragraphs must be perceived by students. Comprehension is the ultimate goal of reading instruction. Subject matter may be understood through reading for a variety of reasons or purposes. These reasons or purposes include reading for facts, sequence of ideas, main ideas, and generalizations. Additional comprehension skills involve critical reading, creative reading, reading to solve problems, as well as recreational reading. Even with all of the above purposes or reasons for reading content, subject matter should not be divided into isolated, fragmented parts. Rather the whole or gestalt of content read is vital. Content is related and does not occur in fragments of pieces.

With IMS and state mandated testing, too frequently reading becomes a means of appraising the achievement of students in acquiring word recognition skills (phonics, syllabication, and structural analysis), as well as diverse comprehension abilities. These skills and abilities are measured very frequently in isolation from the actual act of reading.

The writers would recommend that school system and teachers of reading emphasize increasingly so, the tents of individualized reading. Advocates of individualized reading believe that each person is at a different level of achievement compared to others in the classroom. Library books are utilized as reading materials. Learners individually select their own sequential library books to read. Ideally, each reads at his/her optimal rate of speed. Library books chosen by a student are of personal interest and purpose. Each book selected is on the reading level of understanding of the chooser. After the completion of reading a library book, the student needs to have a conference with the reading teacher to check comprehension, attitude and oral reading abilities. The teacher needs to know the content of library books read by students in order to have a quality conference.

Individualized reading advocates believe that

1. the act of reading is holistic and not fragmented. The entire library book is read by a student, prior to having a conference with the reading teacher;
2. students should select reading materials within a flexible framework. The learner must do the reading. The teacher is a stimulator and guide for students in reading. He/she, however, does not choose reading materials for students. The only exception would be if a student is unable to select a library book to read. If this should be the case, the teacher must select an appropriate book for the student to read;
3. the student is heavily involved in appraising his/her reading performance. To appraise comprehension in reading a library book, open-ended discussions are in evidence. To evaluate word recognition through oral reading, the learner selects the section within the conference framework.

Individualized reading is quite opposite of the measurably stated objectives movement. The former is holistic, the latter tends to be fragmented. The reading curriculum would benefit from being holistic in that students actually read and engage in much reading. A primary goal of reading instruction should be to develop attitudes of appreciation and interest within students to read. Each student should then have a greater intrinsic desire in wanting to read. These attitudes of appreciation and interest should motivate learners to increase their desire to read.

Further Goals in the Teaching of Reading

Holistic means of assisting students in reading stressed within the framework of individualized reading philosophies may also be emphasized with the utilization of basal readers. With carefully chosen, quality basal readers, students must have ample opportunities to read and enjoy the content. If IMS is utilized, time for reading instruction becomes fragmented. Learners then achieve precise, measurable objectives. The specific objectives may be totally unrelated to each other. There may be so many precise goals to attain that little time is left for the actual reading in depth of selected stories in the basal reader. Students learn to read by reading. Isolated skills may be measurable, but can students apply what has been learned? The major objective in reading is to develop quality attitudes which encourage doing more reading on the part of each student.

In a holistic plan in the teaching of reading, students learn to identify new words when they read subject matter. In contextual situations, many new words are recognized by the learner. The teacher or a good reader can give assistance to those students who cannot identify a word while in the actual act of reading. In a stimulating environment, rich with reading materials, students locate content of personal interest. Interest in reading can hurdle many difficulties in word recognition and identification problems. To be sure, selected new words may need to be printed, neatly and legibly, on the chalkboard prior to the actual act of reading. However, these new words must be integrated into a contextual situation involving the actual act of reading.

With measurable stated goals, too frequently the emphasis has been on students learning isolated phonics sounds. Better it would be if each student learns phonics generalizations while reading content. When reading content from library books and textbooks, students may achieve many goals pertaining to phoeneme-grapheme relationships. Becoming a proficient reader is a must in the teaching of reading rather than emphasizing lesson after lesson of phonics instruction. While reading content, students develop and perceive patterns in sound-symbol relationships.

Students should be active participants in learning. Too frequently, passivity is inherent within learners. Teachers raise questions for students to answer pertaining to content read. Rather active learners should do the asking of questions. They tend to see gaps in knowledge and desire to have these deficiencies minimized. With quality questions raised, answers can be generated. Purpose for learning is involved when students identify relevant questions and problems. Intrinsically, a desire is there to secure needed information. Basal reader content, as well as other reference sources, may be utilized to secure needed information. Active involvement of students is preferable to passive recipients in the classroom.

To achieve higher levels of cognition, students need to bring meaning to subject matter. Critical thinking, creative thinking, and problem solving emphasize learners determining and clarifying content read. Traditionally, the perception has been that students passively acquire meaning from subject matter read. Content in the basal reader then moves from the textbook to the student, if the latter secures meaning from what the author has written. Rather, the learner with his/her background experiences should bring understanding and interpretation to facts, concepts, and generalizations read.

In Closing

A fragmented reading curriculum emphasizes isolated measurably stated objectives for students to attain. Rather, reading emphasizes students bringing meaning to subject matter read. Reading involves word recognition and comprehension skills. However, skills must be secured and utilized within the framework of quality holistic reading experiences.

REFERENCES

Alexander, J. Estill (Editor). *Teaching Reading*. Second Edition. Boston: Little, Brown and Company, 1983.

Davis, Gary A. *Educational Psychology*. New York: Random House, 1983.

Harris, Albert, and Edward Sipay. *How to Increase Reading Ability*. Eighth Edition. New York: Longman, Inc., 1985.

Ringler, Lenore H., and Carol K. Weber. *A Language-Thinking Approach to Reading*. New York: Harcourt Brace Jovanovich, 1984.

Rubin, Dorothy. *Diagnosis and Correction in Reading Instruction*. New York: Holt, Rinehart and Winston, 1982.

Motivation and the Learner in Reading

Motivation is a rather persistent problem in guiding students to read well. If a student lacks motivation, a low energy level will be available in learning to read. Through motivation, a learner is encouraged to achieve definite goals in reading. Persistence is there is aid students in goal attainment with adequately motivated behaviour.

Causes and Effects Related to Motivation

Numerous causes can be listed which hinder student motivation in reading. Books that are not on the reading levels of students hinder these learners to achieve optimally. A book that is too complex to read makes for a lack of comprehension of ideas. Or, if the contents are too easy, challenge to read may well be lacking.

Teachers who fail to teach reading minimize the importance of student progress. Teachers need to develop readiness within learners prior to the latter engaging in the actual reading of content. Readiness activities need to be interesting. Otherwise, students' attention may be difficult to secure in an ongoing lesson or unit.

Outdated textbooks that show excessive wear lack appeal for students to read. Textbooks/trade books need to be appealing to students. The appeal helps establish set within students to learn. The student and the reading materials must become integrated. Otherwise, the learner disassociates himself/herself from the reading experience. Motivation in reading then is lacking.

A stimulating room environment with bulletin board displays to encourage reading is important. Jackets from library books on a bulletin board may stimulate many to increase consumption of reading materials. Comfortable, attractive furniture in a reading area may well be a further stimulator to read an increased number of books.

Proper temperature readings with appropriate ventilation is necessary for quality comprehension to occur. The late A.H. Maslow, advocating humanism as a psychology of learning, stressed the importance of meeting needs of students in order that the latter can acquire self-actualization. At the apex, Maslow listed physiological needs which must be met by learners. These included appropriate temperature readings and ventilation, food, clothing, shelter, and water. Students lack motivation to learn if these needs are not met. Maslow further stressed students meet security, love and belonging, and esteem needs. Self-actualization then becomes a possibility. Maslow's hierarchy of needs is known as a theory of motivation. Lower needs must be met before higher level needs become important. Thus, physiological needs generally must be met first before other needs in sequence become significant.

Why Motivation is Lacking?

Numerous reasons are given for students lacking motivation. Frequently, teachers are blamed for learners not being motivated due to poor teaching methods. This may be one reason. Teachers need to feel challenge covering the subject matter being taught. *Enthusiasm* of teachers might be reflected within learners. Thus, a teacher who enthusiastically tells learners what he/she has read and demonstrates interest in reading content, as well as in teaching reading to each student, may well encourage the latter to read proficiently. Certainly, a teacher showing motivation in teaching students to read critically and creatively should have these reading skills reflected with learners. Higher levels of cognition, such as critical and creative reading, must be emphasized in the reading curriculum.

There are numerous other reasons for students lacking motivation in reading. A variety of reading materials, including textbooks, library books, and other print materials must be available for learners to provide for *individual differences*. It certainly is not motivating for learners if the subject matter read is too complex or excessively easy. Each student needs to be ready for reading specific subject matter. Readiness factors include having ample opportunities to see new words in print, attach meaning to each new word, have adequate background information, as well as have a purpose (reason) to read, prior to reading the involved subject matter.

Subject matter to be read should be of *interest* to students. A lack of interesting reading materials can make for inappropriate motivation. With interest in subject matter being read, students possess a high energy level for reading. Motivation is inherent when each student is interested in reading the involved subject matter.

Reading teachers must use a *variety* of methods in teaching students. To learn inductively on the part of students, the teacher needs to ask stimulating questions covering content read. Each question needs to be on the understanding level of students. Questions for students need to lead to higher levels of thinking, such as the levels of analysis (separating facts from opinions, fantasy from reality, accurate from inaccurate content, as well as detecting bias, glittering generalities, and card stacking), synthesis (hypothesizing), and evaluation (appraising subject matter read in terms of quality criteria).

Deductive methods emphasize a teacher modeling behaviour pertaining to analysis, synthesis, and evaluation. Students then apply what has been learned pertaining to higher levels of cognition.

Problems solving methods should also be utilized. Here, students with teacher guidance identify a problem or broad question. Information is gathered through reading and the use of audiovisual materials. A hypothesis or answer to the problem or question should then be in evidence. The hypothesis is tested in action and revised if necessary. Problem solving methods are good to utilize when students elect real, life-like problems in reading pertaining to subject matter read. A variety of reading materials and nonreading activities assist in data gathering, as well as in checking hypotheses. Critical and creative thinking are emphasized in true problem solving experiences. Problems identified are new to involved students. Challenge is involved in choosing learning opportunities to solve the identified problems. If the same methods are utilized continuously, students will tend to dislike reading.

Balance among cognitive, affective, and psychomotor objectives should be emphasized in teaching reading. A single domain of objectives, such as cognitive, is not adequate. The development of the intellect (cognition) is significant in the teaching of reading. Students then need to learn to achieve skills in reading to follow directions, skim, or scan, develop sequence in ideas, as well as achieve main ideas and generalizations. Analyzing what has been read and achieving unique ideas covering subject matter ideas are further relevant cognitive goals.

The affective dimension of objectives is equally important as compared to the cognitive domain. With desirable affective objectives, students learn to select and enjoy quality literature. When ready, a learner then enjoys characterization, setting, plot, irony, and theme of literature read. An individualized reading programme needs to be in evidence in which the student can select the title and achievement level of the library book. Hopefully, challenging library books will be selected by the learner. The teacher in a conference with the student needs to encourage, not force, increased interest in reading. Fascinating questions raised by the teacher and the student can be discussed within the conference setting. Evaluation of the success of each conference would emphasize students doing more reading and appreciating subject matter content.

The psychomotor level of objectives should receive adequate attention in the reading curriculum. With psychomotor goals, students develop proficiency in using the gross and finer muscles, as well as skill in eye-hand coordination. Numerous quality learning opportunities can be stressed by the teacher in the psychomotor domain. Thus, after reading content from basal textbooks or through an individualized reading programme, learners may complete specific projects to reveal comprehension. These projects include

1. developing a mural or pencil sketching;
2. making a diorma;

3. creating a pantomime or creative dramatics presentation;
4. completing a movie set, showing illustrated scenes of subject matter read;
5. writing a different beginning or ending for the story with accompanying illustrations;
6. constructing a model relating directly to ideas contained in a story or reading selection.

Teachers of reading then need to have students attain balance among cognitive, affective and psychomotor objectives.

A further reason why students may lack motivation in reading is that meaningful learning is not present. The reader needs to relate the self to the selection being read. The reading teacher must make certain that students understand subject matter. Students who do not read well enough to benefit from the reading of the textbook need assistance. A good reader could orally read the contents to the disabled reader as the latter follows along in his/her book. He/she can then learn to identify words in the process as well as listen to the ideas read. Attaching meaning to the subject matter listened to is then possible. Gifted/talented readers need to read challenging materials, otherwise a lack of meaning is not possible when subject matter is boring and lacks maturity. These learners must also be assisted to achieve to their optimal which will be well above the grade level they are presently in. If a student with eighth or ninth grade reading abilities is asked to utilize textbooks written for fifth graders, it is no wonder that meaning cannot be attached to subject matter read. Or a fifth grader, reading on the second grade level, will not become an independent reader in understanding the content being read written for average achievers in grade five.

The key to successful reading achievement of students is to match their present level of attainment with materials of instruction that are meaningful and understandable.

Recommendations to Improve the Reading Curriculum

Numerous recommendations have been made by experts to improve reading skills on the part of students. The authors would like to recommend definite quality criteria to assist students to achieve more optimally in reading.

First of all, with the accountability movement in vogue, basic essential skills for students have been identified on the state or local school level. These skills are generally listed as behaviourally stated objectives. The reading curriculum then becomes fragmented. Each student needs to attain the sequential precise ends. Too much time by the reading teacher needs to be spent on having learners achieve each behaviourally stated objective. Little time may be available to have students read subject matter in a holistic approach. Learning of isolated skills becomes relevant, rather than reading sequential ideas in order to learn. Certainly, comprehension of quality literature must be the end result, rather than acquiring isolated reading skills.

Secondly, the writer recommends that students have a greater voice in determining which sources to read from and which problem areas to solve, involving the processes of reading. Student-teacher planning of goals, experiences, and appraisal procedures emphasizes a sound philosophy of education.

Thirdly, well educated and trained teachers should be able to make good decisions in terms of providing for individual differences in reading. With state mandated objectives or local district instructional management systems (IMS), decision making by the reading teacher is minimized. Certainly, a quality teacher should be able to determine scope and sequence better than can be done on the state or district wide level. Each teacher, regardless of age level of students taught or academic area taught, must be a teacher of reading.

Fourthly, state certification departments need to require in teacher preparation programmes that all prospective teachers have adequate course work in the teaching of reading. Schools of education preparing teachers need to be certain that all have demonstrated proficiency in the teaching of reading. Teachers need to possess adequate knowledge and skills in teaching word recognition techniques and diverse kinds of comprehension skills to develop within students.

Fifthly, teachers need to stimulate students to enjoy and appreciate reading. It is a blessing to be a good reader. Nonreaders or those limited in the ability to read suffer grave consequences in society. The level of job attainment is lowered if an adult cannot read at a required proficient level. Enjoyment of life is minimized due to not possessing needed skills in reading.

Sixthly, teachers need to guide students to move to higher education levels, as compared to rote learning and drill experiences. Students should experience needed drill and practice in reading subject matter. However, life itself demands that learners be skillful in problem solving situations.

Seventhly, students should experience life vicariously. It is impossible to experience, in many situations, desirable situations in life. Through reading or vicariously, learners may experience what is good, true, and beautiful. Undesirable situations in life are costly to experience directly. With vicarious experiences in reading, what is undesirable can be experienced in a relatively harmless manner.

REFERENCES

Alexander, J. Estill (Editor), *Teaching Reading*. Second Edition. Boston: Little, Brown and Company, 1983.

Davis, Gary A. *Educational Psychology*. New York: Random House, 1983.

Harris, Albert, and Edward Sipay. *How to Increase Reading Ability*. Eighth Edition. New York: Longman, Inc., 1985.

Ringler, Lenore H., and Carol K. Weber. *A Language-Thinking Approach to Reading*. New York: Harcourt Brace Jovanovich, 1984.

Rubin, Dorothy. *Diagnosis and Correction in Reading Instruction*. New York: Holt, Rinehart and Winston, 1982.

Reform in the Reading Curriculum

Complaints are heard regularly pertaining to the number of illiterate people in society. Rather high percentages are given for individuals who cannot read. The exact per cent will never be known. What constitutes an illiterate person in definition is a further point of debate. Illiteracy will come on a continuum, rather than as given absolute per cents.

There are people in society who, no doubt, fail to learn to read regardless of procedures, subject matter, and methodology. These individuals may even possess, seemingly, the capacity intellectually to learn to read. Those of inadequate capacities would need to be excluded from specific persons who have not learned to read when using per cents in the illiterate segment of the population. Even then, it is difficult to determine who lacks capacity in learning to read. All persons need to achieve as much as possible in the reading curriculum.

In this chapter, the authors will zero in on issues and remediation procedures to improve the reading curriculum.

The Great Debate in the Teaching of Reading

A discussion of diverse procedures in the teaching of reading will need to occur. Presently, most states have identified core competencies and key skills for classroom teachers to emphasize in reading instruction. Location teacher involvement is greatly minimized or nonexistent in selecting the state mandated objectives. It is believed that at the state level, a better job of selecting goals can be in evidence, as compared to teacher decision-making on the local level.

The district level may also identify numerous specific objectives for students to attain in reading. These become known as instructional management systems (IMS) or mastery learning. With IMS or mastery learning, as well as stated mandated objectives, each skill is clearly identified and stated in measurable terms. Either the learner has or has not achieved the skill as a result of teaching. The assumption to back the utilization of measurably stated objectives include:

1. reading skills to become good readers can be identified;
2. each skill can be stated in measurable terms, including an indicator or emphasize minimal levels of achievement;
3. students need to be tested frequently to insure mastery of each specific skill;
4. the end result will be improved reading instruction for each student;
5. all students can become literate individuals.

Too frequently, however, with the use of measurably stated objectives, the reading curriculum becomes fragmented. Isolated skills are taught and measured. Much time is spent on testing to determine if the skills have been acquired by students. Additional time is spent by the teacher on recording the test results of each learner.

Reading skills then are taught and tested frequently. Time spent on the actual of reading is greatly minimized. Learning of isolated skills, like phonics, does not involve the totality or gestalt of reading. Time spent on testing and recording of test results affects the time teachers spend on teaching reading of test results affects the time teachers spend on teaching reading and having students engage in reading content.

To minimize the dilemma of identifying core competencies and key skills, a great debate in the teaching of reading needs to occur. The debate should centre around meeting individual needs of students in reading. These discussions should emphasize tenets and modifications of diverse philosophies in the teaching of reading. Which philosophies then should be emphasized?

Individualized reading has much to offer. A very minimal amount of time is spent in teaching specific skills. Reading is a more holistic enterprize, as compared to identifying and teaching each highly specific skill. In individualized reading, the entire time, as a whole, is spent on the actual act of securing ideas when learning to read. The student selects which library books to read sequentially. A wide variety of books on interesting topics needs to be in the offing. These books also should be on a variety of reading levels to provide for the present achievement level of each student. The teacher is a guide and stimulator to challenge students individually to consume more reading materials. He/she has conferences with students on a one-on-one basis after a library book has been completed. A student may receive assistance on a specific skills, as identified in the conference. Otherwise in the conference, the teacher discusses subject matter that a pupil has read. The student can reveal the quality of reading by selecting content from the library book to read orally to the teacher.

A second holistic procedure to emphasize in teaching reading is the language experience approach. This method of teaching reading can be utilized on all age levels. For young students who do not have a writing vocabulary, the classroom teacher may print the ideas as presented by the former. To secure content, learners need to experience subject matter from audio-visual aids or from a story read to them. After these experiences, young learners present related subject matter to the teacher who in return prints these ideas in neat manuscript letters on the chalkboard. The teacher reads the content on the chalkboard with the involved pupils by pointing to the words and phrases. It does not take long before pupils begin to recognize words and phrases as the content is read with teacher guidance. At any age or grade level, when students have developed their own writing vocabularies, they may write up their own experiences from ongoing lessons and units of instruction. Reading and writing are then correlated, not isolated entities.

A third holistic procedure in learning to read involves the use of basal readers. A minimal amount of time should then be spent on analyzing words, such as the use of phonics, syllabication, and structural analysis. Students must be guided to read sequential stories from the basal reader. The emphasis must be based on reading subject matter, rather than stressing analytic word attack skills.

Why are holistic procedures in the teaching of reading emphasized? Students can hurdle many problems in word recognition if interesting content is being read. Advocates of individualized reading tend to believe that analytic methods of instruction deemphasize interest in students wanting to learn to read. Interest, however, is a powerful factor in learning.

Secondly, if students are to learn to read, they must read and not spend excessive time analyzing words. Reading involves securing meaning from words, phrases, sentences, and paragraphs.

Purpose in reading comes from perceiving reasons for learning. Reading fascinating and challenging content provides sequence in learning. Isolated behaviours, such as achieving measurable reading skills, lacks purpose on the part of students.

Research versus Philosophy in Teaching Reading

Presently, the emphasis in education is to base methods and procedures of teaching upon research results. Research must be emphasized continually to secure data on which methods to use and not use in reading instruction. However, there are many weaknesses in research procedures used in reading. Frequently, with research findings, the following erroneous methods are emphasized:

A professor summarizes research studies in reading and develops selected conclusions, such as all pupils need to have daily, sequential lessons in phonics. The research studies used to develop conclusions may be poorly done indeed. Random sampling procedures for the experimental and control groups are not in evidence. Or, the experimental and control groups were not equated, if randomization was not possible. Other weaknesses in research studies include a lack of adequate numbers used in the study for both the experimental and the control group. Further weaknesses of research include

1. no controls on who teachers the experimental versus the control group;
2. low validity and reliability of measurement instruments used in the study;
3. a lack of utilitarian values of the completed research. External validity then goes downhill.

Truly bad research has been printed in leading scholarly journals. Examples of deficient research are the following;

During the 1960's, two studies received much recognition which concluded that schools had very little affect, if any, on student achievement. One would not need to do a research study to indicate that schools, as well as other institutions, do influence students. If students are in school 180 days in one calendar year which includes a six-hour daily schedule of curriculum and co-curriculum activities, a vacuum does not occur in terms of learners learning something. Here, bad studies were made that tried to prove what the researchers wanted to prove.

A second bad study, among others, was made in the early 1980's which had to do with class size. The researchers concluded that class size had nothing to do with student achievement. One may then conclude that a classroom teacher could teach 100 students in a room without sacrificing student achievement. That is a ridiculous conclusion indeed. All things being equal, adding another student to a classroom makes for an additional student for the classroom teacher to provide for. The only exception might be that an additional motivated student could stimulate others to achieve more optimally in the classroom setting. However, one needs to be careful in adding one more motivated student in a classroom, especially if thirty learners are in the class setting already. One need do no research to indicate that a fifteen to twenty student ratio per teacher is adequate in number. When non-academic students and/or disrupters exist in a classroom, the ratio needs to be lowered.

A third bad method of reporting research is to say "Our data indicate—." These reporters fail to say where they received their information. They do not mention how many responses were made in the data collected, nor the per cent of return. Nothing is said about any controls implemented in the study. Sophisticated writing of these published manuscripts is in evidence. Mixed into the context is "Our data show—."

A fourth defective type of study exists when school administrators in their "research" indicate that "teachers really do not want higher salaries. What they really want is to receive recognition for good teaching." To be sure, good teachers do want these non-monetary rewards, but they also need higher salaries in order to stay on as quality classroom teachers and live a life-style commensurate with a college/university graduate.

Research in education then has not, by any means, answered problems pertaining to increased achievement on the part of students. Those research results that emphasize raising student test scores only, fail to realize the importance of students using what has been learned and applying these ideas in the real world of society. Personal and social developments of students are also lacking when raising test scores becomes the ultimate goal of teaching.

An additional problem of raising test scores pertains to how this is done. The authors have visited schools where teachers teach directly to a standardized achievement test. The test is directly in front of the classroom teacher to teach for. A few articles have been published whereby superintendents were hired in a district to raise test scores of students and thus improve the curriculum. As can be expected, the test scores of students increased lavishly. This, no doubt, will always happen in a like situation.

Teachers and administrators must not give up on conducting and using research results. However, the status of present-day research leaves much to be desired indeed. Critical evaluation of published research is important.

Educators might also look toward a study of philosophy to determine goals, learning opportunities, and appraisal procedures.

The Great Debate in education of the past can provide valuable input into curriculum improvement. William Chandler Bagley (1874-1946) advocated students mastering the essentials. In his *The Essentialist Manifesto*, published in 1938, Dr. Bagley believed that a core of knowledge exists which all should master. In the reading curriculum then, the same essential learnings would be required of all students. Interest in learning would not necessarily be an important criterion to follow in teaching, according to Dr. Bagley. Rather, the students need the will to learn. The learner must reach out and learn regardless of the amount of interest inherent in the reading curriculum.

John Dewey (1859-1952) in his book *Democracy and Education* advocates interest as a powerful factor to create effort in learning. The goals of the student make for interest and effort.

Subject matter is not an end in and of itself. But, it is a means or instrumental to an end, according to Dr. Dewey. In the reading curriculum, students read to secure subject matter to solve problems. The problems must be realistic and life-like. School and society should not be separated from each other. Students might work in committees to gather data from reading, and other activities, to solve problems. John Dewey did not believe that common learnings, or essentials, existed which all students should learn. Rather, problems are unique to the student and the committee. Committees are utilized in society to solve problems. Therefore, the school curriculum needs to emphasize committee work and problem solving.

B.F. Skinner represents the philosophical school of thought of realism. With programmed learning, sequential school of thought of realism. With programmed learning, sequential steps for students to learn are written by the programmer. There is no input into the curriculum from students. Each sequential step of learning is measurable. Either a student has or has not responded correctly to a programmed item.

Realists believe that one can know in whole or in part the real world as it truly is. The reality of the real world in its specifics is identified in terms of behaviourally stated objectives.

In the reading curriculum, precise objectives can be identified according to realists. The chosen objectives can become a part of the instructional management system (IMS) or state mandated core competencies and key skills. IMS and programmed learning emphasize measurably stated word recognition and comprehension skills.

Idealism, as a philosophy of education, emphasizes an idea centred curriculum. Idealists believe one can only know ideas and not know the real world as it truly is. With a reading curriculum emphasizing ideas, students need to do much reading to receive abstract learnings. Audio-visual aids would be used minimally, unless these materials assist students to secure concepts and generalizations in the abstract. The reading textbook, workbook, and worksheets provide major learnings for students. A variety of purposes or comprehension skills need to be taught students so that worthwhile subject matter can be learned. Word recognition skills are important as they assist students to secure abstract content.

Existentialism, as a fifth philosophy of education, emphasizes the individual student making choices and decisions, from among alternatives. To emphasize existentialist thinking, the teacher could have a variety of reading materials at a station. Means of interesting students in the diverse kinds of books and pamphlets should be in evidence, such as appealing bulletin board displays, as well as the teacher introducing selected materials to whet students' appetites for reading.

The sky would be the limit in terms of the numbers of materials read, as well as the complexity of each. Decisions are up to the student. The latter may also determine the methods of appraisal to assess what any one reader got out of the reading materials in terms of comprehension.

Existentialists believe strongly in knowledge being subjective, not objective. The contents of the reading materials, be it biographical, autobiographical, the fine arts, historical, geographical, scientific, among others, should assist students to look at and clarify values. To an existentialist, life consists of choosing from among alternatives in an absorb environment. To be human is to make choices in life. If others make decisions for the self, the latter ceases to be human.

The teacher must be a guide and a stimulator to students. He/she must help learners to make decisions, but not make choices for students.

A study of philosophy may well provide teachers with an excellent basis in making decisions in the reading curriculum. The Great Debate in reading might then centre itself around.

1. Identifying the basics or essentials, as essentialists recommend. These core learnings would be common to all students. The essentials must be identified carefully. Research results can be brought into the identification process. The research could include a basic list of updated words that all students should master in reading for each grade level. However, individual differences must be provided for among slow, average, and fast learners. Each student must achieve optimally;
2. Using problem solving approaches, as experimentalists advocate. Problem solving stresses students reading

subject matter to answer questions and securing solutions to problems;

3. Identifying vital precise objectives for students to attain, as advocated by realists. Critical and creative thinking must not be minimized in the process;
4. Gleaning worthwhile generalizations in reading in an idea centred curriculum, as emphasized by idealists;
5. Attempting to clarify values within dilemma situations, as stressed by existentialists.

The Psychology of Learning

How can each student be assisted to achieve as much as possible in reading? This is a problem for educational psychology to assist in solving. Psychologists would tend to agree on selected broad guidelines in teaching students. These guidelines can be applied to the teaching of reading.

To assist students to achieve optimally in reading, he/she needs to be involved in choosing reading materials which possess personal interest. When objectives for students to attain are identified external to the learner, a lack of interest in reading may be an end result. The student needs to have more control over the reading curriculum. The objectives, learning opportunities, and appraisal procedures should not be handed down, solely or in large part, from the state level, such as in state mandated goals. Neither should IMS procedures of teaching be handed down from the district level to the classroom level. Rather, intrinsic motivation is important in developing the reading curriculum. Being involved in choosing materials to read is important to learners. If students have a desire to read self-chosen materials, intrinsic motivation is then involved. From within, the learner then wants to read. The teacher is a guide and stimulator.

Sequence resides within the student. It does not reside within state mandated objectives or IMS. The student then needs to select stimulating, challenging reading materials. A wide variety of topics based on diverse levels of reading achievement is necessary. Students individually may then select which subject matter to read. The learner selects reading materials based on intrinsic interests. He/she chooses content based on personal interests, needs, and purposes. Intrinsic motivation is then in evidence. Sequentially, the student selects subject matter to read.

Extrinsic motivation procedures in reading should be utilized if intrinsic procedures do not work. Primary (the actual prizes) and secondary reinforcers (tokens to be exchanged for prizes) may be used to encourage reading. Standards for receiving the reinforcers should be announced to students so the latter may be motivated to increase the amount and quality of reading materials consumed. The rewards and extrinsic to the actual act of reading. However, they do serve as reinforces for students to do more reading and on a variety of topics.

There are general criteria for teachers to follow in teaching which all educational psychologists agree with. First of all, students should attach meaning to subject matter read. If learners do not understand what has been read, frustration tends to set in. Meaning theory in learning emphasizes students comprehend content while reading. A lack of meaning in understanding subject matter truly wastes the time of students, as well as of the classroom teacher in teaching-learning situations.

Secondly, learners need to perceive purpose or reasons for learning. If students do not perceive the value of reading, no doubt, limited comprehension and learning will occur. The teacher may explain to students the worth of reading specific selections. A deductive approach is then utilized. Should the teacher utilize a questioning approach to have students perceive the values of reading an inductive method is in evidence.

Thirdly, students should experience interesting learning opportunities. If learners are attracted to reading subject matter, they will attain more optimally as compared to a lack of interest. It behooves the reading teacher to permit students to select more of their very own materials to read. Interest from students will provide for effort in reading. Interest and effort become integrated, not separate entities. Students tend to be interested in content which they selected on an individual basis. Attending to the task at hand is important. Interest will make for the attending to time on task.

Fourthly, individual differences among students need adequate attention. There are slow, average, and fast achievers, on a continuum, in reading. Materials for students to read must be on diverse levels of achievement to provide for each category of achiever. Subject matter contained in the reading materials needs to be varied to provide for diverse interests that learners bring to the reading curriculum. New interests must also be developed within students. The reading teacher's philosophy of teaching must adhere to respecting differences among students. Each person has dignity, much worth, and must be guided to achieve as much as possible in reading.

In Conclusion

Reform in the reading curriculum is needed. A great debate in the teaching of reading is needed. State mandated objectives and IMS with their measurably written goals should be compared with holistic philosophies in the teaching of reading. The writer recommends strongly that a holistic procedure in reading instruction be implemented. Reading involves understanding sentences, paragraphs, and larger bodies of knowledge. Dividing skills into precise objectives for learners to attain violates what the actual act of reading is about.

Quality research in reading must be refined and emphasized. However, research results are indeed confusing. Much negative research has been conducted and has little worth. Improved methods of conducting research must be emphasized. A study of the philosophy of education is very helpful in determining objectives, learning opportunities, and appraisal procedures. Perhaps, achieving a quality philosophy of teaching reading has more worth as compared to conducting and using research results. However, with improved means of doing educational research, their results can continually assist to improve the reading curriculum.

REFERENCES

Cruickshank, Donald R. *Teaching is Tough*. Englewood Cliffs, New Jersey; Prentice-Hall, Inc., 1980.

Henson, Kenneth T. *Secondary Teaching Methods*. Lexington, Massachusetts: D.C. Heath and Company, 1981.

Joyce, Bruce, and Marsha Weil. *Models of Teaching*. Third Edition. Englewood Cliffs, New Jersey: Prentice-Hall, Inc., 1986.

Joycr, Bruce, *et al*. *The Structure of School Improvement*. New York: Longmans, 1983.

National Society for the Study of Education. *Staff Development*, Part II. Chicago, Illinois: The Society, 1983.

National Society for the Study of Education. *The Humanities in Precollegiate Education*, Part II. Chicago, Illinois: The Society, 1984.

National Society for the Study of Education. *Becoming Readers in a Complex Society*, Part I. Chicago, Illinois: The Society, 1984.

National Society for the Study of Education. *Education in School and Nonschool Settings*, Part I. Chicago, Illinois: The Society, 1985.

National Society for the Study of Education. *The Ecology of School Renewal*, Part I. Chicago, Illinois: The Society, 1987.

National Society for the Study of Education. *Society as Education in an Age of Transition*, Part II. Chicago, Illinois: The Society, 1987.

Mathematics in the Elementary School

Mathematics in the elementary school has changed much in the last ten to twelve years. Federal financing of study groups from different colleges and universities devoted to improving the mathematics curriculum has made for many changes in this curriculum area. The following have contributed much to developing what had been called modern mathematics: the Greater Cleveland Mathematics Project; the Madison Project; the School Mathematics Study Group; the University of Illinois Arithmetic Project; and the Minnesota Project.

Many parents of elementary school pupils feel somewhat frustrated in giving their offspring needed help in homework when necessary in the area of elementary school mathematics. The content, methodology, and sequence in mathematics has changed much as compared to one generation ago. No doubt, more changes generally have occurred in this curriculum area as compared to any other curriculum area in the elementary school.

Major Generalizations in Elementary Mathematics

There are certain key ideas that pupils should develop in elementary school mathematics. These key ideas may be called structural properties which are basic to understanding mathematics in the elementary school.

In the kindergarten or first grade level, depending upon the achievement levels of learners, pupils can develop understandings pertaining to the commutative property of addition. For example, the teacher can show pupils three books in one set and two books in a second set. Pupils can, of course, be asked to tell how many books there are in each set. The two sets can then be joined together. Learners can then respond with how many members there are in the new set. Once pupils have responded correctly to these questions, the order of the two sets can be changed. The teacher can ask pupils how many members are in the first set of books. Pupils would respond with "two" if a correct answer is given. Now, learners would be shown the second set of books consisting of three members. They would tell how many books are in the second set. Again, the two sets can be joined together to form a new set, and pupils could then state orally how many members make up the new set of books. Thus, pupils can understand that 3 + 2 = 2 + 3. The order of the sets did not affect the sum. The concept "commutative property of addition" would not be mentioned by the teacher in teaching these early primary grade pupils. The teacher could use the term "changing the order of sets" instead. It is difficult for young children to pronounce the word "commutative" properly. Intermediate grade pupils should utilize the concept "commutative property of addition is a very valuable concept for pupils to understand. In the study of basic addition facts, the number of learnings needed by pupils is cut in half as a result of developing understandings pertaining to the commutative property. Thus, if a pupil understands and attaches meaning to 5 + 4 = 9, he also realizes that 4 + 5 = 9. The commutative property of addition can be used again and again in the elementary school mathematics programme. In dealing with larger values, pupils can understand that 45 + 32 = 32 + 45 or 116 + 235 = 235 + 116.

It is important to have an ample number of learning activities for pupils at the appropriate stage of development to develop understandings pertaining to the commutative property of multiplication. In introductory learnings pertaining to this area, for example, pupils could be shown a set of four marbles. They could be asked how many marbles they would have if two of these sets were in their possession. The number sentence could be written on the chalkboard which would correspond with the set or sets of marbles shown to pupils, such as 2 × 4 = 8. Next, pupils could be shown a set of two marbles; they could be asked how many marbles there would be if 4 sets of marbles existed with two numbers in each set. A number sentence could be written on the chalkboard which could correspond to the concrete situation, such as $4 \times 2 = 8$. Materials should be changed frequently to maintain pupil interest in learning, such as using crayons, markers, children, pencils, chairs, candles, and other objects. The mathematics teacher must use a variety of objects and items within an ample number of learning activities to assist pupils in thoroughly understanding the commutative property of addition and multiplication.

A second major understanding pertaining to structural ideas in elementary school mathematics is the associative property of addition and multiplication. In the associative property of addition, the teacher can again have pupils develop important understandings using concrete materials and eventually have pupils progress to utilizing the abstract. For example, the teacher could call the names of three pupils who come to the front of the classroom. The names of two other learners can be called who would also come to the front of the room representing a second set. Finally, the names of four other pupils can be called and they would come to the front of the room. The teacher can ask how many members make up each of the three sets of pupils. A pupil can volunteer to write the corresponding number sentence on the chalkboard as it is given by pupils. The teacher can ask questions of learners as to how many pupils are in all three sets with the resulting information becoming a part in writing the number sentence, such as $3 + 2 + 4 = 9$. All pupils in the front of the classroom can be asked to take their seats. The teacher then calls the names of four pupils who come to the front of the classroom. This is followed by the teacher calling the names of two other pupils for the second set and three pupils for the third set. A different pupil can volunteer to write the number sentence pertaining to pupils in the front of the classroom prior to and with joining together the members of the three sets to form a new set. Thus, learners will notice that $4 + 2 + 3 = 9$. The teacher can also call pupils to the front of the room whereby the corresponding number sentence when writing the numerals on the chalkboard for each set and the total number of members in all three sets would be the following: $2 + 3 + 4$. Pupils should receive ample practice using a variety of materials whereby they can develop a meaningful generalization pertaining to the associative property of addition. Thus learners will realize that three or more addends can be arranged in any order and it does not affect the sum in addition.

At appropriate stage of development, learners should also realize the associative property of multiplication. Thus learners in their own words would understand that the order of three (or more) factors does not affect the product in multiplication. For example, in introductory learnings pertaining to the associative property of multiplication, pupils could look at two chairs representing the number of members or elements in a specific set. Pupils could be asked a question pertaining to how many members would exist in a new set if three sets of chairs would be considered with two members in each set. To give the student additional assistance in determining the product, a comparison could be made between multiplication and addition. Three sets of chairs could be placed in the room with two members in each set. Pupils could conclude that $2 + 2 + 2 = 6$ or $3 \times 2 = 6$. The pupil should understand the relationship of addition to multiplication. Learnings should be meaningful and make sense to the learner. It generally is very unpleasant to learn that which is not understood or lacks meaning. To proceed with pupils understanding the associative property of multiplication, the six chairs can be taken as members of one set; pupils can then think of 4 sets, for example, each set having six members. To have pupils now enhance their thinking pertaining to the associative property of multiplication, pupils should think in terms of four chairs in a set with six of these specific sets. Chairs in the room could be arranged to have pupils see six sets of chairs with four members in each set. Thus pupils can see and understand that $(3 \times 2) \times 4 = 24$. The order of factors does not affect the product in multiplication. Ample number of experiences using a variety of objects and children should be utilized in guiding learners to understand in a meaningful way the associative property of multiplication. Thus, learners, for example, should realize that $(2 \times 3) \times 4 = (3 \times 2) \times 4 = (4 \times 3) \times 2 = (4 \times 2) \times 3$ by using concrete materials in learning activities which are interesting, understandable and purposeful.

It is important also for learners to understand identity elements. For example, pupils can develop the generalization at a very early age that any counting number plus zero equals the counting number. Seven objects plus zero objects equals the original seven objects. Learning activities which would assist pupils to realize this generalization could include the following:

1. Have six small toys, for example, in a box and ask pupils how many members there are in this set. In a separate

box which has no toys, let pupils respond with the number of members in this set. Then have learners join the two sets together and state how many members there are in the new set. Change the order of the two sets so that pupils can generalize that $6 + 0 = 0 + 6$ (commutative property of addition) and that any counting number plus zero equals that counting number.

2. Three pupils can come to the front of the room; learners can be asked to state how many members there are in this set. A circle can be drawn on the floor which would encircle members of this set. A second circle can be drawn and pupils can tell how many members are in the empty set. Then members of both sets can be joined together to form a new set; learners can then state how many members make up the new set. Thus, the generalization can be developed again that adding zero to a counting number results in a sum which is equal to the counting number.

3. The teacher can state orally a certain counting number; pupils at their desks would then place the corresponding number of members in a set using crayons, chalk, checkers, pencils, books, beads, corn, and other kinds of markers. String or yarn could be used to encircle the members of this set. Next the teacher could have pupils use string or yarn to encircle the set which has no members (if pupils placed six seeds of corn in the first set, then the second set would be any empty set with no corn seeds). The two sets could be joined together and again encircled with yarn or string. Thus, pupils could develop meaningful understandings pertaining to the identity element in addition.

Learners at the appropriate stage of development should also attach meaning to the identity element in multiplication. The teacher, for example, could call the names of four pupils to come to the front of the room. Pupils, of course, could state how many members there are in this set. Learners could then be asked, "If we have one set of four pupils, how many pupils are there?" The basic multiplication fact '1×4' can be written on the chalkboard to guide learners to associate the abstract with the concrete situation where children are involved. Pupils should also, of course, notice the commutative property in that 1 × 4 = 4 × 1. The teacher can ask for a volunteer to come to the front of the room. Pupils can now be challenged and encouraged to think of four sets with one member in each set. Learners can also notice how the number sentence written 4 × 1 = 4 can also be thought of as addition, 1 + 1 + 1 + 1 = 4. In this learning activity, of course, primary emphasis is placed upon pupils realizing that any counting number times one equals that counting number. Too frequently, learners have thought in terms of 8 × 1 = 9; in this situation, pupils are confusing 8 × 1 (or 1 × 8) with 8 + 1 (or 1 + 8). Pupils must attach meaning to what is being learned so they realize that 1 × 8 means one set with eight members in the set, whereas 8 × 1 pertains to eight sets with one member in each set. Once learners understand the identity element in multiplication, they can quickly respond with the counting number being the product if one of the factors is the numeral "one."

The distributive property of multiplication over addition is also important for elementary school pupils to realize at the appropriate stage of development. Thus, in the problem 6(2 + 3) = ——, the six serving as a factor would distribute itself equally over the '2" and the "3." Hence, (6 × 2) + (6 × 3) = 30. The same results would be obtained if the operation of addition were performed first such as 2 + 3 = 5; then six sets of five or 6 × 5 = 30. The distributive property of multiplication over addition is utilized very frequently by pupils when working problems pertaining to multiplication. In the problem 21 × 3 = —— the individual who thinks 3 × 1 = 3 and 3 × 2 tens = 6 tens resulting in a final product of 6 tens plus 3 ones or 63 is using the distributive property of multiplication over addition. Twenty-one times three can be written in the following way illustrating this property more clearly: 3 (20 + 1) resulting in distributing the three equally over the 20 and the 1 or (3 × 20) + (3 × 1) = 63. Pupils need numerous opportunities to understand and apply key ideas pertaining to the distributive property of multiplication over addition.

Providing for Individual Differences

Pupils differ much from each other in mathematics achievement. In a heterogeneously grouped classroom, the range of achievement will be greater in mathematics achievement as compared to homogeneous grouping. In any plan of grouping, however, individual differences in mathematics will be a reality and must be provided for. Too frequently, teachers want to teach all pupils in a class at the same time to keep all learners at the same place using a mathematics textbook. This certainly violates a very important rule of providing for individual differences.

There are numerous approaches to use in providing for individual differences within a class in elementary school mathematics. One approach is to state objective behaviourally and have learners realize these at different rates of speed. Thus, in a class of second grade pupils, learners at different achievement levels could realize the following objectives (only attainable objectives should be stated):

1. Pupils will add correctly nine out of ten problems in addition with each problem having two 2 digit addends and no regrouping involved.
2. Pupils will add correctly nine out of ten problems in addition, regrouping involved, with each problem having two 2 digit addends.

It is quite obvious that the first objective is easier to achieve as compared to the second objective. In mathematical learnings for pupils, proper sequence is of utmost importance. Pupils should be accepted where they are presently and assisted in making continuous progress. With appropriate learning activities which are carefully selected, sequential learnings should become a definite experience for each pupil. Thus, one way of providing for individual pupils within a class is to use behaviourally stated objectives whereby each learner is at a different level of achievement as compared to other children.

A second approach to individualizing instruction in elementary school mathematics could pertain to pupils working at their own optimum rate of speed when utilizing a carefully selected series of elementary school mathematics textbook. Through teacher observation and evaluation, pupils individually would be started at a specific place in the mathematics textbook where learner achievement is presently. A variety of learning activities would be provided to help pupils gain needed mathematical concepts, generalizations, and facts. Adequate guidance must be given each learner as he progresses on a continuum when realizing optimum achievement. The teacher must assist each pupil individually when help is needed to solve problems, to understand structural properties, to understand basic facts, and to stimulate pupils in wanting to achieve. Adequate help must be given teachers in checking papers and other pupil products in elementary school mathematics so that the teacher can devote his time to planning and teaching which is truly a professional responsibility.

To individualize instruction, the teacher of mathematics in a homogeneously grouped classroom could have learners work on the same or similar problem but at varying levels of complexity. With proper readiness activities, let us assume that pupils are working on the following operation: $31\overline{)684}$. Pupils can be asked how many 31's there are in 684. Practical application, of course, can be made of learning activities such as these. For example, if a boy had 684 marbles and he wanted to divide them equally among 31 boys, how many marbles would each boy receive? In receiving answers to this question, many responses basically would be correct. In receiving answers to this question, many responses basically would be correct. If a pupil would say there are ten sets of 31 in 684, this would be correct:

$$
\begin{array}{rl}
31\overline{)684} & \\
\underline{310} & 10 \\
374 &
\end{array}
$$

There are still 374 marbles then which have not been placed into the various sets. Pupils then could be asked how many 31's there are in 374. There are 374 marbles that still need to be divided among the 31 boys. If a pupil responds with 5, the teacher can continue writing the division problem in the following way:

$$
\begin{array}{rl}
31\overline{)684} & \\
\underline{310} & 10 \\
374 & \\
\underline{155} & 5 \\
219 &
\end{array}
$$

There are still 219 marbles that need to be divided equally among the 31 boys. The teacher can continually ask questions of learners until all marbles have been accounted for. Finally, the quotient figures can be added on the right hand side; a remainder will be a part of this problem. It generally is not long before pupils notice that it is tedious to work these kinds of division problems in the way presented. Learners individually will get the largest correct quotient figure ultimately with the first response such as in the following problem:

```
21)857
   840   40
    17
```

Pupils can, of course, also notice that there are not enough left over in the remainder to do further dividing. Ultimately, individual learners can progress to the point of placing the quotient figures correctly above the dividend, such as in the following:

```
    40
21)857
   840
    17
```

At different rates of speed then individuals can achieve to more mature levels of work that is done in working toward optimum achievement in elementary school mathematics. Thus, the teacher is helping to provide for individual differences in elementary school mathematics.

There are many ways which can be utilized to provide for individual differences in elementary school mathematics. The reader needs to study these many approaches carefully and evaluate each thoroughly in terms of acceptable criteria.

Learning by Discovery

Elementary school pupils need to have many opportunities to learn inductively or through discovery. Pupils have turned off frequently when the lecture or explanation approach to teaching is used largely. Educational psychologists have long advocated that pupils do better if they are actively involved in ongoing learning activities as compared to being passive individuals. When pupils learn by discovery, the teacher becomes a good asker of questions rather than a lecturer. Questions asked of pupils should follow good sequence; otherwise the teacher may jump too far ahead of pupils or questions are asked which do not challenge the thinking of learners. The teacher must have a good knowledge of mathematics so that important questions can be asked which will help learners make important discoveries and thus learn inductively.

On any grade level in the elementary school, pupils can develop important learnings in mathematics inductively.

If a first grade teacher wants to have pupils discover the commutative property of addition, the teacher could start with having pupils state orally how many blocks there are in a given set. Let us assume there were two blocks in the set. A second set of blocks could be shown to learners, and pupils could tell how many members there are in the second set. In this second set for example, there were three blocks. If learners responded incorrectly to how many members there were in either set, time may need to be spent in having pupils engage in rational counting (that is learn to count the number of blocks in each set). The two sets of blocks could be joined together to form a new set and learners could now be asked to state orally how many members there are in the resulting set.

The teacher could now place three blocks in the first set and two blocks in the second set. Pupils could be asked to tell how many members there are in each set. Following this, learners could tell how many members there are in the new set which joins together the previously mentioned two sets. Pupils can then realize inductively that the order of the two sets can be changed and yet the sum is not affected. Learners should state the generalization in their very own words which is meaningful to them. Materials need to be changed so that pupils have enough experiences to realize that the commutative property holds true in addition. The teacher, of course, may do some explaining when helping pupils develop learnings inductively.

Drill and the Mathematics Curriculum

The concept "drill" has almost become a bad word in modern educational practices. With the beginning of the 1900's in the United States, drill was being deemphasized more and more in teaching-learning situations. Prior to that time, teachers in many cases would have pupils develop learnings in arithmetic using the drill procedure largely. To be sure, most learners must not have understood what they were learning, and no doubt, interest was lacking in what was being presented. Once learners lost interest in learning, means were utilized to "motivate" students through ways that, of course, would be considered undesirable today. Prior to the 1990's when many faculty members believed that the human mind operated like a muscle, teachers would drill pupils so that the mind would become strong. It was felt that exercising the mind would make it strong. Since them, of course, it has been discovered again and again that pupils may give up in trying if the learning activities are too difficult to be meaningful. Pupils may then develop feelings of inadequacy due to a lack of success in learning.

One would certainly advocate that pupils thoroughly understand and attach meaning to what is being learned in elementary school mathematics. Teachers should also vary learning activities to develop and/or maintain pupil interest in mathematics. The textbook should not be the sole determiner of content and methods. Learners should also "see" purpose in what they are learning. Certainly, it is important to sense reasons for learning something. In initial learnings pertaining to a new process in mathematics, drill does not meet the criterion of helping pupils develop understandings or attach meaning to what is being learned, nor does it meet the criterion of providing interesting learning activities. The chances are in this learning situation, pupils will not see value in drill either.

If pupils are developing introductory learnings pertaining to division as in the following: $2\overline{)4}$, the teacher should use various learning activities to assist learners in developing meaningful learnings. For example, for cookies could be taken to represent the dividend in the previously mentioned division fact. These four cookies could be divided equally between two children. This represents a concrete learning situation since real objects are being used. Social usage is involved in the on-going learning activity since the cookies need to be divided equally between two pupils. These cookies can then be eaten by pupils. There should be ample cookies so that all pupils in the class can have the same satisfying learning experience. Most pupils then will sense that purpose is involved in learning since the cookies needed to be divided equally before they could be eaten. Much interest and enthusiasm can be generated within pupils when learning activities are varied. The teacher can also use among other things, the abacus, sticks, crayons, and pupils when having learners develop understandings pertaining to basic division facts and other operations in elementary school mathematics.

Many pupils, for example, will recall basic addition, subtraction, multiplication, and division facts when appropriate principles of learning have been used in teaching. Most pupils find it too time consuming to continually find what 2)4 is with the use of concrete objects. They realize that being able to recall previously developed learnings quickly is an asset and saves time in computation and in solving problems. There are some pupils who need drill to fix learnings in the mind. However, even in this case, drill procedures should be varied. Flash cards, for example, can be used to help pupils retain learnings previously achieved.

To give another example of pupils engaging in drill pertaining to elementary school mathematics, the teacher could draw and cut pictures of fish on construction paper of different colours. On each of these fish, a paper clip needs to be placed where the mouth is located. A "fishing pole" consisting of a small stick together with the attached string and a magnet can then be used to "catch" the fish contained in a small paper box. The student that catches a fish must respond correctly to the addition, subtraction, multiplication or division fact written on the fish in order to make claims to his success as a fisherman. Once pupils have developed learnings in a meaningful, interesting, and purposeful way, learners should be able to respond quickly to basic facts in addition, subtraction, multiplication, and division. The rate of achievement in this direction will depend upon the pupil's capacity, skill, motivation, and feelings. Each pupil, of course, will realize objectives at a different rate of speed. Learning activities involving drill should be varied to develop and maintain interest as well as provide for individual differences.

The concept "practice" must be treated separately from "drill." It is very important that pupils have ample opportunities to practice that which has been learned previously. Learnings must be transferred from one situation to another. If pupils do not practice what has been learned previously, much forgetting, of course, can occur. Thus, once learners have understood a new process in mathematics, practice needs to be provided to fix learnings in the minds of pupils. There are certain criteria to follow in having pupils engage in practice in elementary school mathematics.

1. The textbook should not be the only source to use in having pupils practice what has been learned previously; activities need to be varied.
2. Periods of time devoted to practice should not be excessively long; time developed to practice must be in harmony with child growth and development characteristics.
3. Not every pupil needs the same amount of practice after understandings have been developed pertaining to a new process in mathematics.
4. Practice sessions definitely must not destroy interest in learning.
5. Pupils should definitely understand and attach meaning to what is being practiced in elementary mathematics.
6. Learners must sense reasons for engaging in learning activities involving practice.
7. Praise needs to be given to all pupils for improved work when engaging in practice.
8. Application of work performed in practice sessions must be related to life outside of school and society in general.
9. Learners must have opportunities to evaluate their own achievement in practice sessions.
10. Pupils with teacher guidance need to diagnose weaknesses in practice sessions devoted to elementary school mathematics and work in the direction of remedying deficiencies.
11. Learners should be accepted by the teacher as human beings having worth regardless of present achievement levels in mathematics.
12. The teacher must work in the direction of having each pupil be successful and thus develop feelings within learners of an adequate self.
13. It is important that pupils enjoy practice sessions devoted to mathematics so that positive attitudes are developed.

Relationship of Knowledge

Elementary school mathematics strongly emphasizes the importance of the relationship of knowledge. Educational psychologists have long stressed the importance of learners sensing that knowledge is related rather than fragmented. It is difficult to recall many isolated bits of information. Content that is perceived as being interrelated can be recalled easier. Thus, mathematics teachers should think in terms of pupils developing appropriate attitudes which would view knowledge as being related.

The modern programme of elementary school mathematics stresses the importance of pupils realizing that subtraction undoes addition. In other words, subtraction is the inverse operation of addition. On the kindergarten or first grade level, depending upon the present stage of development of each learner, individuals can understand that subtraction undoes addition. At their desks, individual pupils can be asked to place four markers in a set. Learners then can be asked to place two markers in a second set. They can write the addition fact that would go along with this problem. The resulting number sentences would be 4 + 2 = 6. Learners can then be asked to make two markers away from the six markers and indicate how many markers are left by writing a number sentence pertaining to the original six markers followed by two markers being taken away leaving four markers: 6 – 2 = 4. Thus, pupils can understand that originally there were four markers in a set in the addition problem with two markers representing a second set being joined together to form a new set of six markers. Six markers in a set with two markers being taken away left the original four markers. In their own words pupils can develop a generalization pertaining to subtraction undoing addition. Thus 4 + 2 = 6 and 6 – 2 = 4.

On the kindergarten or first grade level, pupils should study that subtraction undoes addition as soon as a basic addition fact is understood in a meaningful way using a variety of learning activities. Many learning activities should be utilized to help learners thoroughly understand that subtraction undoes addition. Pupils become frustrated in learning if they do not understand or cannot attach meaning to what has been learned. Much forgetting also will occur if learners do not understand what has been learned.

In proper sequence, pupils can attach meaning to the relationship of addition to multiplication. For example, pupils could be asked how much money they would have if three nickels were owned. The nickels should be shown to pupils. Learners should also be asked to state how many pennies there are in a nickel. They can change each nickel representing a set into pennies. The question can be raised as to how much is 3×5. Pupils can also be led to think in terms of adding $5 + 5 + 5$. Many interesting activities need to be provided whereby pupils sense that addition is related in multiplication and that 3×5 in multiplication is another way of saying $5 + 5 + 5$ in addition. Thus 3×5 means three sets with five members in each set, hence $3 \times 5 = 5 + 5 + 5$.

Mathematics, Algebra, and Geometry

The traditional elementary school curriculum placed much emphasis upon arithmetic and had a tendency to minimize algebra and geometry. The concept of "arithmetic in the elementary school" had to be changed to "mathematics in the elementary school" which included not only arithmetic but also geometry and algebra. In the modern mathematics programme, computation and social usage of arithmetic is not adequate to prepare individuals to live in the latter part of the twentieth century and the twenty-first century.

What was formerly reserved in geometry for the intermediate grade and junior high years has now been brought down, in many cases, to the primary grades. If taught in a meaningful way, first and second graders, for example, can develop understandings in geometry pertaining to lines, line segments, rays, points, closed and open curves, simple and non-simple curves, squares, rectangles, and circles. Better methods of teaching plus better teaching materials have made it possible to bring learnings down to a lower grade level than was formerly thought possible. No doubt, most elementary school pupils have also had a richer background of past experiences as compared to learners a generation ago. Pre-school and public school pupils experience the world of geometry all around them. They see squares and rectangles in buildings when looking at window panes, doors, and the sides of bricks. Squares and rectangles can also be observed in sidewalks. Circles can be noticed in certain window panes in buildings as well as in circle drives or circular gardens. Headlights on cars are also circular in appearance. Thus pre-scholars, as well as elementary school pupils have rich opportunities in building background experiences from their environment pertaining to the world of geometry. The geometry curriculum in the elementary school mathematics programme should have good sequence from the child's point of view. Learners must be successful in achievement so that an adequate self concept is developed as well as an appreciation and liking for geometry.

Pupils on the first grade level, for example, can develop many understandings pertaining to algebra in the mathematics curriculum. Once, these pupils have developed understandings in a meaningful, purposeful, and interesting way in a specific learning situation, to cite an example, that 4 + 3 = 7 and 3 + 4 = 7, the mathematics teacher can have learners think of solution sets to the following open sentences: 4 + — = 7 and — + 3 = 7. The number line can guide pupils in finding the solution set to state a true sentence. Number lines can be purchased commercially; they can also be made for teacher and pupil usage. Modern mathematics textbooks contain many number lines. In the above example of 4 + — = 7, the number line can be used in the following way:

0 1 2 3 4 5 6 7 8

The child can point to the value of "4" on the number line. The pupil can now reason in terms of how many jumps need to be made to reach "7". The sentence can no longer be classified as an open sentence; it is now classified as a true sentence. Markers such as beads, and other manipulative materials can also be used by learners to find the solution set. In this case, pupils can place four beads in a set to represent the first addend in the equation 4 + — = 7. Seven markers can be placed in a set to represent the sum. Thus, individual pupils inductively can determine how many markers should be placed in the space so that a true sentence results. The answer, of course, would be three. If a pupil had decided incorrectly that four markers to into the space, the teacher should merely ask what the sum of 4 + 4 is. Learners could use crayons, sheets of paper, and chalk, for example, to determine the correct answer. At this point pupils could also generalize that 4 + 4 = 7 is false in terms of being a number sentence. Thus, learners would experience true, false, and open sentences.

Pupils should develop meaningful learnings pertaining to relationships between and among numbers. Thus, the concepts of "less than," "greater than," and "equal to," become important. A set of six members is greater than a set of four members. A set of three toys is less than a set of five toys. A set of four balls is equal to a set of four balls. With the use of manipulative materials, pupils should develop these understandings in an interesting, meaningful and purposeful way.

Thus, a modern programme of elementary school mathematics places much emphasis upon some kind of rational balance among arithmetic geometry, and algebra.

Rational Counting

From the previous discussion, it is quite obvious that young pupils can master and apply the concept of rational counting. Kindergarten and first grade pupils need much assistance in this area from teachers of mathematics. Too frequently, faulty methods and materials have been used, and thus learners have not been able to use what has been learned. The teacher can ask questions like the following pertaining to functional situations in life:

1. How many books do you have on your desk (let us assume a library book and a textbook are on the desk of each learner.)
2. How many pupils want milk in the first row? The number of pupils wanting milk in each row can then be counted.
3. How many pupils are in school today in the first row? Second row? Third row? Fourth row?
4. How many pupils are on the committee to feed the fish in the aquarium?
5. How many pupils are on the committee to take care of the plants in the classroom?

The teacher needs to think of numerous learning activities whereby pupils can engage in rational counting. If pupils want to say more numbers than there are members within a set, the teacher could have pupils point to each member as the appropriate number is spoken orally. For example, the learner would point to a book on his desk and say "one"; then he would point to the next book and say "two"; and so on. Thus, the pupil will be developing basic understandings pertaining to one-to-one correspondence. The correct number then is said orally as the child points to a particular member of a set.

A kindergarten or first grade pupil may not have mastered the sequence of numbers when counting. Three pupils, of course, would be working at a lower level of maturity than those that have mastered the proper sequence of numbers through ten, for example. Generally, many pupils in the preschool years become fascinated with numbers; they, in many cases, can say the correct sequence of numbers up to a point when entering the first grade. In a good kindergarten mathematics programme, learners can engage in rational counting. The teacher does not want to frustrate learners when readiness cannot be developed for rational counting. Much harm is done in teaching when pupils are forced to learn that which is not attainable. Emotional problems may then set in where pupils learn to dislike elementary school mathematics.

Evaluating Pupil Achievement in Mathematics

It is essential that proper procedures be utilized to evaluate pupil achievement in mathematics. Evaluation should be a continuous process. Learner achievement must be assessed in terms of objectives. Teacher effectiveness in teaching is thus evaluated. There are certain questions the teacher can ask of herself pertaining to teaching elementary school mathematics. Among these questions could be the following:

1. Did I provide for each pupil in the classroom?
2. Did pupils thoroughly understand what was taught?
3. Was there proper sequence for each pupil in making continuous progress?
4. Did pupils learn to enjoy mathematics more than formerly?
5. Did each pupil achieve at his own unique optimum rate?
6. Are pupils developing more proficiency in computer skills?
7. Do learners volunteer to do additional work in mathematics?
8. Is there balance among geometry, arithmetic, and algebra in the mathematics curriculum?

9. Did I diagnose each pupil's difficulty pertaining to specific problems in elementary school mathematics?
10. Does the mathematics curriculum provide for the needs of individual learners?
11. Did pupils have ample opportunities to evaluate their own achievement?
12. Do pupils develop an appreciation for mathematics?

The teacher and school can use standardized achievement tests to evaluate pupil achievement. These generally are given once a year. Some schools give them twice a year thus giving results of pupil achievement in an approximate pretest and post-test situation. If the test is given approximately two weeks after the school year has started and two weeks before the year is ended, teachers can evaluate the amount of achievement for each pupil as measured by the standardized achievement test. If the standardized test is given only once in year, it would be recommendable to give it about two weeks after the school year has begun. Thus, teachers have an opportunity to notice present achievement levels of each pupil as measured by the standardized test. Results of giving standardized achievement tests are not an absolute. They can be used, however, along with results from other measurement and evaluation devices to determine learner achievement in elementary school mathematics. Standardized achievement tests should always be selected in terms of stated objectives for the mathematics curriculum.

Teacher observation should definitely be used to assess pupil achievement in elementary school mathematics. Teacher observation can be quite continuous and effective. The mathematics teacher can, among others, observe the following:

1. Can pupils complete reasonable assignments that are made on time?
2. Do learners exhibit characteristics of being accurate in work completed?
3. Do individual pupils waste time when working in the area of elementary school mathematics?
4. Do learners have an inward desire in wanting to learn more mathematics?

5. Specifically, what kinds of errors do pupils make whereby additional learning activities are needed to remedy the situation?

6. Which pupils are having difficulty in elementary school mathematics?

7. What kinds of problems do pupils have when utilizing the elementary school mathematics textbook? (Problem in reading, in computation, in problem solving, etc.)

8. Do pupils appear to like mathematics as well as other curriculum areas in the elementary school?

The teacher can also evaluate pupil achievement in elementary school mathematics with the use of behaviourally stated objectives. These objectives must be reasonable for learners to achieve. The following are examples:

1. The pupil will add correctly nine out of ten addition problems.

2. Ninety per cent of the class will multiply correctly eight out of ten multiplication problems.

It is possible to measure if learners have or have not achieved the above stated objectives.

For the first objective, the teacher would select addition problems which would be representative of those that pupils have had ample meaningful practice on. The results of solving these problems would reveal to the teacher what pupils have and have not learned. Additional learning experiences would need to be provided for pupils where mastery has not been in evidence. Learners reveal if they have or have not achieved the stated objective. In the second objective the same procedure would be followed as in the first objective; however, a class minimal achievement level is also stated such as "90 per cent of the class will multiply correctly eight out of ten multiplication problems." In both objectives, the teacher has standards to gauge his or her effectiveness in teaching. If the objectives were too complex for pupils to achieve, necessary adjustments need to be made so the curriculum is adjusted to the learner. The teacher also needs to be aware of teaching that which learners have already mastered. Objectives need to be adjusted which are attainable for learners.

Diagnostic tests can also be administered to determine what pupils do and do not understand. The results of diagnostic tests should pin-point specifically what difficulties and errors learners are making in elementary school mathematics. The diagnostic test may pin-point a lack of understanding on the part of the learners in areas such as the following:

1. structural properties of numbers, such as the commutative, associative, and distributive laws pertaining to addition and multiplication;
2. the union and intersection of sets;
3. other bases, than base ten;
4. the Roman and Egyptian system of numeration;
5. Venn diagrams;
6. use of the number line;
7. addition, subtraction, multiplication and division;
8. true, false and open sentences in elementary school mathematics;
9. perimeters and areas of squares, rectangles, triangles, etc.;
10. equations and relationships between numbers.

In evaluating pupil achievement in elementary school mathematics, the teacher can develop a teacher-made test. This can be a pretest to assess pupil achievement prior to beginning a new unit in mathematics. The teacher-made test can also be developed and given at various intervals when a unit is being taught to assess how well pupils are achieving objectives. The teacher-made test can also be given at the end of a unit to determine achievement from the time the pretest was given. In the post-test the mathematics teacher can evaluate how well learners achieved the objectives at the close of the unit. The teacher's effectiveness as a teacher is thus being evaluated. During the time the unit is taught or at the end of the unit, the teacher-made test must be valid in terms of covering what has been taught. Thus, if learners have had ample opportunity in meaningful, interesting, and purposeful ways to develop learnings pertaining to the following: $32\overline{)640}$, $22\overline{)440}$, $21\overline{)630}$, $12\overline{)480}$, $11\overline{)550}$, $23\overline{)690}$, $41\overline{)820}$, teacher-made tests should contain representative problems pertaining to what pupils have learned previously. It would, of course, not be valid to test pupils in this case pertaining to the following problems in division: $317\overline{)6491}$, $81\overline{)7284}$, $69\overline{)4947}$, $76\overline{)8123}$, $47\overline{)9205}$ and others. Pupils have not had the opportunities to develop understandings pertaining to division problems of this level of complexity. The teacher-made test should also be reliable in that learner's results when taking the test again would be consistent, all things basically being equal or equivalent. If the child is ill physically or emotionally upset, consistency of results on the part of a learner is then not possible.

The Metric System

It is important for elementary school mathematics teachers to teach an ample number of units on the metric system. Pupils, no doubt, will be using the metric system of measurement in functional situations in life in the near future. Thus, the traditional system of measurement using such measures as inches, feet, yards, miles, quarts, gallons, and bushels may be greatly minimized or become obsolete in the near future. Units of study on the metric system stress the following criteria:

1. learnings are relevant for pupils;
2. functional use can be made of learnings gained;
3. concrete objects are used in teaching-learning situations;
4. purpose and interest in learning on the part of pupils is inherent.

In Summary

Mathematics in the elementary school has changed more in the last fifteen years as compared to other curriculum areas. Learners must develop understandings pertaining to structural properties in mathematics such as the commutative property of addition and multiplication, the associative property of addition and multiplication, the distributive property of multiplication over addition, and additive identify, and the multiplicative identity. It is very important to provide for individual differences in the class. Numerous approaches can be used to provide for individual pupils in a class. Learning by discovery or the inductive approach is important to use when providing learning activities for pupils. To fix learnings in the minds of pupils after meaningful, interesting, and purposeful learning activities have been provided, appropriate practice must be provided for learners. Pupils should have ample opportunities to sense the relationship of knowledge. Isolated bits of information, in many cases, may soon be forgotten. The mathematics curriculum must emphasize some kind of rational balance among arithmetic, geometry, and algebra. Algebra and geometry must receive their fair share of emphasis in the total mathematics curriculum. It is important that early primary grade pupils understand the concept of set and develop appropriate skills to be able to engage in rational counting. A variety of approaches should be utilized to evaluate pupil achievement in elementary school mathematics. Evaluation should be continuous and in terms of terms of stated objectives. Thus teacher observation of learner achievement is important as well as the use of standardized achievement and diagnostic tests, and teacher made tests.

REFERENCES

Ballew, Hunter. *Teaching Children Mathematics*. Columbus: Charles E. Merrill Publishing Company, 1973.

Copeland, Richard W. *How Children Learn Mathematics*. Second Edition. New York: The Macmillan Company, 1974.

Fehr, Howard F., and Jo McKeeby Phillips. *Teaching Modern Mathematics in the Elementary School*. Second Edition. Reading, Massachusetts: Addison Publishing Company, 1972.

Grossnickle, Foster E., and John Reckzeh. *Discovering Meaning in Elementary School Mathematics*. Sixth Edition, New York: Holt, Rinehart and Winston, Inc., 1973.

Jensen, Rosalie. *Exploring Mathematical Concepts and Skills in the Elementary School*. Columbus: Charles E. Merrill Publishing Company, 1973.

Kramer, Klaas. *Teaching Elementary School Mathematics*. Second Edition, Boston: Allyn and Bacon, Inc., 1970.

Mahaffey, Michael L., and Alex F. Perrodin. *Teaching Elementary School Mathematics*. Itasco, Illinois: F.E. Peacock Publishers, Inc., 1973.

Riedesel, C. Alan. *Guiding Discovery in Elementary School Mathematics*. Second Edition, New York: Appleton-Century-Crofts, 1973.

Schminke, C.W., *et al. Teaching the Child Mathematics*. Hinsdale, Illinois: The Dryden Press, Inc., 1973.

Swenson, Esther J. *Teaching Mathematics to Children*. Second Edition. New York: The Macmillan Company, 1973.

Science in the Elementary School

Much revision has occurred in the elementary school science curriculum. Perhaps, one can say that the National Defense Education Act passed in 1958 did much to bring on rapid changes and innovations in elementary school science. This Act, among other provisions, provided that the federal government would pay for part of the cost of science, mathematics, and foreign language equipment for school use. This made it possible for many elementary schools to get needed science equipment. Formerly, teachers, as well as pupils, would generally bring all needed equipment to school; experimentation in science could then occur.

Several problems were involved in these situations:

1. Pupils, as well as the teacher, forgot to bring items to school at the time they were needed.
2. It was difficult to find these materials when they were needed.
3. Much inconvenience was in evidence when elementary teachers borrowed science equipment from the high school science laboratory.
4. Teachers found it more convenient to teach elementary school science with very few, if any, experiments.

With more elementary schools obtaining equipment for conducting science experiments either through the National Defense Education Act or by buying it entirely from their own budgeted money, new problems arose. Many elementary schools had more and better science equipment than ever before. However, many teachers had difficulty in using this equipment satisfactorily. Workshops, faculty meetings, college and university level courses, and other forms of inservice education for teachers became necessary.

The Use of Experiments

A modern programme of elementary school science will have much in the area of experiments that pupils will perform with teacher guidance. This will mean that learners should actually be involved in conducting these experiments whenever possible. Almost all units taught in elementary school science can emphasize experimentation. For example, if pupils are studying a unit on "Magnetism and Electricity," the following objects and items can be placed on a learning centre to initiate the unit:

1. containers which contain shreds of paper, pieces of wood, a piece of plastic, and different kinds of cloth;
2. nails, paper clips, different size coins, a piece of copper, and other kinds of metals.

Pupils can notice which objects and items on the learning centre are attracted and which are not attracted by the use of magnets.

Scientists engage in conducting many experiments. This is a way of gaining new knowledge. It is a way of identifying new problem areas. Once these problem areas have been clearly defined, information can be gathered to solve these problems. A hypothesis or hypotheses are then developed which pertain to an answer or a solution to the problem. The hypothesis or hypotheses are tentative and not final or fixed. Only through testing can elementary school pupils develop some degree of certainty as to the correctness or accuracy of the hypothesis. Too frequently when science experiments are conducted, pupils want to jump to hasty conclusions as to the outcomes. An experiment or experiments are conducted to test a hypothesis or several hypotheses. In the preceding example pertaining to the unit "Magnetism and Electricity," pupils could hypothesize as to which kinds of objects and items will be attracted by the magnets. This is only a hypothesis and not a fact. The hypothesis, of course, is based on knowledge. Pupils could then test the hypothesis with the actual using of the magnets. Different kinds of magnets should be utilized to test the hypothesis. Hypotheses are substantiated, modified, or refuted based on testing. As time goes on, with further study and thought, new concepts and generalizations may be developed pertaining to previously held conclusions.

Very early in the experiences of elementary school pupils, the concepts of "experimental" and "control groups" should be emphasized. Pupils on the kindergarten level, for example, may be studying a unit on "Plants in Our Community." The question may arise as to what plants need in order to grow well. On a learning centre, two potted plants can be placed. It is important to have these plants as alike as possible in terms of quality. The soil should be as comparable as possible for the two potted plants. The amount of moisture that each potted plant is to receive should be held constant also. In other words, both potted plants should receive the same treatment except for one variable which will be tested. This variable will be that one of these potted plants has a cardboard box placed over it. This plant will represent the experimental group whereas the other potted plant will be in the control group. Pupils can then test their hypothesis as to what will happen to the plant in the experimental group if it receives no sunshine. The plant in the experimental group can be compared with the plant in the control group at selected intervals. Experiments such as these should be conducted using a variety of kinds of plants. In each case there should be an experimental group as well as a control group. If the outcomes are always the same in this experiment, pupils can achieve accurate generalizations.

In the unit previously mentioned pertaining to "Plants in Our Community," other variables can be tested also as to what plants need in order to grow. Let us again assume for purposes of discussion that the two potted plants are as similar as possible in terms of quality. They receive the same amount of sunshine due to their location. The soil of these potted plants is similar. The one variable that will now be tested will pertain to the amount of moisture that one plant will receive as compared to the other plant. Desert plants would not be involved in this experiment. One of the potted plants will receive no moisture while the other receives a proper amount. Pupils can observe what happens at different intervals when the experiment is being conducted. The plant receiving no moisture for a period of time would be in the experimental group whereas the plant which is receiving the normal treatment is in the control group. Again, pupils should have ample opportunities to observe what actually happens when the one variable is tested. Another variable that could be tested in the experiment would be the soil that is used in the potted plant. All other variables would remain the same. Pupils could use three kinds of soil; sandy soil, clay, and loam. Thus, with several experiments such as these, pupils could generalize as to which kind of soil is most beneficial to plants.

Pupils must have opportunities to identify problems and questions; secondly, information or data needs to be gathered; thirdly, a hypothesis or hypotheses are developed; and finally, the hypothesis or hypotheses are tested and subject to revision and modification. These steps may not necessarily be followed rigidly. However, pupils should use the methods of science in conducting experiments so that results are unbiased and objective.

The importance of Science

More time, no doubt, is devoted to teaching elementary school science than ever before. The authors can well remember attending a five teacher rural elementary school when science was taught once a week on the intermediate and upper grade levels in the later 1930's and early 1940's. The science curriculum then consisted largely of reading about science from a specific series of textbooks. The reading generally was done orally with each pupil taking his turn. Many students in graduate and undergraduate classes of the authors attending the elementary school years in the 1930's and 1940's mention similar learning experiences. The use of experiments in elementary school science has been discussed previously; experimentation should be central in a modern programme of science. The time, of course, devoted to the teaching of science has increased much.

There is much for pupils to learn in science in a scientific age. The space age, jet planes, cars, trucks, buses, ships, refrigerators, ranges, washers, and driers—to mention a few of man's achievements—require that pupils understand and develop major concepts, principles, and generalizations of science. This means that adequate time needs to be given to the teaching of science.

Many elementary schools have adequate time devoted each day to the teaching of science. To be sure, ample time given to teaching a specific curriculum area will not automatically make for optimum achievement on the part of pupils. However, if pupils are to realize carefully selected objectives, the proper amount of time needs to be given to provide for quality learning activities in elementary school science and evaluate if stated goals have been achieved.

Thus, society has realized the importance of science for pupils in the elementary school. If learners are to do well in science on the secondary level, they need to experience an excellent science programme on the elementary level. Young children are curious about their natural environment. Selected pupils have come to school late on the kindergarten and first grade levels due to being curious about insects, rocks, plants, snow, puddles of water, and other natural phenomenon while walking to school.

Teachers have been amazed about the items children will bring to school for a science learning centre. Little or no coaxing needs to be done here. Pupils voluntarily want to bring objects to school pertaining to the curriculum area of science. They may bring rocks, insects in containers, tadpoles in jars, plants, magnets of different kinds, and other items related to science. Pupils can raise many important questions on what has been brought for the science learning centre. Pupils may reveal their interests by asking questions such as the following:

1. What do insects feed on?
2. How are rocks formed?
3. How do tadpoles change into frogs?
4. What do plants need in order to grow?
5. Why do magnets "pick up" certain things but not other materials?

Pupils with teacher leadership can discuss possible answers to these questions. Research also will need to be done to get needed information in solving problem areas. The area of science offers many occasions for pupils to develop interest in and become curious about natural phenomena. It almost appears that pupils are naturally interested in science. Thus, it is no wonder that elementary school science is receiving more emphasis than ever before in the elementary curriculum. Also, in an industrial, automated society, pupils must understand contributions that science has made to improve the quality of living for human beings.

Inservice Education in Science

With more science taught in the elementary school curriculum than ever before, it has become very important to conduct an adequate number of workshops and hold an ample number of faculty meetings to update science in the elementary school.

An elementary school or several elementary schools conducting workshops in the teaching of science must, first of all, determine what facet or facets of the science curriculum need to be emphasized in this approach to inservice education. Cooperatively, then, faculty members should decide upon the theme of the workshop. The theme can be decided upon only by studying trends in elementary school science and evaluating where one's school is presently in this important curriculum area. Thus, a gap will generally exist between where the school is presently, and where it should be in elementary school science. The following areas may represent some of these gaps:

1. objectives of elementary school science;
2. selection of unit titles;
3. proper sequence in the science curriculum;
4. conducting experiments;
5. using science equipment effectively;
6. using a variety of learning activities;
7. assessing pupil achievement effectively;
8. developing a philosophy for teaching science;
9. assisting pupils in reading science content;
10. identifying the scope of the science curriculum;
11. learning by discovery in science.

A general session can then be utilized to pinpoint specifically what participants in the workshop want to stress and emphasize in improving the science curriculum. In the general session, it is good to emphasize tenets of democracy in the decision-making process. The following would be important guidelines to follow:

1. respect the thinking of others;
2. listen carefully to ideas being presented;
3. assess each idea carefully in terms of merit;
4. speak clearly so all can hear the ideas being presented;
5. present ideas to the total group and not to one person alone;
6. do not dominate the discussion or refrain from participating.

Committees can be developed based on decisions made in the general session pertaining to problem areas that need solution in the area of elementary school science. It is excellent if each participant in the general session can select the committee he or she wishes most to participate in. Committee members need to sense purpose in work that is done. In other words, if participants can voluntarily select the committee they wish to serve in and sense that purpose is involved in solving problem areas, energy levels should be high for optimum achievement. The following resources should be available for all committee members:

1. knowledge resource personnel who can work effectively with people;
2. a professional library from which participants can get needed information.

Thus, members of the different committees involved in working to gain more insight into an effective elementary school science programme should have resources available which will help in gaining quality results from effort put forth.

It is necessary for participants in a workshop to work on problems and areas of interest of their very own choosing. This would then provide for individual differences among committee members. It may be that one participant alone has the following problem pertaining to the teaching of elementary school science: assisting pupils in working on committees where responsibility of each member commensurate with ability is in evidence (this teacher may have had difficulty in getting certain committee members to do their share of the work). Thus, the individual participant in the science workshop can work in the direction of solving a relevant problem in the teaching of science. Consultant help and resource materials would be available to help participants on an individual basis.

Faculty meetings in an elementary school should also be devoted to improving the elementary school science curriculum. An agenda committee composed of three or four faculty members can arrange items for discussion at the next faculty meeting. It is good to rotate the members of this committee to provide for a broad base of participation on the part of faculty members of an elementary school. Every faculty member should have equal rights to present items to the agenda committee for discussion at faculty meetings. The agenda should be in the hands of participants two to three days before the meeting is held. This should give all participants ample opportunities to think about the various alternatives and possibilities when discussing solutions to questions and problem areas. Individuals can volunteer or be assigned to serve on committees to solve selected problem areas. Some of the problem areas that may be identified in faculty meetings pertaining to the teaching of elementary school science could be the following:

1. How can the inquiry approach be utilized when teaching science?
2. How does one write objectives which are behaviourally stated?
3. How can pupil achievement be effectively evaluated when using the problem solving approach?

Much thought, research, and discussion can go into the solving of each of these questions or problems. Some faculty members, no doubt, will need to visit other schools and observe teachers, for example, using the enquiry approach in teaching, as well as observe other innovations.

Developing Curriculum Guides

Each public school system should develop curriculum guides which can be utilized by teachers in teaching the different curriculum areas of the elementary school. Curriculum guides should be used in terms of providing suggestions for teaching. They should definitely not be prescriptive. In the early history of curriculum guides, it was felt that these were to be followed rigidly. Today, the emphasis definitely is upon selection, in terms of good criteria or standards, as to what will be utilized from a curriculum guide. The curriculum guide, along with other reference sources, can assist the science teacher to do a better job of planning for teaching elementary school pupils.

The question arises as to what are the salient parts of a good curriculum guide. The format followed in developing these guides may vary from school system to school system. However, there will be some basic agreements as to which essential parts to include in a curriculum guide. The following are important parts of a curriculum guide in terms of the section devoted to elementary school science:

1. statements pertaining to a philosophy of teaching science;
2. suggestions for using the guide;
3. general and specific objectives for teaching different units of study;
4. scope and sequence of science units for each grade in the elementary school;
5. suggested learning activities for each science unit;
6. suggested evaluation techniques to use in evaluating pupil achievement;
7. a listing of child growth and development characteristics;
8. suggestions for implementing committee work, and teacher-pupil planning;
9. suggestions for helping pupils learn inductively, use the problem solving approach, and learn through the inquiry approach;
10. a good bibliography listing teacher references and pupil references.

From the preceding parts that could go into the developing of a curriculum guide, it is quite obvious that the teacher can have a valuable source of ideas to use in planning the science curriculum. For example, the teacher can evaluate and select objectives which pupils should achieve in a specific unit. The teacher also has numerous opportunities to select learning activities from the curriculum guide which should help a given set of learners achieve to their optimum. The evaluation selection of the guide should give the science teacher some new approaches to utilize in effectively evaluating pupil achievement. Again, curriculum guides must be used as guides and not as a holy book which must be followed precisely.

Use of Television in Science

Educational television has made many important contributions in upgrading the science curriculum. Elementary schools that have access to closed-circuit television generally will have listings of programmes which teachers will have well in advance of their showing. These programmes will relate directly to ongoing units being taught in science. For each unit of study, guides have been or should be developed pertaining to the different telecasts. For each broadcast, a listing of objectives for pupils to achieve is important. The teacher can sense then what each broadcast will emphasize in terms of objectives. Suggestions for learning activities are presented in the guide which will provide readiness within learners for viewing the telecast. The teacher can then select which activities would do the best job of providing readiness for learning so that adequate background knowledge will be developed within pupils. If pupils do not have the needed concepts, facts, terms, and generalizations necessary for understanding the telecast, optimum achievement cannot result. The readiness activities should also assist pupils in developing interest in the broadcast. An inward desire should exist on the part of the learner in wanting to watch the telecast. Certainly, learners should have identified some questions which they would want to have answered when viewing the broadcast.

After the telecast, follow-up activities are necessary so that pupils can use what has been learned. Answers to questions raised before the broadcast can be discussed. Experiments may need to be performed in order that pupils can get needed data in answer to questions. Pupils may volunteer to develop reports on selected topics which relate to the broadcast using science encyclopaedias or regular encyclopaedias. Taking an excursion may help to answer additional questions raised after the telecast. In other words, there are many learning activities for pupils which will assist them to "branch out" in broadening their thinking and interests after having viewed a telecast.

Using Knowledge of Children

Science teachers who do a poor job of teaching may not be using knowledge pertaining to important child growth and development characteristics. Teachers need to study each of their pupils carefully so that the best quality of learning activities can be provided. Educational psychologists have long emphasized the importance of providing for individual differences in a class. Too frequently, however, little has been done in this area by practitioners. A very clear violation of providing for individual differences exists when science teachers want to keep all pupils "together" by having the whole group study the same thing at the same time. Perhaps, science has become a reading course where pupils spend much time in reading content from a series of elementary school science textbooks. As educators should be well aware of, this activity will be too difficult for some pupils; for others it is too easy. Very few pupils will find that the content is written on their reading level. Pupils also desire new experiences and want variety in learning activities they are participating in.

Many statements have been written on child growth and development characteristics. Faculty members of an elementary school need to study these contributions written by psychologists and educators realizing that pupils differ from each other in many ways within a class, such an interest, intelligence, abilities, past experiences, motivation, appearance, height, and weight.

Variety in Learning Activities

It is important for the science teacher to provide a variety of learning activities for pupils. This would be important for the following reasons:

1. pupils have different learning styles;
2. different levels of achievement in science exist within any class of pupils;
3. not all pupils, of course, benefit equally from the same activity;

4. teachers have different teaching styles;
5. selected learning activities capture the interests of pupils more than do other kinds of experiences;
6. individuals desire new experiences;
7. monotony in activities hinders pupils in developing proper motivation toward learning.

There are many learning activities in elementary school science which would assist pupils in gaining needed concepts, main ideas, facts, and generalizations. These learning activities could help pupils in the area of problem solving. The following, among others, could become purposeful learning activities for pupils in elementary school science: conducting experiments and demonstrations, taking excursions, reading from a series or several series of elementary school science textbooks, getting information from a set or several sets of general encyclopaedias and / or science encyclopaedias, reading from library books, working at learning centres, using pictures, using transparencies and the overhead projector, constructing objects, making models, utilizing filmstrips and film, listening to tape recordings, interviewing resource personnel, viewing slides, visiting museums, having discussions, giving oral reports to the class, writing reports, engaging in dramatic activities, making dioramas, developing friezes, completing murals, making graphs and charts, developing illustrations, and participating in panel discussions. There are many, many kinds of learning activities for pupils in elementary school science; there should basically be no boredom on the part of pupils when this curriculum area is being taught. It is important to select those learning activities which will help pupils to do the very best possible in elementary school science.

Approach to teaching science can also be varied in terms of using the inductive versus the deductive approach to learning. Much has been written about the advantages of using the inductive approach as compared to the deductive approach. Some of these advantages are the following:

1. pupils have to do much responding so that generalizations and conclusions can truly be discovered;
2. learners reveal where there are presently in achievement when learning by discovery;
3. pupils can become actively involved in ongoing learning activities;

4. it keeps learners "on their toes" when doing much responding in ongoing learning activities;
5. pupils have many opportunities to do critical and creative thinking;
6. a variety of learning activities can be utilized in the inductive approach;
7. pupils can become more self-directed with less reliance on the teacher dominating the classroom situation;
8. teachers become more flexible in their thinking when less reliance can be placed upon how pupils will respond;
9. learners can work more in the direction of using the methods and approaches of scientists; scientists gain much knowledge and information through discovery.

The science teacher can have pupils develop generalizations deductively. For example, in a unit on "Liquids, Solids and Gases," the teacher could perform an experiment whereby a bottle with a narrow opening would be filled with a few inches of water and placed on a hot plate. A balloon would be stretched over the narrow opening of the bottle before it is placed on the hot plate. Pupils would be encouraged to see what will happen. The balloon, of course, becomes larger. The teacher then proceeds to explain to the class why the balloon became larger and what happens when air is heated.

In the inductive approach utilizing the same experiment, the teacher could have pupils hypothesize freely as to what will happen when this same bottle, containing a few inches of water, with the attached balloon is placed on the hot plate. Reasons for the hypotheses can also be discussed thus giving the teacher much information on where learners are presently in achievement pertaining to the area now being taught in the unit "Liquids, Solids, and Gases." Following the discussion, the hypotheses need to be tested using the experiment. The experiment can be performed more than once so that pupils can sense that the outcomes in the experimental will have the same results. The size of the openings of the bottles as well as the size of the balloons can vary when having pupils view the same kind or type of experiment when noticing that the results are similar in terms of generalizations or conclusions realized. Further research can be done using elementary science textbooks, encyclopaedias, films, filmstrips, and other resources to explain conclusions realized from conducting the experiment. In using the inductive approach, the teacher does a very small amount of explaining or lecturing. The teacher sets the stage for learning. Pupils identify problems, gather information develop hypotheses, test hypotheses, and revise them when necessary. Active involvement on the part of pupils is of utmost importance in ongoing learning activities.

A science teacher could tape record his own teaching and evaluate the quality of experiences pertaining to pupils learning by discovery or using the inductive approach. If a portable video-tape machine is available in the elementary school, teaching performance in science can be video-taped. Thus, the teacher in the reply of the video-tape could also observe non-verbal facets of communication such as gestures, facial expressions, and body movements in the teaching-learning situation. Valuable feed-back from learners can come from viewing different facets of teaching on video-tape. The teacher can notice such factors as the following:

1. Do pupils appear interested or bored in the ongoing learning activities?
2. Are all learners actively involved in the lesson being presented?
3. Do a few pupils dominate the discussion while others refrain from participating?
4. Do pupils feel free to hypothesize pertaining to possible outcomes of science experiments?
5. Are pupils using a variety of reference sources in gathering data to develop and/or test hypotheses?
6. Do pupils reveal curiosity in wanting to learn more about any unit of study in elementary school science?

If the teacher has access to video-taping teaching performance, or if a tape recorder is used only, he can analyze what kind of verbal interaction occurred between pupils and the teacher in a classroom situation. The teacher, for example, can notice the following in teaching-learning situations:

1. Do pupils have ample opportunities to hypothesize?
2. Does the teacher ask many relevant questions of learners pertaining to ongoing units of study in science?
3. Are these questions on the present achievement level of pupils?
4. Do pupils have needed background information to develop meaningful hypotheses?
5. Is lecturing minimized much in ongoing learning activities?
6. Is the teacher praising pupils in achieving desired objectives in elementary school science?
7. Do learners identify relevant problem areas?
8. Does it appear that pupils individually are being challenged in developing an inward desire to learn?
9. Does the teacher give pupils adequate time to engage in hypothesizing when being involved in problem solving activities?
10. Does the teacher refrain from scolding or minimizing pupils in the class setting?

Behavioural Objectives in Elementary Science

Elementary school science lends itself very well to having teachers state their objectives behaviourally. Selected educators advocate that objectives be stated precisely. Advantages of behaviourally stated objectives are the following:

1. These objectives very clearly state what learners are to learn.
2. It can definitely be measured if pupils have achieved these objectives.
3. Learning activities can be selected carefully which will guide learners to realize the objectives.
4. Teachers can be held accountable for pupils realizing the objectives.
5. Learners can achieve these objectives at different rates of speed thus providing for individual differences.

6. Parents can notice specifically what their pupils have learned.
7. Principals and supervisors can have a better basis for evaluating teacher performance.
8. Teachers could even be paid on the basis of achievement or lack of it in terms of learner performance (this could be a motivating factor for some teachers).
9. Objectives criteria are used to assess pupil achievement; these criteria are the behaviourally stated objectives.

As in almost any innovation, there are also disadvantages to behaviourally stated objectives. The following, among others, are some of the disadvantages:

1. Too frequently, the trivial or unimportant is taught since the lowest level of cognitive objectives are easiest to write.
2. No one can definitely be sure what pupils actually should learn when stating all objectives precisely prior to teaching.
3. Objectives should come from the learner also and not the teacher only.
4. Affective domain objectives may become minimized if all objectives need to be stated so that it can be measured precisely if pupils have achieved them.
5. Learners become rather passive individuals if all objectives are stated by the teacher prior to teaching.
6. By stating objectives in advance prior to teaching, the teacher is assuming that proper sequence in learning will be in evidence.
7. The teacher should focus more on the learning activity rather than the objectives since it is in this framework that interest and meaning is developed.
8. Behavioural objectives are very time consuming in writing.

The science teacher, the elementary school principal, and the supervisor need to study behavioural objectives carefully to determine if this plan of teaching is really wanted in elementary school science. Workshops and faculty meetings can be devoted to the study and implementation of behavioural objectives. Objectives which pupils are then to achieve should meet the following criteria:

1. they are important or relevant;
2. they stress key ideas or generalizations emphasized by specialists in the different areas of science such as in biology, chemistry, physics, zoology, botany, geology, and astronomy.
3. there is balance among, understandings, skills, and attitudinal objectives or among cognitive, psychomotor, and affective domain objectives.

All behaviourally stated objectives should follow the following standards:

1. the objectives should be clearly written so that little or no room exists in their interpretation;
2. it can definitely be measured if the objectives have been achieved;
3. it states what learners will learn as a result of teaching.

If pupils are studying a unit on "The Solar System," the following objectives may have been identified for pupils to realize:

1. The pupil will list in writing the nine planets in proper sequence from the sun.
2. The pupil will recite orally the names of the largest sequence from the sun.
3. The pupil will write a fifty word paper on the possibility of life as we know it on a planet of his own choice (excluding the planet earth).
4. Pupils in their own words will define the meaning of the following concepts: solar system; universe; planet; satellite; asteroids; theory; hypothesis; magnetic pole; constellation; rotation; and revolution.
5. The pupil will demonstrate and discuss the causes of the different seasons of the year.
6. Learners will predict what will happen in the future in space exploration.

7. A model of the solar system will be made in committees of three; the model will be evaluated in terms of criteria discussed in class.

The first and second behaviourally stated objectives require recall of information which is the lowest level of cognition. Pupils would recall the names of the nine known planets in proper order, and be able to name the largest and smallest of these planets. The third objective may also involve simple recall of what has been learned previously by pupils. Pupils could recall from a discussion if there is or is not life as we know it on one of the planets and write on the selected topic. Pupils individually, however, could also be quite creative when writing a paper of at least fifty words pertaining to the possibilities of life existing on a planet which he chooses to write on. The paper could involve unique, novel, original and constructive ideas which would involve synthesizing of knowledge. The fourth objective goes beyond recall of knowledge. It is true that the child would need to think of definitions he has heard of previously pertaining to such words as solar system, universe, planet, satellite, asteroids, theory, hypothesis, magnetic pole, constellation, rotation, and revolution. The learner, however, would need to reveal his understanding of these concepts by giving definitions in his own words. Comprehension of the meaning of these concepts would be important to pupils when achieving this objective. The fifth objective would generally involve applying what has been learned previously. The knowledge and information the child has developed previously is now utilized in demonstrating the causes of the different seasons of the year. The pupil could use a large globe to represent the earth and a flashlight to represent the sun. The learner could also make drawings on the chalkboard and/or use pictures in clarifying the various causes for the different seasons of the year. In the sixth objective, creative thinking based on much knowledge is involved. Pupils would need to have considerable background information to make predictions as to what will happen in the future as far as space exploration is concerned. The last objective involves a psychomotor domain objective in that a construction activity is involved requiring the use of the muscles. To be sure, much thought and research will go into the making of an accurate model of the solar system. Pupils will need to check the accuracy of their model in terms of standards or criteria developed in class. The latter part of this objective (objective number seven) can involve a very complex level of thinking. Definite criteria will need to be developed in class so that the model of the solar system can be effectively evaluated in terms of these guidelines.

Thus, behaviourally stated objectives can be used effectively in a modern programme of elementary school science. It is important when emphasizing these kinds of objectives that teachers have pupils go beyond the level of recall of information. The science teacher also needs to think in terms of some kind of rational balance among cognitive, psychomotor, and affective domain objectives. Never should one category of objectives dominate teaching-learning situations. One category of objectives does affect the other category or categories.

Adjusting the Science Curriculum to the Child

Too frequently, the teacher has objectives for pupils to achieve which are excessively complex. The science teacher may have felt that this is a way of setting high standards in a specific curriculum area. Many pupils then cannot achieve these objectives and develop feelings of an inadequate self. Pupil achievement goes downhill in situations such as these. Learners think and feel that they cannot do well in elementary school science and this becomes a reality. If pupils perceive that they cannot do well in science, this is the way that learners will behave. The teacher needs to have some kind of pretest in a new science unit to determine where learners are presently in achievement. Once this has been determined, objectives can be developed which are attainable. If objectives are attainable, learners can feel successful and develop feelings of an adequate self. The curriculum is then adjusted to where pupils are presently in achievement in different units of study in elementary school science.

Certainly, there is danger, too, in teaching pupils what they already know in a new unit of study. A pretest can give elementary science teachers data if objectives need to be made more complex. Again, the objectives should be attainable for learners. The science curriculum in this case is again adjusted to present achievement levels of learners.

In Summary

Conducting experiments is a very important type or kind of learning activity in a modern elementary school science programme. Balance among the different curriculum areas in the elementary school must be stressed in teaching-learning situations. Inservice education for teachers, principals, and supervisors is important to update the science curriculum. Curriculum guides can be a valuable source to utilize when selecting objectives, learning experiences, and evaluation techniques in a modern programme of elementary school science. A variety of learning experiences should be provided for pupils in the elementary school. The science curriculum must be adjusted to the present achievement level of each learner. Inductive approaches should be emphasized by the teacher in teaching-learning situations. It behaviourally stated objectives are used in teaching-learning situations, critical and creative thinking as well as problem solving should be emphasized. Attitudinal objectives are important for pupils to achieve. There must be proper balance among the following kinds of objectives for pupils to achieve:

1. understandings, skills, and attitudes or
2. cognitive, affective, and psychomotor domains.

REFERENCES

Esler, William K. *Teaching Elementary Science*. Belmont, California: Wadsworth Publishing Company, Inc., 1973.

Friedl, Alfred E. *Teaching Science to Children: The Enquiry Approach Applied*. New York: Random House, Inc., 1972.

Herman, Jerry J. *Developing an Effective Elementary Science Curriculum*. West Nyack, New York: Parkar Publishing Company, 1969.

Kuslan, Louis I., and A. Harris Stone. *Teaching Children Science: An Inquiry Approach*. Belmont, California, 1972.

Lewis, June E., and Irene C. Potter. *The Teaching of Science in the Elementary School*, Englewood Cliffs, New Jersey: Prentice-Hall, Inc., 1970.

Renner, John W., *et al.*, *Teaching Science in the Elementary School*. Second Edition. New York: Harper and Row, Publishers, Inc., 1973.

Rowe, Mary Budd. *Teaching Science as Continuous Inquiry*. New York: McGraw Hill Book Company, 1973.

Thier, Herbert D., *Teaching Elementary School Science, A Laboratory Approach*, Lexington, Massachusetts; D.C. Heath and Company, 1970.

Washton, Nathan S. *Teaching Science in Elementary and Middle Schools*. New York: David McKay Company, Inc., 1974.

Social Studies in the Elementary School

Since the world is "shrinking" in size due to better transportation and communication, it is more important than ever before for pupils to study justifiable units in the social studies. The following problems on the world scene make it imperative that pupils have the needed understandings, skills, and attitudes to engage in problem solving activities in the classroom.

1. There are wars and threats of war between and among nations such as in the Middle East, North and South, Vietnam, and democratic nations versus nations adhering to communism.
2. New nations are formed and the names of some countries no longer exist due to varying causes.
3. Friendships between and among nations change. Nations which formerly were friends become neutral toward each other; they also may become enemies. Friendship can be developed between countries which in the past had relations which were negative.
4. Selected countries may trade much with each other and engage in very little or no trade with other nations on the face of the world.
5. Certain countries have more of the necessary natural resources which make for a prosperous country as compared to other nations.

6. Technology and inventions change the ways of living of a particular subculture or country.
7. Languages that people speak in the world differ from each other thus making for difficulty in communicating ideas.
8. Differences in religious beliefs and doctrine in different countries of the world can make for misunderstandings among nations.
9. Countries of the world differ much from each other in military strength. Even a small country armed by a world power can become a threat to larger neighbouring countries which have less of the effective kinds of military hardware.
10. Leaders change in different nations of the world. Some of these changes come about through elections. Others come about through revolution and invasions.
11. Many changes occur on the local and state levels in such areas as education, welfare, housing, equality of opportunity, jobs, growth of cities, population changes, pollution, technology and inventions.
12. There are nations of the world which have much influence over other less powerful countries. The more powerful nations of the world include the United States, the Soviet Union, Mainland China, France, Great Britain, and Japan.

Thus, it is important for pupils to have a good understanding of man's relationship to man and of man interacting with his physical and cultural environment. Pupils must learn to get along well with classmates, school personnel, and others in their environment. Human beings in the world must understand others better, along with developing positive attitudes toward others, so that a better life can exist for all. Destroying property and lives through wars and other violent means hinders human beings from realizing their optimum. Too much time is spent in destroying and ruining rather than building up and achieving within a nation as well as within the world. Elementary school pupils need to develop those understandings, skills, and attitudes which will assist them in becoming good citizens in a democratic society.

Objectives of the Social Studies

Each elementary school, as well as the entire school system, should spend an adequate amount of time in identifying important objectives for pupils to achieve in elementary school social studies.

There are numerous skills in the social studies which pupils should achieve to become more proficient as citizens in a democracy. Among others, the following skills would be important for pupils to achieve:

1. Skills Objectives

1. Reading social studies content with understanding.
2. Using the card catalog to locate need reference sources.
3. Using appropriate word recognition techniques to identify new words.
4. Reading for a variety of purposes in the social studies.
5. Using the index and table of contents to locate information.
6. Working effectively together with others in committees.
7. Dramatizing roles and events effectively from various units of study.
8. Using the problem solving approach effectively.
9. Evaluating content through the use of critical thinking.
10. Utilizing creative thinking in coming up with new solutions of problems.
11. Constructing and reading information from picture graphs, line graphs, bar graphs, and circle graphs.
12. Using a variety of reputable sources to gather information, such as encyclopaedias, almanacs, films, filmstrips, tapes, records, models, pictures, slides, and resource persons.
13. Presenting information clearly and effectively to classmates and other individuals in the environment.
14. Reading and comprehending current affairs items from recent newspapers and magazines.

15. Listening effectively to the contributions of others within committees as well as the class as a whole.
16. Comprehending the contents of news broadcasts and television reports pertaining to news items.
17. Being able to disagree politely with others and still present other points of view on a problem or question.
18. Making charts to convey information effectively in the social studies.

2. Attitudinal Objectives

The quality of attitudes that pupils have certainly affects the number of understandings and skills that pupils will be developing. Negative attitudes hinder pupil achievement and a lack of optimum development will thus result. The following attitudes, among others, are important from pupils to achieve:

1. Working harmoniously with others in the environment.
2. Appreciating the problem solving approach in the social studies curriculum.
3. Appreciating the contributions of minority groups in developing the United States.
4. Valuing democracy as a form of government and as a way of life.
5. Appreciating creative ideas suggested by others in the solving of problems.
6. Valuing the inquiry approach and critical thinking in the social studies.
7. Wanting to develop important concepts and generalizations in the social studies.
8. Developing and/or maintaining a desire to read content for leisure time activities as it relates to ongoing units of study.
9. Wanting to utilize a variety of learning activities to solve problems.
10. Having a desire to identify and solve problems in society.
11. Feeling an obligation to participate effectively as a constructive member in society.

12. Respecting the thinking of others.
13. Appreciating, the cultural products of people of other lands, such as art, music, architecture, language, and religious beliefs.
14. Wanting to develop the ability to present information clearly and accurately to others.
15. Desiring to keep up with current events and current issues as they happen in the world.
16. Wanting to utilize the card catalog, index, and table of contents to locate information.
17. Wanting to develop necessary skills to identify new words when reading studies content.
18. Feeling the necessity of reading for a variety of purposes.
19. Wanting to attach meaning to social studies content through pantomiming, role playing, creative dramatics, the use of puppets, and other approaches.
20. Wanting to listen carefully to the thinking of others.

3. Understandings Objectives

Teachers, supervisors, and principals, cooperatively, should spend ample time in determining which objectives pupils are to achieve and realize. This is true not only of skills and attitudinal objectives but also of understandings objectives. Too frequently, no doubt, trivia has been taught pertaining to names, dates, and places in historical units in the social studies. These are vaguely remembered or forgotten by learners as time has moved on. Thus, it is important for understandings objectives to be carefully identified. The "explosion of knowledge" has made it doubly necessary to weed out that which is irrelevant and unimportant.

In many cases, understandings, objectives which pupils are to realize will pertain to specific social studies units. A first grade unit on "The School" will have different understandings that pupils need to achieve as compared to a unit on "Visiting to Zoo" for that some age level of pupils. There are, however, major generalizations which pupils may achieve that cut across different units of study.

The following understandings objectives, among others, could be important for pupils to realize in a unit on Great Britain:

1. Great Britain is a leading manufacturing country in the world.
2. Many agricultural products are imported from other nations of the world to Great Britain.
3. Great Britain has exhibited much influence in world affairs.
4. This nation is a permanent member of the Security Council in the United Nations.

Trends in the Social Studies

Each elementary school should devote ample time to the study of trends in the teaching of elementary school social studies. Too, often, social studies has consisted of pupils reading content from their textbook. Social studies should not be a reading course. Reading social studies content is one learning activity, among others. Reading content is an important learning activity, but it is not the only experience for pupils in the social studies curriculum. What can the elementary school do to keep up with recommendations for a modern programme of social studies?

Scope and Sequence

A modern programme of elementary school social studies places much emphasis upon good sequence among units of study. Too frequently, there has been little or no connection between and among units taught in sequence. One unit of study should be related to and lead harmoniously into the next unit of study. For example, if intermediate grade pupils are studying a unit on the age of discovery pertaining to the New World, a unit that would be related could be entitled "Colonization in the New World." An area of the world, of course, had to be discovered before it could be colonized. The two units would definitely be related to each other. Good sequence could then be a definite possibility between these two units in elementary school social studies. If first grade pupils are studying a unit on "Going to School" at the beginning of a school year, a unit on "Living in the Home" could come in proper sequence with good teaching. The school and its influence cannot be isolated from the home environment. The two environments interact; neither is an island unto itself.

For each grade level, cooperative efforts need to be put forth within an elementary school or several elementary schools to develop proper sequence in social studies units from kindergarten through grade twelve. Thus, the question arises as to which units should be taught first, second, third, fourth and so forth for each of the grade levels in the elementary school.

Good teachers of social studies also need to think of proper sequence of learning activities within a unit. Generally, one would say that learning activities should progress from the simple to those which are more complex. This would be a gradual process. When thinking of sequence in learning activities within a specific social studies unit, which of the following learning activities should come first, second, third, fourth, fifth and sixth pertaining to a unit entitled "Living on the Farm"?

1. Having the country agent present a set of slides and a talk relating to a modern farm.
2. Visiting a modern farm and discussing observations which were made.
3. Viewing and discussing a filmstrip entitled "Lets Visit the Farm."
4. Reading pages 110-115 from the textbook and discussing the contents.
5. Showing and discussing transparencies of farming using the overhead projector.
6. Developing a frieze within a committee of four members; the frieze would pertain to selected scenes on modern farming practices and procedures.

Each of these learning activities must be evaluated in terms of the following standards:

1. being meaningful to learners;
2. developing interest within learners for learning;
3. promoting purpose for learning;
4. providing for individual differences;
5. stimulating pupils in wanting to learn;
6. providing for proper sequence within the specific learning activity.

Using a Variety of Materials in Teaching

The social studies teacher must think of variety in terms of learning activities provided for pupils. Variety in learning activities should assist in providing for individual differences. Pupils differ much from each other in intelligence, past achievement in different curriculum areas of the elementary school, motivation for learning, interest in the unit being studied, and ability to benefit from a given learning activity. Thus learning activities must be varied since each pupil in a class will not benefit equally from an ongoing learning activity whether it be reading of social studies content or developing learning from audio-visual materials. Good readers may enjoy reading social studies materials and gain many important concepts, principles, and generalizations in this kind or type of learning activity. Reading may become the major way of gaining ideas in the social studies from pupils who do much reading and are fascinated with this kind of learning experience. Other pupils may find reading distasteful due to previous encounters in this activity which had negative effects. The negative effects may have been the result of the following influences:

1. the content was to difficult for learners to read;
2. poor methodology was used by the teacher when having pupils read social studies content;
3. adequate readiness was not provided for pupils prior to reading;
4. The teacher was too demanding in terms of purposes pupils were to achieve from reading;
5. too much reading was required of pupils in the social studies programme.

Each pupil has a different learning style just as teachers have different teaching pupils. The teacher needs to select those learning activities which will help each learner achieve to his or her optimum. The following, among others, could help to provide for individual differences among pupils and also vary the kinds of learning activities that are provided:

1. making model villages, famous buildings, and toys;
2. constructing boats, cars, airplanes, and trucks;

3. making relief maps and globes relating to the area being studied in a unit;
4. developing books, scrolls, puppets, marionettes, and musical instruments;
5. making costumes pertaining to people of other lands;
6. making butter and a model diary farm;
7. completing model circus scenes when studying the related unit;
8. making candles, dyeing cloth, and making an oxcart pertaining to units on "Colonization in the New World."
9. developing a pioneer kitchen and covered wagon when studying units on the westward movement;
10. developing dioramas, murals, models, friezes, cartoons, and illustrations pertaining to ongoing units of study;
11. making posters, booklets, and exhibits on important facets of the unit being studied;
12. reading from the textbook or textbooks, selected sections in the encyclopaedia, and library books;
13. viewing films, filmstrips, slides, pictures, and other audio visual media;
14. listening to tapes and records;
15. taking an excursion;
16. interviewing competent resource personnel.

Readiness for Learning

There are several ways in which to think of readiness on the part of pupils to benefit from specific or given units of study in the social studies.

First of all, educators generally believe that pupils can benefit from more complex units of study than was thought possible a decade and longer ago. For many years, it was believed that pupils, for example, should study units on the home and school on the first grade level since these were "close" to the pupil. Pupils experience the home and the school; thus, there is this closeness between the unit being studied and the personal experiences of pupils. On the second grade level, pupils would study units on the city, neighbourhood, or shopping centres as they exist in medium and large size cities. These units would branch out further from pupils' environment as compared to the home and school which were units of study for the first grade level. By the time pupils are in the fifth grade, they may be studying units on Canada, Mexico, and historical units pertaining to the United States. Thus, pupils on these grade levels would be studying units which would be located outside of the United States. Historical units on the United States would deal with the past which is removed in time from the everyday experiences that elementary school pupils have. On the sixth grade level, pupils could be studying units on The Common Market Countries, the Middle East, the Soviet Union, Australia, Japan, South East Asia, and Brazil. These areas would be further removed from the everyday experiences of pupils in the elementary school as compared to social studies units being studied on previous grade levels.

It may be rather arbitrary in some cases as to which grade level specific units in the social studies should be taught. The television set in the home has brought the faraway near to the child. In their homes and in school, pupils can view television programmes which deal with happenings in London, Paris, Moscow, Rio de Janeiro, Buenos Aires, Melbourne, Montreal, Siagon, and other areas of the world. Thus, elementary school pupils today have much more opportunity to view reality on television screens pertaining to faraway places as compared to learners a generation ago or longer. More accurate, colourful, interesting, illustrations in magazines pertaining to faraway places are available to learners than ever before. More pupils in the United States have had opportunities to travel in the United States and abroad to see scenes and sights than was true formerly. It is no wander that pupils in the elementary school may be able to benefit from more complex units of study in the social studies than ever before. Many excellent social studies units on Mexico have been taught on the second grade level. These teachers may be very knowledgeable about Mexico and have the necessary materials and teaching skills to develop interest in this unit. Thus, the social studies curriculum can be adapted to the pupil rather than adjusting the child to the curriculum. Each child should attach meaning to what is being learned as well as have developed interest in the ongoing unit of study.

Educators today generally think that readiness for learning can be hastened. This is not to say, however, that difficult learnings are shoved into the throats of children. However, with a rich background of experiences which interests the pre-schooler, for example, much background knowledge can be developed. If parents then take their children to supermarkets, hardware stores, clothing stores, toy, shops, zoos, circuses, and farms, much meaningful information will be developed. Parents should discuss observations made with their children in a polite, kind, and understanding manner. Pupils will generally raise many questions about experiences which they have had. Answers to these questions should be discussed in a meaningful approach. With quality pre-school experiences for pupils, this should hasten readiness for developing more difficult concepts and generalizations. As learners they enter the elementary school years, more difficult units of study in the social studies can be taught. The teacher must continually strive to provide quality learning activities in various units that are studied, thus helping the child to experience continuous success when building upon experiences from the preschool years. Parents also need to provide a rich learning environment as their children progress through the public school years. In situations such as these, readiness for learning in the social studies is hastened within pupils. Contrast that situation with the following where pupils experience an environment which does not build up background knowledge and where readiness for learning in the social studies would be hindered:

1. a lack of reading materials for pupils in the home;
2. the parent, parents, or guardian ignore the child;
3. food served in the home is low in meeting proper nutritional standards;
4. stability is lacking in the home in that members get along poorly with each other;
5. children are rarely, if ever, taken along to buy groceries and other necessities in life;
6. no visits are made to places of interest in the community;

7. money is very scarce in the home; financial security is completely lacking;
8. vocabulary development is not progressing properly due to a lack of opportunities to communicate with others;
9. nonstandard English is spoken in the home and surrounding environment;
10. an inadequate self-concept exists on the part of these children since success is experienced very rarely.

In situations such as these, it is no wonder that pupils lack background knowledge when entering the elementary school years. The social studies teacher would need to adjust the curriculum for these learners so that important cognitive, psychomotor, and affective domain objectives can be achieved. Learning activities would need to be provided which are at an easier level of understanding as compared to those pupils which come from favourable home environments.

Teaching Units in Depth

Many teachers of social studies have a tendency to teach units utilizing the survey approach. Thus, for example, many units would be taught on the sixth grade level as would be indicated by the following units titles which would need to be completed in a school year:

1. Visiting Japan
2. Living in Australia
3. The Common Market nations
4. Canada—our neighbour to the North
5. Mexico—our neighbour to the South
6. The Soviet Union
7. Mainland China
8. Living in India and Pakistan
9. Islands of the Pacific
10. Brazil—the largest country in South America
11. Spanish speaking countries of South America

12. Countries of Southeast Asia
13. The Antarctic and its future
14. Nations of Central Europe
15. The Middle East
16. Visiting Spain and Portugal.

It is quite obvious from the many unit titles listed that the survey approach to teaching social studies would be utilized. Pupils would get a smattering of content from many units of study rather than developing learnings in depth from a few carefully selected units. The faculty members of an elementary school should rather select six or seven units to be taught in a specific school year. Thus pupils would be able to study in depth each unit that is taught. For example in a unit pertaining to Brazil, the following understandings could be achieved by pupils:

1. the art, architecture, and music of Brazil;
2. the political system of that country;
3. the geography of Brazil such as rivers, plateaus, valleys, and plains;
4. the past which lead to present day happenings (history);
5. the culture of various groups and subgroups of people;
6. Different socio-economic levels and their effects upon group behaviour (sociology);
7. exports and imports of Brazil as well as goods and services produced in that country.

It is certain that pupils will understand various people of the world better if units are taught in depth. Limited understandings can be developed of any unit in social studies, if a teacher needs to hurry through the teaching of many units in a school year. Pupils need to have opportunities to study man by viewing him from the different disciplines that make up the social sciences, namely, history, geography, political science, sociology, anthropology, and economics. It is certain that pupils won't understand the pupil of Brazil, for example, by studying the system of government of that country only. Pupils also need to understand the values, customs, religious beliefs, norms of society and subcultures, vocations and occupations, products and services produced and sold, imports and exports, the history, and geography of Brazil.

The Structure of Knowledge

Educators such as teachers, principals, and supervisors, alone should not determine what is to be taught in social studies. The content of the social sciences is too complex to be selected by educators alone when developing the social studies curriculum. Too frequently, social studies teachers have taught what is unimportant, trivial, and irrelevant. Social scientists should have an important role in selecting social studies content for pupils in the elementary school. This is not to say that social scientists alone would determine content in units of study in the social studies. Certainly, teachers, principals, and supervisors will have a voice in the selection. Elementary school pupils also have an important task in selecting content for different units of study. The social studies teacher must develop pupil interest and purpose in various units of study. Thus, the teacher will have interesting, appealing bulletin boards for pupils to view. If pupils are to begin a unit on Japan, perhaps the following pictures can be placed on the bulletin board with an interesting title or caption:

1. Japanese workers on an assembly line in a modern factory;
2. a home scene which is accurate and representative pertaining to a Japanese family;
3. men in fishing boats which clearly illustrates important facets of this industry;
4. a representative urban scene in Tokyo or other large city in Japan;
5. farmers in a rural area taking care of their crops and livestock.

The teacher's goal is to get pupils in wanting to ask many questions about Japan when viewing the bulletin board display. The following questions may be asked by pupils:

1. How are cars assembled on an assembly line in Japan?
2. What are some leading products manufactured in Japan?
3. Who buys these products?

4. How do Japanese and American homes differ from each other? How are they alike?
5. How important is the fishing industry to Japan's economy?
6. How does Tokyo differ from New York City or Chicago? How are they alike?
7. What products are produced on Japanese farms and how are they sent to market?
8. How do farm products in Japan eventually get to the consumer?
9. How important are the following concepts to the Japanese economy?
   (a) imports;
   (b) exports.

If the social studies teacher is teaching this same unit on Japan, individually or cooperatively with pupils, interest centres can be developed. These items could be placed on a table in several tables in the classroom. As an example, the following objects pertaining to Japan could be placed on an interest centre:

1. toys representative of what Japanese children play with;
2. traditional dress of Japanese people;
3. models of Japanese made cars;
4. a relief map of Japan;
5. a model farm scene in rural Japan.

Pupils individually could ask questions of each other and of the teacher pertaining to these items on the interest centre. A good class discussion could follow the identification of these problem areas or questions. Pupils, as an example, may ask the following questions pertaining to the interest centre:

1. How are Japanese toys different from those that American children play with?
2. How have patterns of dress changed in Japan during the years?
3. How are Japanese cars assembled?

4. What is the land like in Japan and what kinds of crops are grown there?
5. How does farming in Japan differ from that in the United States?

Much research could be done by pupils using a variety of resources such as reference books, tapes, records, interviews, slides, filmstrips, maps, globes, and films to get needed information to answer these questions.

In the preceding examples, it is noticed that pupils should be ample opportunities to identify questions and problems for which information can be gathered. The interests of pupils are very important when thinking of learning activities which should be provided for learners in elementary school social studies. However, social scientists also have an important contribution to make in helping to determine key ideas or structural ideas which pupils should develop inductively pertaining to each social studies unit. These social scientists would specialize in their area of speciality from one of the following disciplines in the social sciences:

1. anthropology;
2. geography;
3. history;
4. sociology;
5. political science or civics
6. economics.

Balance in Unit Titles

An important question that an elementary school must answer pertaining to the social studies curriculum is which unit titles should be taught in the different grade levels so that balance exists among the different areas of the world that pupils study. To be sure, pupils could devote most of their time in the social studies studying about the contributions and development of the Western World. This is important for pupils. However, pupils also need to become thoroughly familiar, among other areas, with the Middle East, the Far East, India and Pakistan, and nations of Africa. In fact, many major important happenings are occurring in these areas. Thus, pupils need to have a thorough understanding of the

Western World, but the changes, development, and contributions of the non-western world need also to be adequately emphasized in a modern elementary school social studies programme.

Faculty members in an elementary school and the total school system involved in teaching the social studies should make a thorough study as to units taught presently in the different grade levels of the elementary school. Do revisions need to be made so that some kind of rational balance exists in different units that are taught in the social studies? Based upon diagnosis as to the units presently taught in the social studies in an elementary school, faculty members can make rational decisions pertaining to pupils obtaining a world view which is comprehensive in the social studies.

Stating Objectives Precisely

There is a trend in elementary school social studies in stating objectives precisely. This means that observers generally would agree as to what is to be taught by looking at a statement of objectives. Thus pupil achievement can be measured if objectives are stated behaviourally. Objectives which are written behaviourally state what the learner is to do as a result of teaching. Consider the following objectives:

1. The pupil will write a fifty word paper on the Amazon River.
2. Pupils will develop democratic behaviour.

In the first objective pupils will, as a result of teaching, develop understandings, concepts, and generalizations pertaining to the Amazon River. Ultimately, pupils will be able to write a fifty word paper on the Amazon River. In the second objective, much vagueness exists as to what will be taught. There are various interpretations as to what democratic behaviour is. The objective does not state how much of this behaviour pupils are to develop. Thus, it cannot be measured if learners are achieving the objective.

Teachers must be precise in writing their objectives so that it can be determined what will be taught. In educational literature today much emphasis is placed upon teacher accountability. The teacher is then held accountable for what pupils are to learn. Thus, clearly written objectives state what pupils are to learn. Principals and supervisors can then determine what will be taught to pupils. Also, it is easier to select learning activities which will guide learners in achieving objectives if each objective is clearly written. It is difficult to select appropriate learning activities if vague, ambiguous objectives are written. The final question arises as to how pupils are to be assessed if the objectives lack clarity. In situations like these it cannot be determined if objectives have been achieved.

A word of caution is necessary here. To be sure trivia and unimportant learnings can be stated precisely when writing specific objectives. The following objectives can be written precisely where no room exists in interpretation as to what will be taught:

1. The pupil will list in writing the capital city of each country in South America.
2. Pupils will recite orally five leading farm crops of each country of South America.
3. Pupils will list four leading manufactured products of each South American country.

In the above objectives pupils have used the lowest level of cognition only and that is recall of facts. To be sure, there are important facts for pupils to learn. These facts, however, must be selected very carefully since there is much content that needs to be learned in different disciplines of knowledge. The teacher needs to have pupils engage in critical thinking, creative thinking, and problem solving. To be sure pupils engage in recall of facts when engaging in critical and creative thinking as well as problem solving. However, pupils do something with the facts when engaging in higher levels of thinking. Comparing statements and evaluating them, coming up with unique, new, novel ideas, and the solving of problems is very important in a modern programme of elementary school social studies. A democratic society demands that pupils become proficient in higher levels of thinking so that individuals become more effective in decision-making.

Continuous Comprehensive Evaluation of Achievement

If teachers are to evaluate pupil achievement well, continuous evaluation needs to be in evidence. Pupils need to be evaluated comprehensively so that all facets of achievement are assessed.

A teacher who does not continuously evaluate pupil achievement will not know at what point or points pupils are not making continuous progress. One can think of pupil achievement as being represented by points on a line or line segment. For pupils to achieve continuously on this line, evaluation needs to be done continuously. Otherwise, the social studies teacher definitely cannot know if pupils are achieving well. If pupils have not developed a particular concept or generalization, they may not be successful in moving on to more complex learnings. Teachers of social studies must think of proper sequence for pupils in learning; otherwise continuous progress may not come about in learner achievement. Sequential learnings on the part of children can come about only when teachers assess learner progress continuously.

Too often, it has been thought and felt that paper-pencil tests alone can adequately assess pupil achievement. To be sure, in many situations, good evaluation can come about with the use of true-false, multiple-choice, completion, matching, and essay test items. This would be true, especially, of understandings or cognitive domain objectives. To evaluate skills objectives and attitudinal objectives, other forms of assessment need to be utilized. If a pupil is to develop skill in gathering information from using a set or several sets of reputable encyclopaedias, hardly would a paper-pencil test alone evaluate pupil achievement effectively in this area. It would be good to actually observe pupils to determine if they can do the following when looking up information from encyclopaedias:

1. the pupil can identify the correct topic heading for the information he is to gather. For example, if the pupil is to gather information on opium in a unit on the harmful use of drugs, which heading would he look under in the appropriate reference book;
2. the pupil knows the letters of the alphabet and can find the appropriate place in the encyclopaedia from which information is to be gathered;
3. the learner can comprehend the contents well when gathering information;
4. the child can take notes over what he reads and develop an outline in proper sequence when utilizing the notes;

5. the pupil can write a summary of the ideas read from the encyclopaedia using topic sentences, proper sequence in paragraphs, unity within paragraphs, and the necessary skills in the mechanics of writing (capitalization, punctuation, spelling, handwriting, and sentence structure);
6. the learner can present ideas, gained from research, effectively to the class. Listeners then have an inward desire in wanting to get major concepts and generalizations presented by the speaker;
7. the presenter utilizes appropriate audio-visual materials, such as pictures, slides, drawings, and the overhead projector, when presenting his findings to the class.

When utilizing these guidelines to evaluate pupil achievement, the present level of achievement of each child must be assessed and then assist each learner to progress continuously to realize optimum achievement. The following is of utmost importance to remember: no two pupils will be at the same place in achievement when realizing these guidelines or standards. Each pupil is at a different level of achievement.

It is important also to think of comprehensive evaluation in the social studies. Too frequently, pupil achievement has been evaluated pertaining to understanding objectives only. Tc be sure, these are very important objectives to achieve. Secondly in frequency of evaluation in terms of objectives, assessing skills which pupils have developed has been given some consideration. The category of attitudinal objectives, no doubt, is least often evaluated.

It is indeed very difficult to write a paper-pencil test to evaluate pupil attitudes. There are standardized tests which evaluate pupils in the area of attitudes or the affective domain. The social studies teacher must always observe pupils to notice changes in feelings, values and beliefs. Is there a positive change in this area from day to day, or for longer periods of time? Generally, longer periods of time are needed to see growth in the affective domain. It may, of course, take years to change some attitudes. The teacher needs to evaluate himself in terms of the following criteria when thinking of assisting pupils in attitude development:

1. Are pupils interested in learning activities provided for them? If not, what kinds of activities should be selected so that positive attitudes may develop toward learning?
2. Do pupils understand what is taught? If learnings are not meaningful for pupils, much turning off will occur by pupils in realizing objectives.
3. Does the teacher assist each learner to be successful in the school situation? It is no wonder that pupils develop negative attitudes if they feel unsuccessful.
4. Are pupils being guided in social development so that they like working with others in committees, the class as a whole, and others in the larger environment?
5. Is the pupil developing and/or maintaining feelings of an adequate self concept? If learners feel inadequate to the tasks at hand, they will generally lack in total school achievement.
6. Does the teacher respect all pupils regardless of socio-economic levels, colour of skin, religious beliefs, and status within the class setting?
7. Are pupils assisted in developing respect for each other? Too frequently, pupils call each other mean names which cause feelings of resentment and reprisal.
8. Are pupils realizing desired understandings and skills through carefully selected units which assist in developing positive attitudes? No doubt, some units in the social studies would be eliminated and others would be added when answering this question. More social studies units need to be taught which will guide learners in personal and social development.

Thus, it is necessary to evaluate pupil achievement in all facets of development using a variety of evaluation technique. One very important evaluation technique to utilize is teacher observation. Teacher observation needs to become objective in evaluating pupil achievement. Through reading, study, thought, empathy, and understanding, teachers can guide pupils in personal and social adjustment as well as other facets of development.

Being A Democratic Human Being

In a society which emphasizes democracy as a form of government, it is important for schools to stress a philosophy of education which is in harmony with ideals of democratic living. American society and its schools should emphasize a consistent philosophy which would pertain to democracy as a form of government and also as a way of life. Teachers of social studies have gone to extremes when providing a psychological environment which was to assist pupils in developing to their optimum. Unfortunately these extremes did not harmonize with basic ideas of democratic living, nor did they help learners achieve to their highest possible capabilities. Consider the teacher on one end of the continuum who expects a pin-drop quiet classroom. Pupils are asked to speak only when the teacher asks the questions. The question asked at a given time may be directed to one pupil only. The answer required is factual and a "right" answer is wanted. Critical thinking, creative thinking, and problem solving would not be stressed. Each pupil would constantly face the front with little or no interaction with other pupils. Pupils would be reprimanded in front of others for "infracture" of strict rules and regulations. The teacher may strictly play the role of a policeman and disciplinarian in the classroom.

Contrast the autocratic teacher described above with one who is anarchic. The anarchic teacher would represent the other extreme on the continuum. This teacher would permit pupils generally to do as they wish with few, or perhaps, no restraints. The anarchic teacher would be the leader in the class situation if requested by pupils. Pupils could roam around the room freely with little or no purpose involved in these movements. Pupils would visit with each other whenever and wherever they wished with little or no respect for others.

Democracy as a way of living in the class situation would stress that there is mutual respect between and among pupils and faculty members.

Using Maps and Globes in the Social Studies

Ample opportunities should be given to pupils in the use of maps and globes. With a "shrinking world" due to better transportation and communication, it is more important than ever before for pupils to develop necessary skills to use maps and globes effectively. It is difficult to say in which country of the world a crisis will develop that would affect the interests of leading countries in the world such as the United States and the Soviet Union. India and Pakistan, Berlin, and the Cuban missile crises, and the Middle East have been critical areas in the world which could have involved major world powers in a confrontation. It is important for pupils to have ample knowledge pertaining to place geography whereby important areas of the world can be located on maps and globes. It is also important for pupils to develop more complex understandings such as how climate affects the kinds of crops grown in a given area, or how latitude affects the kind of temperature reading a given area of the world will have.

The following represent some major understandings that pupils should develop pertaining to the use of maps and globes.

1. Pupils should realize that distances can be computed by using the scale given on the map or globe. Maps and globes vary as to the number of miles that would be represented by one inch as given in the scale of miles.
2. Specific places on the earth can be located using the concepts of "latitude" and "longitude."
3. North latitude refers to distance in degrees north of the equator while south latitude refers to distance in degrees south of the equator.
4. East longitude has reference to distance in degrees east of the prime meridian while west longitude relates to distance in degrees west of the prime meridian.
5. Distances north and south of the equator are measured along a meridian while distances east or west of the prime meridian are measured along a parallel.
6. The earth rotates from a west to east direction once each 24 hours (causes for day and night can be shown by using a flashlight, a darkened room, and a globe which represents a model of the planet earth). The imaginary line on which the earth rotates is called its axis.
7. The earth revolves around the sun approximately once in 365¼ days. On March 21 and September 21,

approximately, the sun is directly overhead at noon on the equator. Whereas on June 21, approximately, the sun is directly overhead at noon on the Tropic of Cancer located 23½ degrees north of the equator; on December 21, the sun is overhead at noon on the Tropic of Capricorn located 23½ degrees south of the Equator. Other factors involved in determining temperature readings include elevation of land being considered, ocean currents, and nearness to bodies of water.

8. The axis of the earth on a globe points toward the north star. (On a bright day at noon each pupil can look directly at his shadow; he is facing north at this time. Pupils while facing north can be shown the position of the North Star as it would be at night).

9. Maps do not represent as accurately the surface of the earth as compared to globes. With the use of maps, however, a certain continent, country, or area can be studied more conveniently than on a globe since it will be represented on a larger area.

10. Some of the symbols used in legends on maps and globes are standard symbols. For example, symbols on maps which represent hospitals, railroad tracks, and paved roads are standard symbols. There are also symbols which vary from legend to legend on different maps and globes that are used.

11. Any circle has 360 degrees. There are 24 time zones in the world thus making each time zone have an approximate value of 15 degrees of longitude.

12. A hemisphere is represented by half of the earth; four hemispheres can be referred to—southern, northern, western and eastern.

13. The direction of north on a map pertains to going directly to the North Pole; whereas the direction of south means to go directly to the South Pole. There are different projections of maps so the direction of north may not always "up" on the map.

14. Low, middle, and high latitudes refer to specific areas or parts of maps and globes, such as the low latitudes lying

north and south of the equator while the high latitudes are located around the north and south poles. The middle latitudes refer to those parts lying between the low latitudes and the high latitudes.

Current Affairs in the Social Studies

To keep the social studies curriculum updated, each elementary school should have good current affairs programmes in all grades. Units which deal with history, geography, economics, sociology, anthropology, and political science may become outdated unless recent happenings, events, and issues are brought in to the social studies programmes. If the teacher is teaching a unit on "The United States Today," certainly the unit can become somewhat obsolete unless current affairs are brought into the ongoing unit of study. Too frequently, social studies teachers in teaching historical units have delved too thoroughly, no doubt, in units that deal with early American history such as "The Age of Exploration," "Colonization in the New World," The Beginning of the United States," and others. Units which deal with the present one then slighted or, perhaps, even omitted. The present is very important to elementary school children since this is the world they live in now and understand better than any other period of time in American history. The pupil needs to understand present trends, issues, problems, and strengths in the United States if he is to become a participating member in society working toward identifying problems and solving them. Certainly, a democratic citizen is one who greatly appreciates the positive in American society and yet works for an even stronger democracy as a form of government as well as a way of life.

Boundaries of countries change. Only with keeping up with the news can one be knowledgeable of new nations which arise and those which no longer exist. Witness the great number of new countries that have arisen on the continent of Africa after World War II! It is difficult for any individual to become thoroughly familiar with each country in Africa. Well educated people have discovered to their amazement that they didn't know the names of certain countries on that continent that came up on news broadcasts. The surface of the earth has also changed in terms of geographical features. Earthquakes, volcanoes, folds, and faults have altered the surface of the earth. Current affairs can help pupils keep up-to-date in terms of happenings in the field of geography. Certainly, space feats and explorations have done much to change our knowledge of the moon and Mars, in particular.

There are many important current issues and events in the field of economics. The rate of employment and unemployment vary in per cent from time to time within most countries. Many countries have problems in balancing imports with exports. This situation can change from time to time. Thus, much emphasis can be placed upon economics in a modern programme of current affairs instruction. The total amount of money involved in the gross national product (GNP) of any country can vary from year to year. Current affairs item could also assist learners to understand the meaning of inflation as it pertains to buying goods and services in any country.

In the area of sociology, many current affair items need to be studied to keep this area of the social sciences updated. Overpopulation, of course, has not always been a problem on the face of the earth. Today, it is a major problem in many countries of the world. Norms of a subculture change are modified due to reevaluating of beliefs, values, and ideals. Norms also change as a result of borrowing ideas from other subcultures and societies. New inventions also help to bring on changes within any group of people.

In the area of anthropology, current events and issues can and do become a part of news broadcasts. A subculture is discovered for the first time and this group is in the stone age. New excavations release findings pertaining to a particular tribe of Indians or civilizations of long ago. Recommendations for improving schools, homes, and other institutions in society are made by leading anthropologists in the United States.

Political science and current affairs instruction have much in common. The Security Council, General Assembly, and the Office of the Secretariat of the United Nations continually make news headlines in terms of decisions and recommendations made which affect various nations of the world. The United Nations, of course, is an attempt made at some kind of world government. It is rather common for listeners to news broadcasts on radio and television to hear of political leaders of different nations having left their positions for various reasons and a new government has stepped in. This presents opportunities for pupils to learn more about the forms of government of different nations of the world. When pupils study such units as "Living in Great Britain" or "Visiting Canada," they may be developing learnings in depth pertaining to Parliament, the Prime Minister, and other facets of government of these two countries. When listening to news broadcasts, one hears of decisions made by Parliament of either Great Britain or Canada. Thus, items pertaining to political science can well become an important part of the current affairs programme in the modern elementary school.

Using the Bulletin Board in Current Affairs

The social studies teacher needs to think of ways to stimulate pupil interest in current affairs instruction. To be sure, some pupils have little or no interest in this area. Thus, the teacher must provide interesting learning activities which will capture the interests of pupils. One way to do this would be to develop a bulletin board display pertaining to pictures of current happenings. An appealing caption should be a part of the display. The caption orientates the reader to the contents on the bulletin board. As an example, pictures pertaining to the following happenings can be neatly placed on the bulletin board:

1. conflict in the Middle East;
2. the President of the United States presenting the state of the union message;
3. the Security Council in session at the United Nations headquarters in New York;
4. the energy crisis.

Pupils with teacher guidance may ask the following questions pertaining to these pictures:

1. What will eventually happen in the Middle East between competing and opposing sides?
2. What recommendations did the President make in his annual state of the union message?
3. How are decisions made in the Security Council?
4. How can the energy crisis be solved?

Answers to the above problems should be discussed in an informal atmosphere. Respect for the thinking of others is of utmost importance. All pupils should participate in the discussion if possible. Pupils who dominate the discussion or participate excessively should be guided in sensing the importance of all pupils participating in the ongoing learning activity. The self-concept of each pupil is very important. Each pupil should be praised even if there is a very, very slight degree of improvement in performance. This helps pupils in developing self-confidence and in wishing to participate in current affairs programmes. By getting pupils interested in the ongoing current affairs programme in the elementary school, learners will transfer these learnings to situations involving listening to news broadcasts on radio and television in the home.

In Summary

Teachers, principals, and supervisors must study the following in working toward a modern social studies curriculum:

1. objectives in the social studies;
2. trends in teaching social studies;
3. scope and sequence;
4. materials used in teaching;
5. readiness for learning;
6. number of units taught in a year;
7. emphasis to be placed on the structure of knowledge;
8. balance in unit titles;
9. the use of specific objectives;
10. thorough evaluation of pupil achievement;
11. democratic living in the classroom;
12. the use of maps and globes in social studies units;
13. current affairs in social studies units;
14. developing pupil interest in current affairs.

REFERENCES

Clements, H. Millard, and others. *Social Study: Inquiry in Elementary Classrooms*. New York: Bobbs-Merrill Company, Inc., 1966.

Douglass, Malcolm P. *Social Studies from Theory to Practice in Elementary Education*. New York: J.B. Lippincott Company, 1967.

Herman, Wayne L. *Current Research in Elementary School Social Studies*. New York: The Macmillan Company, 1969.

Hoffman, Alan, J., and Thomas F. Ryan. *Social Studies and the Child's Expanding Self*. New York: Intext Educational Publishers, 1973.

Jarolimek, John. *Social Studies in Elementary Education,* Fourth Edition. New York: The Macmillan Company, 1971.

Michaelis, John U. *Social Studies for Children in a Democrary*. Fifth Edition. Englewood Cliffs: Prentice-Hall, Inc., 1972.

Nerbovig, Marcella H., and Herbert J. Klausmeier. *Teaching in the Elementary School*. Third Edition. New York: Harper and Row, 1969. Chapter Twelve.

Ploghoft, Milton E., and Albert H. Shuster. *Social Science Education in the Elementary School*. Columbus: Charles E. Merrill Publishing Company, 1971.

Preston, Ralph C., and Wayne L. Herman, Jr. *Teaching Social Studies in the Elementary School*. Fourth Edition. New York: Holt, Rinehart and Winston, Inc., 1974.

Shaftel, Fannie R., and George Shaftel. *Role-Playing for Social Values: Decision-Making in the Social Studies*. Englewood Cliffs: Prentice-Hall, Inc., 1967.

16

Evaluation of Pupil Achievement

There are many ways to assess learner achievement in the different curriculum areas of the elementary school. Not all approaches to evaluating pupil achievement evaluate in the same facets of development. For example, using sociometric devices evaluates learners in social development. It does not assess pupils in general intellectual development. A standardized achievement test evaluates pupils in growth pertaining to different curriculum areas in the elementary school. It would not evaluate personal and social development of pupils. Thus, a variety of evaluation devices must be used to assess learners intellectually, socially, emotionally, and physically.

Using Work Samples of Pupils

A very effective way of assessing pupil achievement is through the saving of work samples of pupils. These samples can be placed in a folder for each child. The work products should be dated so that comparisons may be made between and among earlier work of pupils compared to later work. Thus, the teacher, parents, and the child can notice improvement over previous attempts in school work. If a fifth grade pupil, for example, has developed a written report on "Manufacturing in Great Britain" when a unit on that country is being studied, the final product can be placed in the child's folder with the date on it. Reports that are written later can also be dated. Thus, comparisons can be made of earlier attempts at writing with later attempts. Too frequently, the teacher has felt that pupils are not achieving satisfactorily until he sees objective evidence by examining work products.

If pupils are giving oral reports to the class the reports can be tape-recorded. A date can be placed on the tape which is then ultimately stored. Later tapes on pupil reports can also be dated. The teacher, parents, and the child could listen to these tapes and notice if pupils are achieving. The reports would, of course, be evaluated in terms of acceptable criteria. The objectives to be achieved by pupils in the oral reports should harmonize with the present achievement level of each child. Certainly, it is unwise teaching to expect that which pupils cannot achieve.

It would be good if more pupil products could be stored satisfactorily than what is possible. For example, if pupils are studying a unit on "Toys Around the World," they should have ample opportunities to make accurate toys of selected nations around the world. The final products could be dated and stored. Comparisons can then be made of other constructed objects and items that pupils have completed. However, many elementary schools are overcrowded and lack the necessary space to store selected objects and items of what pupils have constructed.

Thus, work samples of pupils should be collected, dated, and stored after it has served its purpose in the teaching-learning situation. Cooperatively, those involved in evaluating pupil achievement can notice if progress is being made by learners when comparing present efforts with those of the past. Too frequently, the teacher is very close to the child on a day-to-day basis and is not aware of the small gains learners are making in the different curriculum areas of the elementary school. By making comparisons of each pupil's achievement, earlier efforts with later efforts, it can be noticed of a child is making progress.

Using the Checklist

Many teachers have successfully used checklist in evaluating pupil achievement. The teacher must determine which behaviours to write on the checklist. The teacher can, of course, forget what learners have achieved unless records are kept. Thus, different approaches to evaluation should be used; recording the result of the evaluation becomes important to notice patterns of learner achievement and behaviour when comparisons are made from one evaluation to the next.

In the checklist the teacher needs to carefully evaluate if learners are realizing the desired goals which are stated in writing.

Objective observation by the teacher is necessary to evaluate pupil achievement in terms of the standards written on the checklist.

The following standards could be written on a checklist, for example, and the teacher could check the area or areas pupils are weak in:

Name of Pupil .... Date ....

1. The pupil presents ideas clearly when giving an oral report.
2. More information needs to be obtained to substantiate ideas presented in the oral report.
3. More guidance is needed in organising ideas for the report.
4. Audio-visual aids should be used to capture listener interest in the report.
5. The pupil has distracting mannerisms when presenting the oral report.

The above criteria could be written so that little or no interpretation exists as to the meaning of these guidelines. It is important for the teacher to emphasize only those objectives which pupils can achieve.

The teacher can make comparisons of checklist results from an earlier observation to later observations. Feelings of teachers, of course, change when using the checklist at different intervals to assess pupil achievement. Being aware of the fact that feelings change when evaluating pupils at different intervals will assist the teacher in realizing that the checklist has its weaknesses as an evaluation instrument. This device should be used along with others to evaluate learner progress.

Rating Scales

An evaluation device that is closely rated to the checklist approach is the rating scale. The teacher should carefully select those behaviours pupils will be rated on. A five-point scale can be used in the evaluation such as giving a pupil a five, four, three, two, or one rating on each behaviour being evaluated. The categories of "Very good," "Good," "Average," Below average," and "Poor" can also be utilized. Each child should be evaluated in terms of what he can reasonably achieve. A learner should not be compared with others since unfair comparison may be made when one child is compared with another child. Pupils, of course, differ from each other in capacity and achievement. It is only normal that some children achieve at a more rapid rate as compared to other learners.

The following is given as an example in terms of listing behaviours and indicating ratings that can be given to pupils:

	Very good	*Good*	*Average*	*Below average*	*Poor*
The child gets along well with others on a committee.					
The child does his share of the work.					
The child uses references sources well.					
Information is evaluated carefully.					

The above categories pertain to having children work on committees. Behaviours can be listed which would relate to many facets of pupil achievement such as in giving oral reports, participating in teacher-pupil planning, and doing a research project.

The teacher needs to be aware that his perception of a child's behaviour will not always be the same when using the rating scale. Feelings of a given teacher change from time to time, as the rating scale is used as an evaluation device to assess learner achievement.

Sociometric Device

The sociometric device may be used in evaluating pupil achievement in the area of social development. This procedure in evaluating pupil achievement does not, of course, assess learners in intellectual and physical development. The teacher should use the sociometric device at justifiable intervals during a given school year. The reason for utilizing this procedure at various intervals during a given school year is that pupils' attitudes toward each other change. For example, two pupils may be very close friends until a disagreement occurs which can result in changes of preferences as far as friendships are concerned. Friendships can also be quite lasting in duration.

The teacher can ask the following questions of pupils:

1. If you had a chance to select three pupils to work on a committee with you in preparing a report pertaining to the unit now being studied in social studies, who would be your first choice, second choice, and third choice?
2. If you could pick three children in learning to play a new game, who would be your first choice, second choice, and third choice?

Pupils would write their responses to the above questions on paper. They would need to have complete assurance that the completed information would be held confidential by the teacher. The teacher can use the acquire information in developing committees for pupils to be involved in. The teacher must realize that pupils' feelings toward others change. Careful attention should be given to identify those pupils who have no friends, or are on the fringe area of having friends. These pupils must be given assistance in becoming accepted better by other children in a class. Perhaps, the child who is an isolate or on the fringe area of being an isolate can best function on a committee where other members are highly accepting.

Conferences to Evaluate Pupil Achievement

It is of utmost importance for teachers to get to know their pupils well. This information must be used to improve the teacher-learning situation. The teacher should take time to have conferences with each pupil in the class. It is important to set aside, perhaps, five minutes of time during each school day to have a conference with a child. No doubt, in most cases then, each pupil in a class could have a conference with the teacher before a month and a half of school has elapsed.

The teacher should prepare well for the conference in terms of possible questions to discuss with the child. This does not mean that the teacher will dominate the conference. Rather, the teacher should be a good listener to each pupil's questions, comments, and responses. The teacher, however, must be well prepared in terms of providing leadership and direction when conducting conferences with pupils.

The teacher should record observations made during the conference. This should be done after the conference has been completed. Comparisons can be made for each pupil then of observations made of earlier conferences with those conducted later.

An atmosphere of freedom to express ideas on the part of each pupil should be inherent when conferences are conducted. The teacher will not get valuable data from a child to be used in teaching if a rigid, formal atmosphere exists during the time a conference is conducted. If a pupil feels he must exhibit behaviour which the teacher desires from him during the conference, the time spent in using conferences as an evaluation technique is largely wasted.

Thus, the teacher must strive to have good rapport with each child so that conferences held with pupils can be successful. Good teachers are interested in each child's welfare and achievement. A teacher definitely should not threaten a child for exhibiting negative behaviour during the time a conference is held. If this is done, a child will not reveal his thoughts, feelings, and beliefs to the teacher.

Parent-teacher conferences can also be an excellent way to evaluate pupil achievement. Parents generally hold their children in high esteem and want the best of them. They definitely should be involved in planning for the welfare of their children. Pupils learn much from their parents during the pre-school and public school years. Learners spend much time with their parents and the restaurant effects are important. There are certain guidelines that teachers should follow in conducting parent-teacher conferences:

1. The teacher should listen very carefully to comments made by parents when conferences are conducted. Parents have goals which they have want their children to achieve. These goals could be realistic or unrealistic. Parents also reveal feelings that they have toward their children.
2. It is good to have samples of pupil's work to show to parents. Parents can then ask questions over their child's

achievement when viewing these products as well as over general achievement in the elementary school on the part of the learner. The classroom teacher then needs to be well prepared prior to conducting a parent-teacher conference.

3. The teacher definitely should not criticize remarks made by parents during a conference. It remarks by parents are criticized, hostile feelings may result during the time the conference is conducted. Or, parents may not reveal their feelings during a conference.
4. It is very important that parents and the teacher make decisions cooperatively which will help each child to achieve to his highest potential.
5. Decisions made cooperatively pertaining to the welfare of a child should not be used as a club or lever. For example, the teacher and/or parents can place pressures on pupils which definitely have detrimental affects.

Diary Entries

Individual pupils or a committee of learners can record on a daily basis major generalizations that were developed from various units of study. If pupils, for example, are studying a unit on astronomy, records can be kept on a daily basis in terms of main conclusions that have been achieved. The teacher can evaluate if pupils are gaining important, relevant understandings. All pupils in a class should have ample opportunities to be actively involved in writing the diary entries on a daily basis. Illustrations can also be drawn which would relate directly to these written entries. Pictures could also be collected by learners which would help pupils to understand the contents of the diary entries in a more meaningful way.

Anecdotal Records

Teachers need to gather much information pertaining to each child's growth and development. The quality of teaching should improve if knowledge about the growth and development of each child is used in teaching. Observations that are made by the teacher should be recorded periodically; otherwise these observations can be forgotten or become hazy in the mind of the teacher.

Before writing anecdotal records the teacher should make careful observations of pupil behaviour. The teacher then should record exactly what was observed. A representative random sample of each pupil's behaviour should be recorded at intervals. Thus, the teacher can ultimately observe a pattern of behaviour on the part of each pupil after having studied and analyzed these anecdotal records.

A word of caution needs to be given pertaining to the writing and using of anecdotal records. The teacher should record exactly what was observed and not used loaded words. Words such as "troublemaker," "delinquent," "lazy," "indifferent," and "dumb bell" do not describe pupil behaviour accurately. Infrequent records of observation do not give an overview of a child's behaviour. Pupils behave differently under the guidance of different teachers. For example, teacher A may have considerable difficulty in working with a specific child. Next year, teacher B finds this same pupil to be a delightful person.

Teacher-made Tests

It is important for teachers to evaluate pupil achievement in terms of objectives. These objectives can be developed cooperatively between the teacher and pupils. The teacher may write test items on the developmental level of pupils to determine if the objectives have been achieved.

Teacher-made tests should assist in determining what learners have and have not learned. That which was not learned provides the teacher with ample opportunities to provide additional learning activities for pupils which will assist in getting needed understandings, attitudes, and skills not obtained originally. Thus, the teacher is diagnosing pupils' strengths and weaknesses when using teacher-made tests.

Writing Essay Items

The teacher can write essay items in evaluating learner achievement in the elementary school. Essay items should only be utilized in evaluating learner achievement if it assists in determining if pupils have achieved objectives. The items written should be on the understanding level of pupils; learners must have an adequately developed writing vocabulary in order to respond in a proficient manner to essay items.

The teacher must write essay items which cover content taught during a unit or part of a unit. Thus, it is of utmost importance that essay items are valid. Criticism has been made of the subjectivity factor involved in grading responses pupils made to questions on an essay test. Subjectivity can be greatly minimized if the items are delimited so that more precision is required when learners make responses. The following essay item pertaining to a unit on Great Britain would be too vague and needs to be delimited: Discuss life in Great Britain. Pupils would not know what facet of life in Great Britain to discuss in writing. Instead, the teacher could be more specific in terms of desired learners' responses by writing the following essay item: List in writing four leading farm crops grown in Great Britain and tell how each is produced. Essay tests should be long enough so that pupils can exhibit a random sample of what has been achieved during a specific interval of instruction. They should not be excessively lengthy whereby pupils become tired and lose interest in the ongoing learning activity involving evaluation. Subjectivity in grading essay items can be greatly minimized by writing out answers to questions by the teacher at the time the test items are written. Credit must be given, of course, to pupils' responses if they are correct and yet do not conform to the teacher's key for grading the essay items. The teacher should evaluate all learners' responses to essay item one before evaluating essay item number two and so on.

One major advantage in giving essay tests is that the teacher can notice not only the understandings that pupils have gained but also the students' ability to organise information with proper sequence. The teacher can also evaluate pupil achievement in the mechanics of writing such as spelling, handwriting, usage, and punctuation. The mechanics of writing, however, should be evaluated separately from understanding that pupils have gained.

Writing True-False Items

The teacher can write true-false items to evaluate pupil achievement. The true-false test should be long enough to measure what pupils have achieved. It, however, should not be too lengthy whereby fatigue sets in on the part of the child. True-false items should be clearly written so that they are on the understanding level of the child who is taking the test. Vague items should be omitted from a true-false test. Items that lack clarity on a true-false test do not measure learner achievement. Guessing generally results if test items are not written clearly.

When writing true-false items, the teacher should not use statements that come directly from a textbook. Thus, rote learning would not be emphasized when assessing learner achievement.

Specific determines should not be used when writing true-false items. Thus, words such as "all," "never," "none," and other similar words would indicate the statement is false. Words which are confusing it learners should also not be utilized when writing true-false items. The teacher should want to determine what pupils have or have not learned rather than confusing learners.

Generally, there should be an equal number of test items which are true as compared to those which are false. This is important in terms of results not being biased if a pupil would answer "true" to all items and the teacher having written most true-false statements which actually are true. Answers to true-false items should not follow a pattern such as every other item being "false" or every other item being "true."

When writing true-false items, the teacher must be aware of factual statements versus opinions. In other words, if statements on a true-false test deal with opinions held by the teacher or other persons, the items should mention whose opinions are being considered. Pupils may become confused when responding to true-false items if they are to respond to opinions as if these are statements which can be verified by using reliable reference sources.

Multiple Choice Items

The teacher may wish to write multiple-choice items in noticing if learners are achieving objectives. Generally, three or four alternatives are written as possible responses from which to select. Sometimes, responses to a multiple choice item are ridiculous to the point where the learner senses that only one response can be right; this can be determined without having learned anything about the unit being considered in the evaluation. Each alternative should be plausible. Thus, each response must be considered by the learner in determining which would be correct. If two responses are reasonable only, the test item becomes more like a true-false item rather than a multiple choice item.

Clues should not be given in the stem of the multiple choice item as to which is the correct response. The following multiple-choice item would indicate to the pupil which would be the correct response without the learner needing any knowledge basically in selecting the correct answer:

Hawaii is an

(a) bay;

(b) peninsula;

(c) cape;

(d) island.

The only correct response would be the following: Hawaii is an island.

Responses in a multiple choice item should be somewhat equivalent in length so that no clues are given as to the correct answer. Consider the following multiple choice item:

The Middle East

(a) consists largely of countries made up of Israel and the Arab World;

(b) is an island;

(c) is a part of the United States;

(d) is unimportant in world happenings.

In the above test item, response "a" is considerably longer than the other responses. This may give a clue to the student as to which is the correct response.

Too frequently, multiple choice items have evaluated learner achievement in factual knowledge or recall of information. The student should also be evaluated in the areas of problem solving, creative thinking and critical thinking when responding to multiple choice items.

Matching Items

Matching items can be used to evaluate pupil achievement in terms of stated objectives. One column should have more items than the second column in a matching test as is true of the following example:

A.	Gerald Ford	...	famous General of World War II
B.	Lyndon Johnson		
C.	John F. Kennedy	...	President during World War II
D.	Dwight Eisenhower		
E.	Franklin D. Roosevelt	...	former senator from Massachusetts
		...	most recent President of the United States

The student cannot guess the remaining matchings through the process of elimination when more items exist in one column as compared to the second column. For example, if a pupil has matched correctly all items except one, he can determine the final matching merely through the process of elimination if columns one and two have the same number of items. If the above listed matching test on "Presidents of the United States," pupils can write in the correct letter from the response alternatives of the first column to the blank space in front of the items of the second column.

In writing matching items, the teacher needs to think of homogeneity in terms of content. For example, the following matching test items would pertain to homogeneous content:

Colonies in the New World

A.	Massachusetts Bay	...	begun by the Pilgrims
B.	Plymouth Rock	...	headed by John Smith
C.	Jamestown	...	started by Puritans
D.	Georgia	...	led by Thomas Hooker
E.	Connecticut		

The matching items above come under the category of "Colonies in the New World." Thus, the items are homogeneous in terms of content. If an item has been put in dealing with a recent president of the United States, a generalization could be realized pertaining to unrelated content being a part of the matching test.

Teachers need to be aware of having an excessively large number of items in a matching test. This makes it difficult for learners to wade through two columns of information when attempting to match items in one column with items in the second column. The number of items put in a matching test would depend upon a child's present level of achievement. The test items should also be on the reading level of learners. The teacher in a matching test is attempting to determine what pupils have learned rather than evaluating the reading levels of individual pupils.

Pupils experience much difficulty in taking a matching test if both columns contain lengthy phrases or sentences. One of the two columns as a minimum must contain short phrases or words.

It is important that the teacher refrain from writing matching test items where the correct answer is obvious. In the following example, one item is quite obvious in terms of correctness of response:

A.	President of the United States during World War I	... ...	1917 Woodrow Wilson
B.	Year of entry of the United States into World War I	... ...	Great Britain John J. Pershing
C.	Famous American General during World War I		
D.	Was an ally of the United States during World War I		

In the above example, it is quite obvious that "Year of entry of the United States into World War I" matches with "1917." There is no other rational matching that would be correct.

Completion Items

Pupil achievement in terms of objectives can be evaluated with the use of completion items. Selected standards must be adhered to when writing completion test items.

The teacher should write items, which are meaningful to learners. Completion items have been written which contain too many blank spaces; thus, pupils do not understand what is wanted in terms of responses. Consider the following example.

......and......is the......of......

There, of course, are too many blank spaces for the learner to attach meaning in what is wanted in terms of responses. The teacher must want to evaluate learner progress rather than the pupil's ability to guess at vague test items.

The teacher should develop a key as to the correct response(s) for each item as the completion test is being developed. As the response, of each pupil are being checked, the key can be utilized. The evaluator also must be aware of additional correct answers that pupils may write other than those listed in the key.

Answers to completion items can be written on the right hand side of the page, where appropriate blank spaces are provided. This saves time in scoring completion items.

Completion items should assess pupils on important concepts and generalizations which have been achieved. The mechanics of writing, such as spelling, should be evaluated separately from the information which is supplied by the pupil in completion items. Generally, textbook wording should not be utilized by the teacher when writing completion items. Pupils should reveal understandings developed rather than recall of factual information.

Using Standardized Tests

The teacher can also evaluate pupil achievement through the use of standardized tests. Standardized tests generally are administered once or twice during a given school year. They can give teachers valuable information in terms of how a given child in class compares with the norms of the standardized test. Standardized tests should adhere to the criteria of being valid and reliable. For a test to be valid, it should cover what has been taught. It would be ridiculous, for example, to have items in a unit test in social studies which would cover technical terms in music. This would especially be true if these terms had not been taught in the unit of study. The teacher needs to be certain that what is being evaluated in terms of pupil achievement has been taught in the unit. It is difficult, however, for the teacher to know precisely what should be taught in different units of study so that the contents of a standardized test are valid. Thus, validity is lacking in degrees when pupils are engaged in the taking of a standardized test. How valid any standardized achievement test is will depend upon the consistency of its objectives with those of the participating elementary school. Too frequently, teachers may have taught isolated facts when pupils are engaged in ongoing learning activities, whereas the standardized test being utilized evaluates learners in terms of problem-solving skills and abilities. The opposite situation could prevail also where the teacher emphasized the importance of problem solving, and yet the standardized achievement test assesses pupils in terms of facts achieved.

Reliability is also important when selecting standardized achievement tests. When standardized tests are reliable, pupil results from having taken the test are consistent. For example, if 1,000 pupils have completed taking form A of a standardized test and then a few days later take form B under comparable circumstances, the results should be quite consistent in terms of grade equivalency or percentile rank. A standardized test, for example, would not be reliable if pupils in the above named group averaged 5.6 grade equivalency from form A and 3.1 grade equivalency from form B. The question then arises as to where are these pupils in achievement pertaining to different curriculum areas in the elementary school. However, if these same pupils averaged a 5.5 grade level equivalency on form A and a 5.6 or 5.7 grade equivalency for form B, one could say that the results were quite consistent providing that consistency of results were also inherent on the part of each child's test results. Teachers then should think of the concept of reliability when developing teacher-made tests.

Self Evaluation by the Teacher

One of the best ways to evaluate pupil achievement is for the teacher to assess his own strengths and weaknesses. There are numerous questions the teacher can ask of the quality of his or her own teaching.

1. Did I try to get pupils interested in ongoing learning activities?
2. Did it appear that individual differences were provided for?
3. Did pupils see a purpose or purposes for learning, or were learners forced to learn that which lacked purpose?
4. Were a variety of activities used in teaching so that individual differences among learners were provided for?
5. Were pupils given adequate chances to develop major generalizations inductively?

6. Did it appear that learners were motivated in desiring to achieving stated objectives?
7. Were diagnostic approaches utilized in determining pupil strengths and weaknesses in ongoing units of study?

REFERENCES

Collier, Calhoun C., *et al*. *Teaching in the Modern Elementary School*. New York: The Macmillan Company, 1967, Chapter 12.

Crosby, Muriel. *Curriculum Development for Elementary Schools in a Changing Society*. Boston: D.C. Heath and Company, 1964, Chapter 17.

Dutton, Wilbur H., and John A. Hockett. *The Modern Elementary School*. New York: Holt, Rinehart and Winston, 1959. Chapter 17.

Ediger, Marlow. *Social Studies Curriculum in the Elementary School*. Kirksville, Missouri: Simpson Printing Company, 1971. Chapter 8.

Frost, Joe L., and G. Thomas Rowland (Eds.). *The Elementary School, Principles Practices*. Boston: Houghton-Mifflin Company, 1969. Chapter 19.

Hass, Glen, *et al*. (Eds.). *Readings in Curriculum*, Second Edition. Boston: Allyn and Bacon, Inc., 1970. Part 2.

Joyce, William et. al. (Eds.). *Elementary Education in the Seventies*. New York: Holt, Rinehart and Winston, Inc. 1970.

Lee, J. Murray, and Doris May Lee. *The Child His Curriculum*. New York: Appleton-Century-Crofts, Inc., 1960. Chapter 15.

Michaelis, John U., *et al*., *New Designs for the Elementary School Curriculum*. New York: McGraw-Hill Book Company, 1967. Chapter 13.

Nerbovig, Marcella H., and Herbert J. Klausmeier. *Teaching in the Elementary School*. Third Edition. New York: Harper and Row Publishers, 1969. Chpater 17.

Saylor, J. Galen, and William M. Alexander. *Curriculum Planning for Schools*, New York: Holt, Rinehart and Winston, Inc., 1974. Chapter 7.

Shuster, Albert H., and Milton E. Ploghoft. *The Emerging Elementary Curriculum*. Columbus: Charles E. Merrill Publishing Company, 1970. Chapter 14.

Reporting Pupil Progress to Parents

Most parents are highly interested in the achievement of their offspring. They want to know how well their children are doing in school. Parents also want to know what they can do to help their offspring achieve to the best degree possible. Thus, faculty members of an elementary school must find the best ways to communicate pupil achievement to parents. This presents a difficult problem.

The curriculum of an elementary school should continuously be evaluated and modified if evidence warrants the making of changes. One way to improve the curriculum is to study, evaluate, and change the approaches used to report pupil achievement to parents. Certainly, the methods used to report pupil progress to parents does affect learner achievement. In some cases, parents have used information obtained from conferences with teachers as a club against their children. The club is used as a lever to get pupils to work "harder" and achieve at a higher level. Perhaps, parents misinterpreted statements made in the evaluation of their child's progress. If a teacher says that child is not working up to potential, the parent may pressure the child to "work up to capacity." It is difficult to determine which pupils are or are not working up to their highest potential. First of all, it is difficult to assess what the capacity of individual pupils are. Intelligence tests are not perfect determinants of the capacity of any child. Even if one could evaluate the capacity of a child with no flaws involved, a further problem would be to evaluate if a child is working toward his revealed intelligence level. Achievement tests which are standardized have their weaknesses thus making the problem complex indeed in determining if a child is working up to capacity. Teacher observation, of course, also has its many weaknesses in determining if a child is working to capacity.

If parents are pressuring a child to work "up to capacity" the pupil presently could really be trying to do his best work. Thus, parental pressures upon the child could have negative consequences. There are a number of reasons why a pupil is not doing better than it appears his mental maturity would permit.

1. The child faces personal problems which reflect upon his being able to benefit more from ongoing learning activities. He worries much about these problems and thus loses out on valuable learnings that could be achieved.
2. Parents are not as accepting of a particular child as compared to other children in the family. Perhaps, the child's total personality development is not what the parents appreciate as compared to other children in the family.
3. Perhaps, poverty or low income is a problem in the home. A child then does not receive the benefits from living an enjoyable life due to inadequate income in the home.
4. Illness, death, divorce, and separation of parents can take its toll of a child being able to benefit from the curricular offerings of an elementary school.
5. Cruel and/or unusual punishment given by one or both of the guardians can do much to hinder pupils from achieving to their highest potential. A guardian using abusive language, hitting pupils physically, screaming at the child, and sending a child to his room frequently as punishment can only assist the child in disliking the home, and what it stands for.
6. Teachers using outdated methods of teaching and emphasizing the irrelevant and unimportant can definitely keep pupils from doing well in an elementary school.
7. Instructors who are in poor mental or physical health which is not conducive in helping learners to achieve

can definitely take its toll in learner performance in the school setting.

8. Administrators emphasizing "quiet classrooms as being good learning environments" can influence the classroom teacher into thinking that continually clamping down on children is the major objective to be achieved in teaching. Pupils then can become passive learners who lack interest, curiosity, purpose, and zest for learning.

9. The child may lack friends. An elementary school is a social institution. There are many human beings in the school setting. Thus, it is important that learners enjoy being together with each other. The teacher must assist learners in developing good human relationships. Teachers should enjoy children and have a desire to help all learners achieve to their optimum. A prejudiced, biased, emotionally unstable classroom teacher has no business in the classroom attempting to teach children!

An approach must be developed whereby pupil achievement and progress can be reported in an objective way. The method used should help pupils to achieve at their own highest unique rate possible. It should emphasize the total growth of the child which includes the following facets— intellectual, social, emotional and physical. If parents use information properly of reported learner achievement, the child should develop positive attitudes toward himself and others. Reporting to parents of learner achievement should assist pupils to achieve to their maximum development intellectually. Punishment given by parents to offspring based on information obtained from report cards, for example, will not help pupils to develop positive attitudes toward self and others. It will not help pupils, generally, in achieving at a higher level intellectually. Instead the pupil may learn to dislike the different curriculum areas of the elementary school as well as teachers and the entire school setting. Thus, different methods of reporting pupil progress to parents should not defeat its own purpose. The purpose should be to keep parents informed of their child's achievement in terms of the total growth of each individual learner. The home and the school should work together in which a curriculum will be developed to fit the needs, interests, and abilities of each individual child. In a democracy, the individual is of utmost importance. Democratic living stresses the importance of all human beings being respected by others. It emphasizes the importance of the uniqueness of each human being.

Using Report Cards to Report Pupil Achievement

Many elementary schools use report cards in reporting pupil progress to parents. Educators have long questioned the values of reporting learner progress in this way. Many disadvantages can be given for reporting pupil progress with the use of report cards.

1. It is difficult to do a thorough job of reporting pupil progress covering all facets of development.
2. Parents, in many cases, perceive the marks given in the report card differently from the way they are perceived by the teacher.
3. If a child is given an "A" grade in reading, it is difficult to determine what this means. For example, this could mean that the child is one of the best readers in the class. It could also mean that the child reads poorly, but he is improving over previous efforts. It could also mean that the child is achieving to his optimum efforts. The best reader in a class could get grades below an "A" if he is goofing off or is lacking in effort.
4. A single grade given in a curriculum area is not sufficient to determine how well a child is doing. For example, if a child gets an "A" grade in social studies, what does this mean? Is the child doing well in getting factual information? Is he doing better in social development or working in committees? Or, is he achieving at an optimum rate in using reference materials? There are many more questions that could be raised as to what the one letter grade would mean in elementary school social studies as well as the other curriculum areas in the elementary school.
5. Negative attitudes have been developed by the pupil when he or she perceives marks received as unfair.
6. Parents have used the results of the report card as a lever to pressure pupils to higher levels of achievement.

7. Parents have become dissatisfied with teachers and the school as a result of having observed the report card of their child.
8. It is difficult and arbitrary to determine the marks or grades that a particular child should receive.
9. Sometimes there are too many categories for a teacher to evaluate pupil achievement in. For example, reading could be divided into many categories in which pupils could be assessed such as using context clues configuration clues, phonetic, analysis, syllabication, and picture clues. The teacher could check how well the learner is doing in each of these areas. Further divisions, other than using word recognition techniques, could be made of the curriculum area of reading. These could include different purposes in reading such as being able to read for facts, main ideas, generalizations, a sequence of ideas or events, directions, and being able to skim content. The reader will readily notice that there are too many areas for teachers to evaluate pupil achievement in reading when reporting many categories of information to parents. Other curriculum areas of the elementary school would add to the number of categories. Parents, no doubt, would not understand the meaning of all these different categories.
10. Many complaints reach the school due to marks or grades that have been given on report cards. The time spent in handling grievances had report cards not been issued could have been given to improving the total elementary school curriculum.
11. It is a oneway street of communication.

Report cards have existed for a long time in American educational history to report pupil achievement to parents. The philosophy back of using the report card has changed over the years as has the different categories or areas that students are assessed in. Thus, report cards also have their many advantages.

1. This is one way that the school can communicate pupil achievement to all parents.

2. Report cards can be used with other approaches in reporting pupil progress to parents. This then has a tendency to minimize some weaknesses that report cards have.
3. If reports cards convey information incorrectly as perceived by parents and guardians, the faculty of an elementary school should invite reactions to categories that learners have been evaluated in.
4. No approach in reporting pupil achievement to parents is perfect. Thus, report cards also have their strengths and weaknesses.
5. Parents should feel free to come to school and inquire about their child's achievement if the marks or grades received were perceived to be low.
6. Facilities of elementary schools should continuously revise the report cards used in order that weaknesses can be eliminated or minimized. Important facets of a pupil's achievement and development should appear on the report card.

No doubt, report cards will be with us for some time to come in reporting pupil achievement to parents. Thus, it behooves faculty members of an elementary school or several elementary schools to provide the best and most important information about each child's progress on the report card. The following questions are important to answer when revising or modifying the report card as it is presently being utilized in a public school system:

1. Does the report card reflect up-to-date thinking in terms of what facets of each child's achievement is being reported to parents?
2. Are the contents of the report card too difficult for parents to interpret?
3. Could the report card convey misinformation to parents?
4. Can the report card be filled out by teachers in a reasonable amount of time?
5. Are the categories for pupils to be evaluated in free from duplication?

6. Is the philosophy of the school clear pertaining to basic ideas in back of the issuing of grade cards?
7. Have parents been informed as to the meaning of each of the categories pupils are being evaluated in on the report card?
8. Is the terminology used in the report card clear, concise, and free from ambiguous statements?
9. Is space available on the report card for parents to respond to marks or grades given to pupils?
10. Does the report card invite parents to come to school to confer with the teacher and principal about their child's progress?
11. Could teachers justify the grades or marks given to pupils which appear on the grade card?
12. Is there adequate justification in terms of how frequently pupil achievement should be reported to parents when using report cards?
13. Should other approaches be used simultaneously with the grade card when reporting pupil progress? Should parent-teacher conferences occur at the same time report cards are issued?
14. Do the contents of the report card clearly convey to parents needed information about each child's progress?
15. Has the faculty of an elementary school studied and evaluated an adequate number of report cards from various school systems to determine what a good report card should contain?

Improving the quality of report cards can be one approach, among others, in which an elementary school can improve the curriculum.

Having Parent-Teacher Conferences to Report Pupil Progress

Many elementary schools conduct parent-teacher conferences at least once a year. This gives parents opportunities to ask questions of the teacher in a face-to-face situation. Problems and questions can be identified by parents as well as the teacher. It is not a one-way street of communication. Both the parent or parents as well as the teacher can be actively involved in the parent-teacher conference. There are certain standards that the teacher should follow in conducting parent-teacher conferences.

1. The ideas of parents must be respected since good communication comes about in an atmosphere of positive consideration for the thinking of others.
2. The teacher should be well prepared prior to conducting each parent-teacher conference. Otherwise, parent-teacher conferences can be a waste of time. The teacher should have important knowledge about the child's general capacity and achievement, home background information, and general emotional and physical health.
3. It is good to show parents work samples of their child's achievement. Thus parents can get some data about the achievement of their children. Teachers and parents must understand that all materials used in teaching pupils should be on the instructional level of the child. Objectives must be reasonable so that they can be achieved by pupils. Thus learning activities need to be on the instructional level of pupils and not the frustrational level.
4. After report cards, if used, have been issued for the first time in a given school year, results can be discussed with parents in a parent-teacher conference.
5. Agreed upon criteria should be established with teacher-parent cooperation in a conference to help in improving the curriculum for each child.
6. If a second parent-teacher conference is held somewhat toward the end of a given school year, these criteria could be referred to in the conference when making comparisons from the first to the second conference.
7. The teacher must use terminology which parents understand. Technical vocabulary used only by educators has no place in a parent-teacher conference. If these terms are used, they should be explained to parents. Parents must sense that meaningful communication is taking place in a parent-teacher conference.

8. The teacher should jot down some major generalizations and conclusions from the conference. The summaries can be placed in a folder for each child. It is important that the date appear on the papers which are filed for each child in a folder.
9. Information obtained from a conference should be kept strictly confidential. The purpose of the conference is to guide learner achievement to the optimum.
10. All conferences should have a positive emphasis to provide for a free flow of ideas.

Parent-teacher conferences have many advantages over the report cards as a means of reporting pupil progress.

1. The plan is good psychologically in that a one-to-one relationship exists between parent or parents and the teacher.
2. If the atmosphere provides for freedom of expression, many misunderstandings could be minimized due to being able to clarify ideas between parents and the teacher in a face-to-face situation.
3. Numerous opportunities exist for the identification and solution of problems pertaining to each child's achievement.
4. Parent-teacher conferences can be held whenever it is feasible and appropriate. There is no limitation on the number of conferences that can be held in a given school year. The school should invite parents to discuss their child's achievement with the teacher whenever it is desirable.

Using the Telephone in Reporting Pupil Progress

The telephone can be used effectively in reporting pupil progresses to parents. To often, the negative is reported to parents about their child's achievement. Thus, parents and the child may come to feel that the school has nothing positive to report on learner progress. The telephone can be used quickly to compliment a given child on his performance on a particular lesson or test. It can also be used to compliment a selected child's attitude toward others in a specific situation. Thus, the telephone can be used to communicate ideas rapidly and effectively.

The giver of information on the telephone cannot see the receiver of the message. This, of course, is a disadvantage in using the telephone. However, there is a one-to-one relationship between the sender and the receiver of the message. The following standards are important in conducting a parent-teacher conference using the telephone:

1. Politeness is important in conducting the conference.
2. The teacher, principal, or supervisor should listen carefully to the thinking of others.
3. A pleasant tone of voice should be used.
4. Ideas that are communicated should be to the point.
5. Words and sentences used should be on the understanding level of parents.

It is important that more elementary school teachers use the telephone to communicate ideas quickly in a parent-teacher conference. Parents, of course, do not need to come to school in order to use this approach to communicate ideas. Thus, much time is saved in the scheduling and conducting of conferences of this kind.

Writing Letters to Report Pupil Achievement

Some schools have adopted the practice of writing letters to parents in order to report pupil achievement. Guidelines to follow in writing letters to report pupil progress cold be the following:

1. Ideas must be communicated accurately when putting statements in writing.
2. The mechanics of writing are important, such as spelling, handwriting or neat typing, punctuation, and capitalization.
3. Statements must be written which are meaningful to the reader.
4. Respect for the parent and child must be an inherent part of ideas to be communicated.
5. Due care must be taken to refrain from putting in content which can be misinterpreted.

6. Ideas in the letter should pinpoint learner achievement being reported to parents.

There are numerous advantages of written statements pertaining to pupil achievement which is reported to parents.

1. Content can be written down just the way it is desired before mailing the letter to parents. In speaking to parents, ideas are expressed and cannot be changed unless verbal clarification occurs.
2. Letters can be written to parents at any point during a given school year.
3. Any facet of pupil achievement can be put in the letter, not just the categories as they appear in a report card.

Disadvantages of writing letters pertaining to reporting pupil progress to parents are quite in evidence.

1. Once content has been sent out, it cannot be revised by the sender.
2. Misinterpretation of content in the letter is definitely a possibility.
3. It is difficult for many to put ideas in written form which communicate ideas clearly to readers;
4. Seeing content in written form leaves much room for a variety of interpretation pertaining to words, phrases, and sentences. Ample time must be taken to evaluate what has been written at the time the information is sent.

In Summary

There are numerous ways to report pupil achievement to parents. The grade card or report card is, perhaps, the most common approach used. There are advantages and disadvantages in using this method of reporting pupil progress to parents. It is difficult to convey accurately to parents what grades mean on a report card. Teachers differ much in their thinking pertaining to how pupils should be evaluated. In other words, should the top achievers in a class get A's, the next best achievers receive B grades, and so on? Or, should learners be evaluated in terms of effort? This would mean that pupils doing poor quality work could get A grades if they are trying to do the best work possible in terms of their capacity and past achievement. A major problem in using report cards to report pupil achievement relates directly to the number of categories in each curriculum area that teachers would assess pupil progress in.

Parent-teacher conferences can be an excellent means of reporting pupil progress depending upon the quality of interactions between and among those involved. Respect for human beings is important in these conferences. The teacher must be a good listener to understand the concerns, goals and aspirations that parents have for their children. Parents should be involved in solving problems pertaining to their child's achievement. The home and the school should be brought together in cooperative planning so that the best curriculum can be developed for each child.

The telephone can be a good means to inform parents about learner progress. This approach can be used at different intervals when necessary and desirable. It is an inexpensive approach to use which takes a minimum amount of time. Parents then do not need to take time in making arrangements to come to school. Neither do teachers need to arrange a time schedule as to when parents should come to school for conferences. Parents should be informed about their child's achievement at numerous intervals.

Letters can be written to inform parents of their child's achievement. Numerous problems exist here. A major problem is that it is difficult to write ideas clearly. Secondly, words, phrases, and sentences leave considerable room, in many cases, for a variety of interpretations. Thirdly, once content has been written down and mailed, it cannot be revised.

REFERENCES

Frost, Joe L., and G. Thomas Rowland. *Curricula for the Seventies*. Boston: Houghton Mifflin Company, 1969. Chapter One.

Hicks, William Vernon, and others. *The New Elementary School Curriculum*. New York: Van Nostrand Reinhold Company, 1970, Chapter Eleven.

Hyman, Ronald T. *Ways of Teaching*. Second Edition. Philadelphia: J.B. Lippincott Company, 1974.

Regan, William B., and Gene D. Shepherd. *Modern Elementary Curriculum*. Fourth Edition, New York: Holt, Rinehard and Winston, 1971. Chapter Sixteen.

Shuster, Albert H., and Milton E. Ploghoft. *The Emerging Elementary Curriculum*. Second Edition. Columbus, Ohio: Charles E. Merrill Publishing Company, 1970. Chapter Fourteen.

Additional Reading

Bhaskara Rao, Digumarti (1994). *Scientific Aptitude*, New Delhi: Ashish Publishing House. pp. 100. ISBN 81-7024-658-X.

Bhaskara Rao, Digumarti (1995). *Animal Kingdom*. New Delhi: Discovery Publishing House. pp. 135. ISBN 81-7141-274-2.

Bhaskara Rao, Digumarti (1995). *Batracology*. New Delhi: Discovery Publishing House. pp. 174. ISBN 81-7141-279-3.

Bhaskara Rao, Digumarti (1996). *Scientific Attitude vis-à-vis Scientific Aptitude*. New Delhi: Discovery Publishing House. pp. 143. ISBN 81-7141-308-0.

Bhaskara Rao, Digumarti, Editor (1996). *Encyclopaedia of Education for All*, 5 Volumes. New Delhi: APH Publishing Corporation. pp. 1460. ISBN 81-7024-759-4 (set).

Vol. I *Education for All: The World Conferences*. pp. 440. ISBN 81-7024-760-8.

Vol. II *Education for All: The EPA-9 Summit*. pp. 340. ISBN 81-7024-761-6.

Vol. III *Education for All: Quality Education for All*. pp. 250. ISBN 81-7024-762-6.

Vol. IV *Education for All: Planning and Monitoring*. pp. 170. ISBN 81-7024-763-4.

Vol. V *Education for All: The Indian Scenario*. pp. 260. ISBN 81-7024-764-0.

Bhaskara Rao, Digumarti, Editor (1996). *Global Perceptions on Peace Education*, 3 Volumes. New Delhi: Discovery Publishing House. pp. 980. ISBN 81-7141-319-6.

Bhaskara Rao, Digumarti, Editor (1996). *National Policy on Education.* 2 Volumes. New Delhi: Anmol Publications Pvt. Ltd. pp. 710. ISBN 81-7488-323-1.

Bhaskara Rao, Digumarti, Editor (1997). *Care the Child*, 2 Volumes. New Delhi: Discovery Publishing House. pp. 616. ISBN 81-7141-394-3.

Bhaskara Rao, Digumarti, Editor (1997). *Education for the 21st Century*. New Delhi: Discovery Publishing House. pp. 288. ISBN 81-7141-389-7.

Bhaskara Rao, Digumarti, Editor (1997). *Reflections on Scientific Attitude.* New Delhi: Discovery Publishing House, pp. 980. ISBN 81-7141-319-6.

Bhaskara Rao, Digumarti (1997). *Scientific Attitude.* New Delhi: Discovery Publishing House. pp. 120. ISBN 81-7141-381-1.

Bhaskara Rao, Digumarti, Editor (1997). *Success Story of a Primary Education Project.* New Delhi: APH Publishing Corporation. pp. 260. ISBN 81-7024-850-7.

Bhaskara Rao, Digumarti, Editor (1997). *World Food Summit.* New Delhi: Discovery Publishing House. pp. 153. ISBN 81-7141-386-2.

Bhaskara Rao, Digumarti, Editor (1998). *Adolescence Education.* New Delhi: Discovery Publishing House. pp. 238. ISBN 81-7141-432-X.

Bhaskara Rao, Digumarti, Editor (1998). *Community and School Nutrition Education.* New Delhi: Discovery Publishing House. pp. 425. ISBN 81-7141-435-4.

Bhaskara Rao, Digumarti, Editor (1998). *District Primary Education Programme.* New Delhi: Discovery Publishing House. pp. 506. ISBN 81-7141-396-X.

Bhaskara Rao, Digumarti, Editor (1998). *Earth Summit*, 2 Volumes. New Delhi: Discovery Publishing House. pp. 930. ISBN 81-7141-435-4.

Bhaskara Rao, Digumarti, Editor (1998). *National Policy on Education: Towards an Enlightened and Humane Society*, New Delhi: Discovery Publishing House. pp. 542. ISBN 81-7141-426-5.

Bhaskara Rao, Digumarti, Editor (1998). *Reforming School Education*. New Delhi: Discovery Publishing House. pp. 575. ISBN 81-7141-403-6.

Bhaskara Rao, Digumarti, Editor (1998). *Teacher Education in India*. New Delhi: Discovery Publishing House. pp. 424. ISBN 81-7141-406-0.

Bhaskara Rao, Digumarti, Editor (1998). *World Summit for Social Development*. New Delhi: Discovery Publishing House. pp. 278. ISBN 81-7141-420-6.

Bhaskara Rao, Digumarti, Editor (2000). *Education for All: Achieving the Goal*, 3 Volumes, New Delhi: APH Publishing Corporation. pp. 830. ISBN 81-7648-152-1.

Vol. I *The Global Consensus*. pp. 285. ISBN 81-7648-155-6.

Vol. II *Mid-Decade Review Reports of Regional Seminars*. pp. 198. ISBN 81-7648-154-8.

Vol. III *Issues and Trends*. pp. 346. ISBN 81-7648-155-6.

Bhaskara Rao, Digumarti, Editor (2000), *International Encyclopaedia of AIDS*, 11 Volumes in 13 Parts. New Delhi: Discovery Publishing House. pp. 676. ISBN 81-7141-6 (Set).

Vol. 1 *Introduction to HIV/AIDS*. pp. 246. ISBN 81-7141-523-7.

Vol. 2 *HIV/AIDS—Issues and Challenges*, 2 Parts. pp. 805. ISBN 81-7141-524-5.

Vol. 3 *HIV/AIDS—Socio Economic Realities*. pp. 436. ISBN 81-7141-524-3.

Vol. 4 *HIV/AIDS—Law Ethics and Human Rights*, 2 Parts. pp. 589. ISBN 81-7141-526-1.

Vol. 5 *AIDS and NGOs*. pp. 215. ISBN 81-7141-527-X.

Vol. 6 *AIDS and Home Care*. pp. 183. ISBN 81-7141-528-8.

Vol. 7 *STD Case Management*. pp. 223. ISBN 81-7141-529-6.

Vol. 8 *HIV/AIDS Prevention and Care—Teaching Modules for Nurses and Midwives*. pp. 183. ISBN 81-7141-530-X.

Vol. 9 *HIV Prevention Education for Education for Educational Institutions*. pp. 75. ISBN 81-7141-531-8.

Vol. 10 *Instructional Modules for AIDS Education*. pp. 111. ISBN 81-7141-532-6.

Vol. 11 *School Health Education to Prevent AIDS and STD—A Package for Curriculum Planners*. pp. 298. ISBN 81-7141-5338-4.

Bhaskara Rao, Digumarti, Editor (2000). *International Encyclopaedia of Science and Technology Education*, 11 Volumes. New Delhi: Discovery Publishing House. pp. 4892. ISBN 81-7141-548-2 (Set).

Vol. 1 *Science and Technology Education*. pp. 557. ISBN 81-7141-568-7.

Vol. 2 *Science Education in Developing Countries*. pp. 334. ISBN 81-7141-570-9.

Vol. 3 *Organisational Structure of Science*. pp. 334. ISBN 81-7141-570-9.

Vol. 4 *Science Education in Asia and the Pacific*. pp. 249. ISBN 81-7141-571-7.

Vol. 5 *Science and Technology Education for All*. pp. 464. ISBN 81-7141-572-5.

Vol. 6 *Values, Ethics, Talent and Girls in Science and Technology Education*. pp. 463. ISBN 81-7141-573-3.

Vol. 7 *Popularization of Science and Technology Education*. pp. 334. ISBN 81-7141-574-1.

Vol. 8 *Science, Power and Society*. pp. 357. ISBN 81-7141-575-X.

Vol. 9 *Information Technology*. pp. 442. Rs. 775. ISBN 81-7141-576-8.

Vol. 10 *Teacher Training in Science and Technology Education*. pp. 536. ISBN 81-7141-577-6.

Vol. 11 *Teacher Training in Science and Technology: A Curriculum Framework*. pp. 642. ISBN 81-7141-578-4.

Bhaskara Rao, Digumarti, Editor (2001). *Distance Education in Different Countries*. New Delhi: APH Publishing Corporation. pp. 574. ISBN 81-7648-229-3.

Bhaskara Rao, Digumarti, Editor (2001). *Decentralised Management of Education (Management of Education in Panchayati Raj and Municipal Bodies)*. New Delhi: Discovery Publishing House. pp. 116. ISBN 81-7141-617-9.

Bhaskara Rao, Digumarti, Editor (2001). *Electrochemistry for Environmental Protection*. New Delhi: Discovery Publishing House. pp. 208. ISBN 81-7141-619-5.

Bhaskara Rao, Digumarti, Editor (2001). *Global Educational Studies*. New Delhi: Discovery Publishing House. pp. 145. ISBN 81-7141-616-0.

Bhaskara Rao, Digumarti, Editor (2001). *Global Synthesis of Educational Assessment*. New Delhi: Discovery Publishing House. pp. 152. ISBN 81-7141-613-6.

Bhaskara Rao, Digumarti, Editor (2000). *International Encyclopaedia of Human Rights*. 7 Volumes in 13 Parts. New Delhi: Discovery Publishing House. pp. 6500 (Royal Size). ISBN 81-7141-567-9 (Set).

Vol. 1 *International Instruments of Human Rights*, 2 Parts. ISBN 81-7141-595-4.

Vol. 2 *Regional Instruments of Human Rights*. ISBN 81-7141-604-7.

Vol. 3 *Human Rights and the United Nations*, 2 Parts. ISBN 81-7141-605-5.

Vol. 4 *Fact Files of Human Rights*, 3 Parts. ISBN 81-7141-605-3.

Vol. 5 *Study Stories of Human Rights*, 3 Parts. ISBN 81-7141-607-3.

Vol. 6 *International Meetings on Human Rights*, 2 Parts. ISBN 81-7141-608-X.

Vol. 7 *Professional Training in Human Rights*. ISBN 81-7141-609-8.

Bhaskara Rao, Digumarti, Editor (2001). *Jomtein Decade of Education*. New Delhi: Discovery Publishing House. pp. 106. ISBN 81-7141-618-7.

Bhaskara Rao, Digumarti, Editor (2001). *Nuclear Materials: Issues and Concerns*, 2 Volumes. New Delhi: Discovery Publishing House. pp. 1100. ISBN 81-7141-611-X.

Bhaskara Rao, Digumarti, Editor (2001). *World Conference on Education for All*. New Delhi: APH Publishing Corporation. pp. 380. ISBN 81-7141-274-9.

Bhaskara Rao, Digumarti, Editor (2001). *World Conference on Higher Education*, New Delhi: Discovery Publishing House. pp. 306. ISBN 81-7141-610-1.

Bhaskara Rao, Digumarti, Editor (2001). *World Conference on Science*. New Delhi: Discovery Publishing House. pp. 85. ISBN 81-7141-612-8.

Bhaskara Rao, Digumarti, Editor (2004). *Chernobyl: Never Again*. New Delhi: Discovery Publishing House.

Bhaskara Rao, Digumarti, Editor (2004). *Habitat Agenda*. New Delhi: Discovery Publishing House.

Bhaskara Rao, Digumarti, Editor (2003). *Inspiring Experiences in Teacher Education*. New Delhi: Discovery Publishing House. pp. 256. ISBN 81-7141-656-X.

Bhaskara Rao, Digumarti, Editor (2003). *International Studies in Education*, 3 Volumes. New Delhi: Discovery Publishing House. pp. 912. ISBN 81-7141-647-0 (Set).

Bhaskara Rao, Digumarti, Editor (2003). *Military Conversion: Impact on Science and Technology*, New Delhi: Discovery Publishing House. pp. 200. ISBN 81-7141-578-4.

Bhaskara Rao, Digumarti, Editor (2004). *Virology and Immunology*. New Delhi: Discovery Publishing House.

Bhaskara Rao, Digumarti, Editor (2003). *United Nations Millennium Summit*. New Delhi: Discovery Publishing House. pp. 112. ISBN 81-7141-632-2.

Bhaskara Rao, Digumarti, Editor (2003). *World Assembly on Aging*. New Delhi: Discovery Publishing House. pp. 88. ISBN 81-7141-637-3.

Bhaskara Rao, Digumarti, Editor (2004). *World Conference on Human Rights*. New Delhi: Discovery Publishing House.

Bhaskara Rao, Digumarti, Editor (2003). *World Education Forum*. New Delhi: Discovery Publishing House. pp. 336. ISBN 81-7141-639-X.

Bhaskara Rao, Digumarti, Editor (2004). *Education Employment and Human Resource Development*. New Delhi: Discovery Publishing House.

Bhaskara Rao, Digumarti, Editor (2004). *Learning to Live Together*, 3 Volumes. New Delhi: Discovery Publishing House.

Bhaskara Rao, Digumarti, Editor (2004). *Successfully Schooling*. New Delhi: Discovery Publishing House.

Bhaskara Rao, Digumarti, Editor (2004). *European Education and Teachers*. New Delhi: Discovery Publishing House.

Bhaskara Rao, Digumarti, Editor (2004). *Teachers in a Changing World*. New Delhi: Discovery Publishing House.

Bhaskara Rao, Digumarti, Editor (2003). *All for Education: Sharing Strategies and Experiences in Education*. New Delhi: APH Publishing Corporation.

Bhaskara Rao, Digumarti, C.A.P. Swamy and B.S.V. Dutt (1997). *Self-Evaluation in Student Teaching*. New Delhi: Discovery Publishing House. pp. 762. ISBN 81-7141-374-9.

Bhaskara Rao, Digumarti and Digumarti Pushpa Latha (1994). *Achievement in Biology*. New Delhi: Discovery Publishing House. pp. 102. ISBN 81-7141-264-5.

Bhaskara Rao, Digumarti, C. Sridevi and K. Vijaya (1995). *Achievement in Social Studies*. New Delhi: Discovery Publishing House. pp. 102. ISBN 81-7141-281-5.

Bhaskara Rao, Digumarti and Digumarti Pushpa Latha (1995). *Achievement in English*. New Delhi: Discovery Publishing House. pp. 214. ISBN 81-7141-283-1.

Bhaskara Rao, Digumarti and Digumarti Pushpa Latha (1994). *Achievement in Science*. New Delhi: Discovery Publishing House. pp. 159. ISBN 81-7141-280-70.

Bhaskara Rao, Digumarti and Digumarti Pushpa Latha (1995). *Achievement in Mathematics*. New Delhi: Discovery Publishing House. pp. 125. ISBN 81-7141-278-5.

Bhaskara Rao, Digumarti and Digumarti Pushpa Latha, Editors (1998). *International Encyclopaedia of Women*. 5 Volumes. New Delhi: Discovery Publishing House. pp. 2172. ISBN 81-7141-410-9.

Vol. 1 *Status of World's Women*. pp. 427. ISBN 81-7141-494-X.

Vol. 2 *Women, Education and Empowerment*. pp. 467. ISBN 81-7141-498-1.

Vol. 3 *Women Challenges and Advancement*. pp. 354. ISBN 81-7141-497-4.

Vol. 4 *Women and Family Health*. pp. 470. ISBN 81-7141-497-4.

Vol. 5 *Women and International Action*. pp. 453. ISBN 81-7141-498-2.

Bhaskara Rao, Digumarti, Digumarti Pushpa Latha and Digumarti Harshitha, Editors (2001). *Biological Warfare*. New Delhi: Discovery Publishing House. pp. 422. ISBN 81-7141-597-0.

Bhaskara Rao, Digumarti, Digumarti Pushpa Latha and Digumarti Harshitha, Editors (2001). *Women as Educators*. New Delhi: Discovery Publishing House. pp. 112. ISBN 81-7141-602-0.

Bhaskara Rao, Digumarti, Digumarti Pushpa Latha and Digumarti Harshitha, Editors (2001). *Education in India*. New Delhi: APH Publishing Corporation. pp. 280. ISBN 81-7141-207-2.

Bhaskara Rao, Digumarti, Digumarti Pushpa Latha and Digumarti Harshitha, Editors (2001). *Assessing Learning Achievement*. New Delhi: Discovery Publishing House. pp. 128. ISBN 81-7141-601-2.

Bhaskara Rao, Digumarti, Digumarti Pushpa Latha and Digumarti Harshitha, Editors (2001). *Energy Security*. New Delhi: Discovery Publishing House. pp. 564. ISBN 81-7141-598-9.

Bhaskara Rao, Digumarti, Digumarti Harshitha and K.R.S.S. Rao, Editors (1999). *Advanced Biotechnology*. New Delhi: Discovery Publishing House. pp. 335. ISBN 81-7141-516-4.

Bhaskara Rao, Digumarti and D. Sridhar (2002). *Job Satisfaction of School Teachers*. New Delhi: Discovery Publishing House. pp. 104. ISBN 81-7141-652-7.

Bhaskara Rao, Digumarti and K.R.S. Sambhasiva Rao, Editors (1996). *Current Trends in Indian Education*. New Delhi: Discovery Publishing House. pp. 234. ISBN 81-7141-311-0.

Bhaskara Rao, Digumarti and K. Vijaya (1995). *A Text Book of Evaluation*. Ambala Cantt: The Associated Publishers. pp. 100.

Bhaskara Rao, Digumarti and N.V.M. Mohana Rao (2002). *Problems of Mentally Handicapped Children*. New Delhi: Discovery Publishing House. pp. 96. ISBN 81-7141-645-4.

Bhaskara Rao, Digumarti and S. Chandra Mohan (2002). *Student Participation in Sports and Games*. New Delhi: APH Publishing Corporation.

Bhaskara Rao, Digumarti and S. Chandra Mohan (2002). *Student Participation in Sports and Games*. New Delhi: APH Publishing Corporation.

Bhaskara Rao, Digumarti, V.V. Rao, V.V. Lakshmi and V.V. Krishna, Editors (1999). *Status and Advancement of Women*. New Delhi: APH Publishing Corporation. pp. 570. ISBN 81-7648-169-6.

Babu, P.C. Author and Digumarti Bhaskara Rao, Editor (2004). *Flowers of Wisdom*. New Delhi: Discovery Publishing House.

Bhagya Lakshmi, Lingineni, Author and Digumarti Bhaskara Rao, Editor (2000). *Reading and Comprehension*. New Delhi: Discovery Publishing House. pp. 108. ISBN 81-7141-543-1.

Bhuvaneswara Lakshmi, Gadde, Author and Digumarti Bhaskara Rao, Editor (2000). *Attitude Towards Science*. New Delhi: Discovery Publishing House. pp. 128. ISBN 81-7141-541-6.

Devraj, T.A.S., Author and Digumarti Bhaskara Rao, Editor (1997). *Trace Analysis of Uranium and Thorium*. New Delhi: Discovery Publishing House. pp. 195. ISBN 81-7141-375-7.

Durga Rani, K., Author and Digumarti Bhaskara Rao, Editor (2000). *Educational Aspirations and Scientific Attitudes*. New Delhi: Discovery Publishing House. pp. 130. ISBN 81-7141-555-55.

Dutt, B.S.V. and Digumarti Bhaskara Rao (2001). *Empowering Primary Teachers*. New Delhi: Discovery Publishing House. pp. 283. ISBN 81-7141-615.2.

Ediger, Marlow and Digumarti Bhaskara Rao (1996). *Science Curriculum*. New Delhi: Discovery Publishing House. pp. 309. ISBN 81-7141-321-8.

Ediger, Marlow and Digumarti Bhaskara Rao (2000). *Teaching Mathematics Successfully*. New Delhi: Discovery Publishing House. pp. 179. ISBN 81-7141-552-0.

Ediger, Marlow and Digumarti Bhaskara Rao (2001). *Teaching Science Successfully*. New Delhi: Discovery Publishing House. pp. 320. ISBN 81-7141-600-4.

Ediger, Marlow and Digumarti Bhaskara Rao (2001). *Teaching Social Studies Successfully*. New Delhi: Discovery Publishing House. pp. 296. ISBN 81-7141-596-2.

Ediger, Marlow and Digumarti Bhaskara Rao (2002). *Philosophy and Curriculum*. New Delhi: Discovery Publishing House. pp. 224. ISBN 81-7141-631-4.

Ediger, Marlow and Digumarti Bhaskara Rao (2002). *Improving School Administration*. New Delhi: Discovery Publishing House. pp. 240. ISBN 81-7141-633-0.

Ediger, Marlow and Digumarti Bhaskara Rao (2002). *Elementary Curriculum*. New Delhi: Discovery Publishing House. pp. 490. ISBN 81-7141-658-6.

Ediger, Marlow and Digumarti Bhaskara Rao (2003). *Language Arts Curriculum*. New Delhi: Discovery Publishing House. pp. 348. ISBN 81-7141-657-8.

Ediger, Marlow and Digumarti Bhaskara Rao (2001). *Pilgrimage: The Holy Land*. New Delhi: Discovery Publishing House.

Ediger, Marlow and Digumarti Bhaskara Rao (2004). *Psychology and Curriculum*. New Delhi: Discovery Publishing House.

Ediger, Marlow and Digumarti Bhaskara Rao (2004). *Teaching Language Arts Successfully*. New Delhi: Discovery Publishing House.

Ediger, Marlow and Digumarti Bhaskara Rao (2004). *Psychology and Curriculum*. New Delhi: Discovery Publishing House.

Ediger, Marlow and Digumarti Bhaskara Rao (2004). *Teaching Mathematics in Elementary Schools*. New Delhi: Discovery Publishing House.

Ediger, Marlow and Digumarti Bhaskara Rao (2004). *Teaching Science in Elementary Schools*. New Delhi: Discovery Publishing House.

Ediger, Marlow and Digumarti Bhaskara Rao (2004). *Teaching Social Studies in Elementary Schools*. New Delhi: Discovery Publishing House.

Ediger, Marlow and Digumarti Bhaskara Rao (2004). *School Curriculum and Administration*. New Delhi: Discovery Publishing House.

Ediger, Marlow and Digumarti Bhaskara Rao (2004). *Elementary Curriculum Improvement*. New Delhi: Discovery Publishing House.

Ediger Marlow, B.S.V. Dutt and Digumarti Bhaskara Rao (2004). *Teaching English Successfully*. New Delhi: Discovery Publishing House.

Jayasree, Kandi, Author and Digumarti Bhaskara Rao, Editor (1999). *Correlates of Socialisation*. New Delhi: Discovery Publishing House. pp. 160. ISBN 81-7141-517-2.

John Babu, Chikati, Author and T.J.R. Prasad, G.M. Madhukar and Digumarti Bhaskara Rao, Editors (1996). *Problem Solving in Mathematics*. New Delhi: APH Publishing Corporation. pp. 125. ISBN 81-7648-273-0.

Jyothi, Nirmala M., Author and Digumarti Bhaskara Rao, Editor (2003). *Non-Detention System in School Education*. New Delhi: Discovery Publishing House. pp. 400. ISBN 81-7141-654-3.

Marja, Talvi and Digumarti Bhaskara Rao, Editors (1996). *Educational Leadership and Social Change*. New Delhi: Discovery Publishing House. pp. 236. ISBN 81-7141-320-X.

Prabhakaram, K.S., Author and Digumarti Bhaskara Rao, Editor (1998). *Concept Attainment Model in Mathematics Teaching*. New Delhi: Discovery Publishing House. pp. 122. ISBN 81-7141-424-9.

Prasanth Kumar, J., Author and Digumarti Bhaskara Rao, Editor (1998). *Effectiveness of Distance Education System*. New Delhi: Discovery Publishing House. pp. 152. ISBN 81-7141-437-0.

Ramatulasamma, K. Author and Digumarti Bhaskara Rao, Editor (2002). *Job Satisfaction of Teacher Educators*, New Delhi: Discovery Publishing House. pp. 160. ISBN 81-7141-655-1.

Rama Krishnaiah, D., Author and Digumarti Bhaskara Rao, Editor (1998). *Job Satisfaction of College Teachers*, New Delhi: Discovery Publishing House. pp. 251. ISBN 81-7141-438-9.

Rathaiah, Lavu and Digumarti Bhaskara Rao, Editors (1996). *International Innovations in Education*. New Delhi: Discovery Publishing House. pp. 513. ISBN 81-7141-359-5.

Ramesh, Ganta and Digumarti Bhaskara Rao, Editors (1998). *Environmental Education: Problems and Prospects*. New Delhi: Discovery Publishing House. pp. 324. ISBN 81-7141-423-0.

Rathaiah, Lavu and Digumarti Bhaskara Rao (1997). *Achievement Correlates*. New Delhi: Discovery Publishing House. pp. 116. ISBN 81-7141-385-4.

Reddy, Sudhakar Y., Author, and Digumarti Bhaskara Rao, Editor (2003). *Creativity in Adolescents*. New Delhi: Discovery Publishing House. pp. 430. ISBN 81-7141-659-4.

Reddy, M.S., Author and Digumarti Bhaskara Rao, Editor (2004). *Creativity in College Students*. New Delhi: Discovery Publishing House.

Radramamba, B., Author and Digumarti Bhaskara Rao, Editor (2003). *Problems of Teaching*. New Delhi: APH Publishing Corporation. pp. 203. ISBN 81-7648-462-8.

Sanjeeva Rao, P.C., Author and Digumarti Bhaskara Rao, Editor (1996). *A Text Book of Geology*. New Delhi: Discovery Publishing House. pp. 320. ISBN 81-7141-313-7.

Satya Narayana V., Author and Digumarti Bhaskara Rao, Editor (2001). *Physical Education, Social Attitudes and Leadership Qualities*. New Delhi: Discovery Publishing House. pp. 296. ISBN 81-7141-593-8.

Srinivasulu Reddy, M., and K.R.S. Sambasiva Rao, Authors and Digumarti Bhaskara Rao, Editor (1999). *A Text Book of Aquaculture*. New Delhi: Discovery Publishing House. pp. 296. ISBN 81-7141-482-6.

Srinivasa Rao, Mandalapu, Author and Digumarti Bhaskara Rao, Editor (2004). *Achievement Motivation and Achievement in Mathematics*. New Delhi: Discovery Publishing House.

Vanaja, M., Author and Digumarti Bhaskara Rao, Editor (1999). *Inquiry Training Model*. New Delhi: Discovery Publishing House. pp. 189. ISBN 81-7141-515-6.

Veleri V. Koustiouk, Author and Digumarti Bhaskara Rao, Editor (2002). *A Text Book of Cryogenics*. New Delhi: Discovery Publishing House. pp. 288. ISBN 81-7141-642-X.

Veleri V. Koustiouk, Author and Digumarti Bhaskara Rao, Editor (2004). *Refrigeration and Environment*. New Delhi: Discovery Publishing House.

Veena Kumari, Balusu and Digumarti Bhaskara Rao (1996). *Operation Black Board*. New Delhi: Ashish Publishing Corporation. pp. 140. ISBN 81-7024-711-X.

Veena Kumari, Balusu, Author and Digumarti Bhaskara Rao, Editor (2000). *Psycho-Social Correlates of Achievement*, New Delhi: Discovery Publishing House. pp. 36. ISBN 81-7141-547-4.

Venkata Rao, P. and Digumarti Bhaskara Rao (1989). *A Text Book of Zoology—Junior Intermediate*. Guntur: Vignan Publishers. pp. 370.

Venkata Rao, P. and Digumarti Bhaskara Rao (1989). *A Text Book of Zoology—Senior Intermediate*. Guntur: Vignan Publishers. pp. 480.

Venugopala Rao, K., Author and Digumarti Bhaskara Rao, Editor (2000). *Teacher Morale in Secondary Schools*. New Delhi: Discovery Publishing House. pp. 300. ISBN 81-7141-551-2.

Vidya, C., Author and Digumarti Bhaskara Rao. Editor (1996). *A Text Book of Nutrition*. New Delhi: Discovery Publishing House. pp. 438. ISBN 81-7141-309-9.

Vidya Bharathi, D., Author and Digumarti Bhaskara Rao, Editor (2000). *Educational Philosophies of Swami Vivekananda and John Dewey*. New Delhi: APH Publishing Corporation. pp. 200. ISBN 81-7648-309-9.

Books in Telugu Language

Bhaskara Rao, Digumarti (1986). *Dhrushya Sravana Bodhanapakaranalu* (Audio Visual Teaching Aids). Guntur: Nagarjuna Publishers.

Bhaskara Rao, Digumarti (1993). *Jeevasashtra Bodhana* (Teaching of Biology). Guntur: Nagarjuna Publishers.

Bhaskara Rao, Digumarti (1995). *Vignanasasthra Bodhana* (Teaching of Science) Guntur: Nagarjuna Publishers.

Bhaskara Rao, Digumarti (1997). *Vidya Manovignana Seshtram* (Educational Psychology). Guntur: Creative Press. pp. 434. Rs. 79.

Bhaskara Rao, Digumarti (1998). *DSC Study Material*. Guntur: Nagarjuna Publishers.

Bhaskara Rao, Digumarti (1998). *Upadhyayudu Vidya*. (Teacher and Education). Guntur: Nagarjuna Publishers.

Bhaskara Rao, Digumarti (1998). *Vidya Drukpadalu* (Prespectives of Education). Guntur: Nagarjuna Publishers.

Bhaskara Rao, Digumarti (1999). *EdCET Teaching Aptitude*. Guntur: Nagarjuna Publishers.

Bhaskara Rao, Digumarti (2001). *Bharata Samajamulo Upadyayudu Vidya* (Teacher and Education in Emerging Indian Society). Guntur: Nagarjuna Publishers.

Bhaskara Rao, Digumarti (2001). *Bhoutika Sastra Bodhana Paddathulu* (Methods of Teaching Physical Science). Guntur: Nagarjuna Publishers. pp. 324.

Bhaskara Rao, Digumarti (2001). *Jeeva Sastra Bodhana Padhathulu* (Methods of Teaching Biology). Guntur: Nagarjuna Publishers. pp. 224.

Bhaskara Rao, Digumarti (2001). *Vidya Manovignana Sastram* (Educational Psychology). Guntur: Nagarjuna Publishers. pp. 344.

Bhaskara Rao, Digumarti (2003). *Patsala Yajamanyam/Paripalana* (School Management and Administration). Guntur: Nagarjuna Publishers.

Bhaskara Rao, Digumarti (2004). *Vidya Sanketika Sastram mariyu Computer Vidya* (Educational Technology and Computer Education). Guntur: Nagarjuna Publishers.

Index

G

I

K

L

R

S

T

U

W